Students' English Grammar Exercises
with answers

Jake Allsop

PHOENIX
ELT

incorporating
PRENTICE HALL MACMILLAN

New York   London   Toronto   Sydney   Tokyo   Singapore

Published 1995 by
Phoenix ELT
Campus 400, Spring Way
Maylands Avenue, Hemel Hempstead
Hertfordshire, HP2 7EZ
A division of Prentice Hall International

First published 1983 by Cassell Publishers Ltd
Published 1993 by Prentice Hall International

Printed and bound in Great Britain by
The Bath Press, Bath

ISBN 0-13-856055-2

5 4 3 2
99 98 97 96 95

Contents

Introduction

This book of exercises is a companion to *Students' English Grammar*, but my hope is that it will stand on its own. All the exercises have been tried out at the intermediate level with groups of students. At the same time, there is no reason why a student should not work through the exercises alone. A key to the exercises is provided for those who do so.

The exercises are of various types, and lead to a variety of classroom activities. Exercises which ask the students to describe the different situations in which similar pairs of sentences would be used are particularly good for stimulating group discussion and activity. It is gratifying to see how well intermediate students do, even when faced with such subtleties as the difference between *get something done* and *have something done*, once they start to share ideas in class discussions.

I make no apology for including several sections called *Just for Fun*, which contain activities which some would not regard as 'serious'. These sections are included for those occasions when the students feel like a bit of relaxation – although they will find some of the *Just for Fun* exercises quite searching!

I am extremely grateful to Mione Ieronymidis for all her help in weeding out unsuitable items, and for testing so much of the material in classes at various levels. It is a better book as a result of her efforts, but I take sole responsibility for any defects which remain.

I dedicate the book to Joy McKellen, not because of her excellent editorial assistance, but because I wish to refute her opinion of herself that she is 'no good at grammar or puzzles'.

Jake Allsop
Bournemouth
August, 1982

Unit 1 Nouns

1.1
Which of these words should be written with an initial capital letter?

1	month	6	tuesday	11	the *moonlight sonata*	15	tolstoy's *war and peace*
2	the bank	7	the duke of kent	12	princes and princesses	16	holidays
3	star	8	easter sunday	13	the daily mirror	17	new year's eve
4	miss jones	9	a symphony	14	politicians	18	the first sunday in june
5	tomorrow	10	grammar				

1.2
Complete this table. (We have done the first one to help you)

	Singular	Plural		Singular	Plural
1	office	offices	16	penny	
2		loaves	17		feet
3	loss		18	cupful	
4		potatoes	19	son-in-law	
5	roof		20		lives
6		mice	21	manservant	
7	solo		22	traffic warden	
8	key		23	spoonful	
9		teeth	24	passer-by	
10	sandwich		25	rabbit	
11	city		26		species
12	child		27	sheep	
13	tomato		28	salmon	
14	stepson		29	trout	
15		women	30		series

1.3
The plural ending may be pronounced [s], [z] or [ɪz]. Put these plural nouns into the correct column according to the way the ending is pronounced. (We have done the first one to help you.)

	[s]	[z]	[ɪz]			[s]	[z]	[ɪz]
1 teacups	✓				13 handkerchiefs			
2 bones					14 wages			
3 hedges					15 garages*			
4 roads					16 rings			
5 eyes					17 prices			
6 lights					18 works			
7 combs					19 babies			
8 eyelashes					20 paragraphs			
9 eyebrows					21 lengths			
10 books					22 designs			
11 sizes					23 ankles			
12 chairs					24 paths			

*The ending -*age* is pronounced [ɪdʒ] or [ɑːʒ] in *garage*

1.4   'Odd man out'

In the set *dog cat cow sheep book horse mouse*, the 'odd man out' is *book*: all the others are animals. In the following sets of words, there is one 'odd man out' – there is one word in each set in which the plural ending is pronounced differently from the others. Can you find the odd words?

1	houses	horses	matches	lines	ages	
2	ropes	safes	roads	gifts	bikes	chips
3	knees	days	grapes	donkeys	flies	rows
4	stores	chairs	hearts	wires	ears	
5	paths	months	mouths	youths	baths	

1.5

Complete the table. Note that some of these words of foreign origin have regular plurals.

	Singular	Plural		Singular	Plural
1		cacti	13		memoranda
2	analysis		14	stadium	
3		stimuli	15	museum	
4		strata	16		addenda
5	datum		17		radii
6		vertebrae	18	drama	
7	basis		19	genius	
8	fungus		20		appendices
9		genera	21	axis	
10	index		22		media
11		crises	23	album	
12		criteria	24		phenomena

1.6
Which of the following words are singular in meaning (i.e. would be used with *is*); which are plural (would be used with *are*); and which can be used either singular or plural (i.e. could be used with either *is* or *are*)?

1	the news	10	statistics
2	people	11	gymnastics
3	measles	12	underpants
4	trousers	13	headquarters
5	the team	14	the government
6	the police	15	mathematics
7	billiards	16	Manchester United*
8	cattle	17	thanks
9	scissors	18	the clergy

*Remember that Manchester United is a football team.

1.7 'Something in common'
The words *dog, cat, cow, horse, squirrel, pig,* have all got something in common: they are all singular nouns. What have the following groups of words got in common? (We are concerned with grammar rather than with meaning.)
1 information luggage news advice furniture
2 family council committee crowd government staff the public
3 customs minutes outskirts thanks lodgings
4 bread rice ink wool iron sugar salt wood
5 knickers trousers tweezers binoculars pyjamas scissors

1.8 Matching
To match things is to put together those things which usually go together. For example, there are three matching pairs of words in the following:
   chair saucer table knife fork cup
The pairs are: cup and saucer, table and chair, knife and fork

Can you match words from group A with words from group B using the pattern A(n)[A] OF [B]? For example, *loaf* goes with *bread* to form the expression *a loaf of bread.*

Group A: blade grain sheet loaf drop lump speck bar strand item slice

Group B: paper dust grass news meat water sand coal soap bread hair

1.9
Match words from group A with words from group B using the pattern A(n)[A] OF [B]. For example, *bottle* goes with *milk* to form the expression *a bottle of milk.*

Group A: box bottle bunch flock packet crowd tin pack bundle herd

Group B: flowers people matches clothes cows birds milk cigarettes sardines cards

1.10
Complete the table. We have done the first one for you.

1	brother	~~sister~~	10	duke
2		mother	11	emperor
3		wife	12	countess (2 possibilities)
4	uncle		13	queen
5		niece	14	lord
6	son		15	usher
7	hero		16	manager
8		spinster	17	lass
9	waiter		18	Dear Sir,

1.11
If you are interested in animals, try matching the pairs (male and female) of these ten kinds of animal:

Male: bull boar buck stag fox dog gander drake stallion cock

Female: hind goose cow mare hen vixen sow bitch duck doe

If you have managed to find the pairs, can you now match their young?
   fawn cub calf foal pup piglet gosling chick fawn duckling

1.12
Using the endings -ist, -er, -or, -ian, give the names of people who do the jobs connected with these words. Changes of spelling are needed in

some cases, and note that numbers 28, 29 and 30 have other ways of forming the noun describing the person who does the job.

e.g. drum – drummer

1	drum	16	football
2	engine	17	science
3	physics	18	organize
4	economics	19	library
5	survey	20	comedy
6	violin	21	type
7	law	22	trombone
8	chemistry	23	photograph
9	drama	24	music
10	telephone	25	instruct
11	supervise	26	accounts
12	attend	27	flute
13	technology	28	democracy
14	cello	29	athletics
15	trumpet	30	gymnastics

1.13

Form abstract nouns from these verbs, using the endings **-tion, -(s)sion, -ance, ence, -ure,** or **-ment**. To make it interesting, we have included six verbs (marked*) which form abstract nouns using different endings!

add, agree, amuse, apologize*, appear, associate, assume, authorize, arrive*, attend, compare*, complete, conceive, concentrate, conclude, confer, confuse, deceive, decide, declare, defend, defy, depart*, differ, disappoint, distinguish, divide, employ, endure, enjoy, entertain, explain, explode, explore, fail, inform, imitate, interfere, intervene, irritate, judge, multiply, observe, offend, permit, persist, prefer, proceed, provide, receive, refer, refuse*, repeat, revise, sign, simplify, solve, sympathize*, transmit, vary.

1.14

The words on the left are written separately. Look at the definitions on the right and decide whether the words on the left are the parts of a compound noun, or whether they are simply of the pattern ADJECTIVE + NOUN. Then write them out correctly and show where the stress falls.

A a | green | house = a place where young plants are grown

B a | green | house = a house which has been painted green

A is a compound noun and should be written *a 'greenhouse*; **B** is simply a noun (*house*) described by an adjective (*green*), and should be written *a green 'house*.

1	i)	A | dark	| room	=	a place where films are developed
	ii)	A | dark	| room	=	a room which is dull and without light
2	i)	A | light	| house	=	a building which warns ships of dangers
	ii)	A | light	| room	=	a room which is bright and airy
3	i)	A | country	| house	=	a house which is situated in the country
	ii)	A | country	| man	=	a man of the same nationality as you*
4	i)	A | brief	| case	=	a case for carrying documents
	ii)	A | brief	| meeting	=	a short meeting
5	i)	A | gold	| watch	=	a watch with a gold case
	ii)	A | gold	| fish	=	a type or species of fish, related to the carp
6	i)	A | school	| boy	=	a pupil, a boy who goes to school
	ii)	A | school	| building	=	a building which is part of a school
7	i)	A | paper	| bag	=	a bag which is made of paper
	ii)	A | paper	| back	=	a kind of book with soft covers
	iii)	A | paper	| weight	=	a heavy object for keeping loose papers in place

8	i)	A | cash	| offer	= an offer to pay in cash
	ii)	A | cash	| box	= a box where cash is kept
	iii)	A | cash	| book	= a special book where you record cash paid in and out
9	i)	A | working	| model	= a small-scale model of a machine
	ii)	— | working	| mothers	= mothers who go out to work
	iii)	— | working	| hours	= the hours for which employees are paid to work

*It can also mean *a man who lives in the country, not in the town.*

1.15

Put the possessive ending 's or ' in the space marked [   ] in the following expressions:

1   the girl[   ] dresses
2   the girls[   ] clothes
3   the boss[   ] announcement
4   ladies[   ] night
5   policemen[   ] uniforms
6   children[   ] education
7   the country[   ] problems
8   secretaries[   ] working hours
9   an actress[   ] professional life
10 actresses[   ] opportunities
11 Mr Davies[   ] office
12 France[   ] foreign policy
13 a greenfinch[   ] nest
14 greenfinches[   ] nests
15 a lady[   ] handbag

1.16

Complete these sentences using the appropriate possessive form.

e.g. The dog which belongs to my neighbour = _____ dog.

Answer: my neighbour's dog

1   The scheme sponsored by the Duke of Edinburgh is called _____ .
2   The office where the managing director works is called _____ .
3   The car which belongs to my sister-in-law is _____ .
4   A school for boys only is called _____ .
5   The union which represents railwaymen is _____ .
6   The law which was discovered by a man called Murphy is known as _____ .
7   A holiday which lasts a fortnight is _____ .
8   The home where the nurses live is called _____ .
9   The car which belongs to Mr Brown's wife is _____ .

1.17

The possessive ending 's may be pronounced [s], [z] or [ɪz]. Can you say how the following should be prounounced?

1   the *Pope's* visit
2   *women's* liberation
3   St *George's* Hall
4   the *water's* edge
5   a *year's* time
6   *Jack's* dinner
7   *Frances's* dress
8   a *month's* time
9   *Nature's* way
10 the *Church's* work
11 your *money's* worth
12 the *horse's* mouth
13 The *Devil's* Disciple
14 *Mike's* place
15 the *teacher's* opinion
16 the *princess's* wedding dress
17 for *Pete's* sake
18 the *monarch's* role

1.18

If you want to buy some food, you go *to the grocer's.* Where do you go if you want to do the following?

1   buy some vegetables
    go to the g_____
2   have your teeth examined
    go to the d_____
3   have your eyes examined
    go to the o_____
4   buy some medicine
    go to the c_____
5   buy some screws and some nails
    go to the i_____
6   buy some meat
    go to the b_____
7   get your hair cut
    go to the h_____

8   buy some flowers
    go to the f_____
9   have some clothes cleaned
    go to the c_____

1   to lead a dogs life
2   'Thursdays child works hard for a living.'
3   'It is part of Lifes rich tapestry.'
4   'A fair days pay for a fair days work.'
5   wolves in sheeps clothing
6   'A womans work is never done.'
7   'One mans meat is another mans poison.'
8   For goodness sake!
9   *Loves old sweet song*

1.19

Can you put the possessive apostrophe (') in the correct place in the following expressions?

Just for fun

1.20

Look at this family tree and then answer the questions.

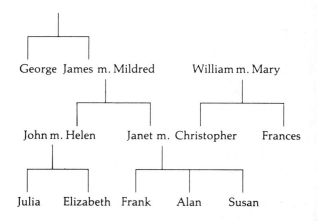

1   What is the name of James's brother?
2   What is the name of William's wife?
3   How many nephews has Frances got?
4   What relation is Janet to John?
    Answer: 'She is his _____'
5   What is the relationship of Julia and Elizabeth to James?
    Answer: 'They are his _____'
6   What is the name of John's mother-in-law?
7   What is the name of John's wife's sister?
8   What is the name of Christopher's father-in-law's brother?
9   What are the names of Julia's aunt's husband's parents?

10   What is the name of William and Mary's granddaughter?
11   How many cousins has Julia got?
12   How many people are likely to call George 'Uncle'?

1.21 Word square

The words in the list are hidden in the word square. They may be horizontal, vertical or diagonal, and may be written forwards or backwards. How many can you find? (We have done the first one to help you.)

biking   gliding   pot holing (*two words*)
bowling   golfing   racing
dancing   hitchhiking   sailing
diving   horseriding   singing
driving   hunting   skiing
fencing   jogging   trekking
fishing   ping pong (*2 words*)

Note:

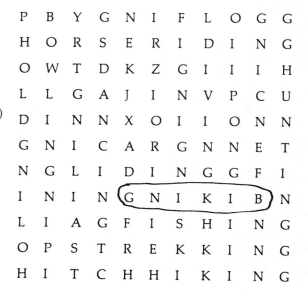

horizontal   vertical   diagonal

Unit 2 Articles and demonstratives

2.1

Rewrite this story, putting in **the, a** or **an** if necessary.

_____ **Elephant and** _____ **Mouse**

_____ elephant and _____ mouse fell in love and decided to get married.

When _____ elephant told her father, he said 'Don't be silly, _____ elephant cannot marry _____ mouse.'

When _____ mouse told his mother, she said 'Don't be silly, _____ mice do not marry _____ elephants.'

So _____ elephant, who was very musical, became _____ pianist, and _____ mouse, who had _____ good voice, became _____ singer. They toured _____ world together for _____ many years, giving _____ concerts and bringing _____ pleasure to everyone who heard them.

Moral: There is more than one way to live in _____ harmony.

2.2

Which of these place names are written with **the**?

1	Brussels	16	Great Britain
2	West Indies	17	Table Mountain
3	Philippines	18	Sahara
4	Siberia	19	South Pole
5	New Zealand	20	South America
6	Isle of Man	21	Pennines
7	East Africa	22	Los Angeles
8	Sicily	23	Atlantic
9	Lake Constance	24	North Island
10	Black Sea	25	Atlantic Ocean
11	River Thames	26	Athens
12	Pacific	27	USA
13	Arctic	28	USSR
14	Pyrenees	29	Middle East
15	Long Island	30	Straits of Gibraltar

2.3

Put **the, a** or **an** into these sentences if necessary:

1 'Is this _____ book you were telling me about? 'Yes, it is about _____ life of Queen Victoria.'

2 It is _____ interesting book. It gives _____ wonderful picture of what _____ life was like in _____ Victorian times.

3 'Is there _____ newsagent's near here?' 'There are several; _____ nearest one is just down _____ road on _____ left.'

4 We always stay at _____ Palace Court Hotel because it is _____ only one with _____ facilities for _____ disabled.

5 _____ Playhouse is _____ old theatre, but it puts on _____ modern plays.

6 _____ Swiss Alps are _____ good place to go if you like _____ skiing. There is usually plenty of _____ snow during _____ winter months.

7 'Just look at _____ snow! It seems to be just _____ right kind of _____ snow for _____ skiing.'

8 _____ English people are forever complaining about _____ weather, but in _____ fact _____ British Isles have _____ reasonable climate on _____ whole.'

9 'This is _____ toughest steak I have ever eaten. It is _____ last time I eat in this restaurant.'

10 _____ otter used to be _____ common animal, but is now found only in _____ north of _____ Britain.

11 In _____ old days, you used to see
    _____ otters all over _____ place, but
    now you can only find them in _____
    certain parts of _____ country.

12 Robin Hood is _____ legendary hero that
    _____ children learn about from _____
    story books. He used to take _____
    money from _____ rich and give it to
    _____ poor.

13 Martin King lives in _____ little village
    on _____ edge of _____ New Forest.
    He writes _____ books about _____
    natural history in _____ general, and
    about _____ natural history of _____
    New Forest in particular.

14 I have just bought _____ copy of his
    latest book, _____ *Close Look at*
    _____ *Nature*. It contains some of
    _____ finest photographs of _____
    wildlife subjects that I have ever seen.

15 Martin's book deals with _____ wide
    range of animal species, from _____
    blackbirds to _____ rare animals like
    _____ otters.

16 We have just been on _____ holiday to
    _____ Lake District. At _____ first we
    thought of _____ camping, but then we
    decided to stay in _____ hotels instead.

17 It is _____ wonderful part of England
    and _____ scenery reminds you of
    _____ mountainous countries like
    _____ Switzerland. As _____ matter
    of _____ fact, we had such _____ good
    time that we have decided to have _____
    holiday there again _____ next year.

18 We also paid _____ short visit to _____
    Scotland. We went to Edinburgh to see
    _____ usual sights, including _____
    Castle and _____ Prince's Street. Then
    we spent _____ week in _____
    Highlands.

2.4

Use the patterns WHAT . . .! or WHAT A(N) . . .! to
make exclamations from the following.

Example: good advice   What good advice!
             good idea   What a good idea!

1 terrible weather   7 clever people
   terrible climate   clever person

2 beautiful luggage   8 difficult job
   beautiful suitcase   difficult work

3 elegant clothes   9 fresh bread
   elegant dress   fresh loaf

4 heavy rainfall   10 delicious food
   heavy shower   delicious meal

5 healthy cow   11 horrible tune
   healthy cattle   horrible music

6 awful rubbish   12 tough beef
   awful mess   tough steak

2.5

Can you match these words to the definitions
given below?

Example

glass   a substance used, for example, in
         windows
a glass a container for drinking out of

Words

1	glass	19	language
2	a glass	20	a language
3	paper	21	tin
4	a paper	22	a tin
5	wood	23	study
6	a wood	24	a study
7	iron	25	light
8	an iron	26	a light
9	string	27	air
10	a string	28	an air
11	coffee	29	duck
12	a coffee	30	a duck
13	cloth	31	gold
14	a cloth	32	a gold
15	rubber	33	play
16	a rubber	34	a play
17	lamb	35	thought
18	a lamb	36	a thought

Definitions
the activity of learning
a substance used for making a stimulating drink
the stuff we breathe in order to stay alive
a kind of bird which lives on or near water
the part of a guitar, for example, which you
    pluck in order to make a note
The Times or the *Daily Mirror* for example
a substance used, for example, in windows
a material from which car tyres, for example,
    are made
a tune or melody; also used to describe
    someone's manner or appearance
a metal, chemical symbol Fe, from which steel is
    made
a group or clump of trees
a story performed on stage by actors
a kind of meat which we get from a young sheep
a metal, chemical symbol Sn, used in the
    manufacture of food containers
popular name for the medal awarded to the best
    performer in an Olympic event
a device which we switch on in a room when it
    goes dark
a container into which food is put before it is
    sold
something which you use to get rid of a pencil
    mark
an animal, the young of a sheep
something which you use for tying up parcels,
    for example
meat from a particular kind of bird
a container for drinking out of
the faculty or ability by which human beings
    communicate with each other
a precious metal, chemical symbol Au
an activity performed purely for pleasure; not
    work
a device for taking unwanted creases out of
    clothes; also the popular name for a kind of
    golfclub
the material obtained from trees with which we
    make furniture, for example
material for writing on
a form of energy from the sun which enables us
    to see
English, Spanish, Arabic or Japanese, for
    example
a piece of material used for wiping or cleaning
    things

a material from which clothes are made, for
    example
refers to a cup containing a drink made from this
    substance
a quiet room where you go to think or to work
a mental process
an idea

2.6
Put **the** into these sentences if it is necessary.

1 'I don't take _____ sugar, thank you.'

2 Although _____ brown rice is better for
   you, _____ most people prefer _____
   white rice.

3 Roger knows a lot about _____ classical
   music. He seems to like _____ string
   quartets of Beethoven best.

4 I studied _____ modern history at
   _____ University. In _____ last year I
   specialized in _____ history of _____
   American Civil War.

5 'What can you tell me about _____
   history of this town?' 'Well, I can tell you
   that _____ Cathedral was begun in
   _____ twelfth century and that it is
   supposed to be a fine example of _____
   early Gothic architecture.'

6 Do you think that I could ever learn to
   speak _____ Japanese _____ way
   _____ Japanese speak it?

7 They say that _____ Japanese language is
   particularly difficult for _____
   Europeans.

8 The two kinds of _____ dog that I detest
   most are _____ show dogs and _____
   lap dogs.

9 What an interesting piece of _____
   furniture! _____ top is made of _____
   Spanish mahogany, and _____ legs are
   made of _____ iron.

10 Here is a picture of _____ village where I
   was born. It is about ten minutes by
   _____ car from Wellington, _____
   nearest big town.

11   I have just heard on _____ radio that _____ Boltavian ambassador has asked _____ American government for _____ political asylum.

12   I have noticed that _____ English people do not seem to shake _____ hands as much as people do on _____ Continent.

13   They both joined _____ army at _____ same time. After _____ war, they met quite by _____ accident when they were both on _____ leave in _____ Cyprus.

14   Because _____ sun was so strong, they decided to sleep during _____ day and travel by _____ night.

15   Did you know that _____ English children start _____ school at _____ age of _____ five? Those who want to go on to _____ university have to stay on at _____ school until they are eighteen.

16   Her husband is ill in _____ hospital so she has to stay at _____ home to look after _____ children instead of going to _____ work.

17   It seems to me that _____ worker participation in _____ industry is an excellent idea in _____ theory, but it is very difficult to put into _____ practice.

18   She works in _____ hospital as personal assistant to Mr Read, _____ Senior Registrar.

2.7

Match a phrase from the first column with an expression from the second column.

Example
The expression *from scratch* matches (goes with) the word *start* to form the expression *start from scratch*.

1   send a letter
2   deliver the parcel
3   learn a poem
4   recite a passage
5   keep your current account
6   take somebody
7   call something
8   agree
9   drive
10   know someone
11   cancel an appointment
12   slice an apple
13   suddenly burst
14   call the workforce out
15   put the accused
16   have the matter
17   start
18   fall madly

a)   at great speed
b)   to mind
c)   in credit
d)   into tears
e)   on strike
f)   by hand
g)   in love
h)   from memory
i)   by airmail
j)   by surprise
k)   from scratch
l)   in principle
m)   at short notice
n)   by sight
o)   in half
p)   by heart
q)   under consideration
r)   on trial

2.8 Definitions
Make up definitions on the pattern

A(N)	A	IS A(N)	B	FOR / WHO	C	.

Use the information given in colums **A**, **B** and **C** to complete the pattern. You may be able to use more than one alternative from column **B** (e.g. a camera could be described as a *machine* or as an *instrument*).

Example:

A	B	C
screwdriver	tool	driving in screws

Answer: 'A screwdriver is a tool for driving in screws.'

	A	B	C
1	screwdriver		runs a school
2	computer	tool	making holes
3	ruler		controlling temperature
4	telescope		measuring time
5	butcher	instrument	driving in screws
6	mechanic		controlling the flow of gas or liquid
7	headmistress		drawing straight lines
8	valve	man	writing with
9	camera		sells meat
10	saw		measuring temperature
11	accountant	woman	cutting wood
12	drill		processing information
13	pen		pulling heavy loads
14	tractor	machine	acts in plays and films
15	clock		taking photographs
16	thermometer		checks figures
17	actress	device	making distant objects appear bigger
18	thermostat		repairs cars and other machines

2.9

Replace the underlined part of each sentence by an expression on the pattern VERB + NOUN. The noun in each case is given in brackets at the end of the sentence. Add any prepositions that may be needed and make any other changes (e.g. of tense) that may be necessary.

e.g. Will you <u>look after</u> the house while I am away? (care)

Answer: the expression with *care* is **take care of**. Therefore: Will you take care of the house while I am away?

1 Please <u>listen carefully</u> to what I have to say. (attention)
2 Her behaviour <u>caused</u> a lot of gossip. (rise)
3 British Steel is a good company to <u>deal</u> with. (business)
4 I think she <u>was very offended</u> by what you said. (offence)
5 He has decided to <u>leave his present job and get another one.</u> (jobs)
6 Poor Martin! His wife is forever <u>criticizing</u> him. (fault)
7 <u>I believe you can succeed.</u> (confidence)
8 The bridge <u>collapsed</u> under the weight of the snow. (way)
9 The other boys <u>laughed</u> at him. (fun)
10 He worked hard and <u>improved a lot.</u> (progress)
11 The protest meeting <u>was held</u> in the Caxton Hall. (place)
12 I rarely <u>need</u> to go to London nowadays. (occasion)
13 We <u>enjoyed ourselves</u> at Edith's party. (fun)
14 He used to belong to the Labour Party, but he has now <u>joined the SDP.</u> (sides)
15 <u>I can no longer remember</u> the number of times I have said this. (track)
16 The Princess has <u>had</u> a baby daughter. (birth)
17 It is a good idea to <u>become friendly</u> with your neighbours. (friends)
18 I will try to <u>organize</u> your transfer to another section. (arrangements)

2.10

Which of these sentences could be written in the singular without any important change of meaning? That is, which would be better in the singular?

1 Cars parked at owners' risk. (*Notice in a car park*)
2 Passengers are requested to remain seated until the plane has come to a standstill. (*Announcement on a plane*)
3 In future, private cars must be fitted with seatbelts. (*Announcement of a new regulation*)
4 Dogs make wonderful pets. (*from a magazine article*)
5 Russian citizens cannot travel abroad without a visa. (*overheard in a conversation*)
6 Refrigerators are essential pieces of equipment in modern kitchens. (*taken from an advertisement*)
7 Examinations for second-year students take place at the end of May. (*from a university prospectus*)
8 Men who drink and drive are more than just fools; they are criminals. (*said during a debate on TV*)
9 Students who have not yet received their results should get in touch with their tutors at once. (*announcement on a noticeboard*)

Just for fun

2.11 'Where's the post office?'

From the plan of the village you can see where twelve important buildings are situated. Describe their position using the pattern below.

| The | | is on the $\frac{\text{left}}{\text{right}}$ | just after
just before
, next to
opposite
near | the | |
| | | | between the | and the | |

Plan of the village

| Police Station | Bank | Post Office | Bus Stop | Telephone Booth | Red Lion (Pub) |

-- ← ⟩

You are standing here

| Church | Village Hall | Butcher's | Grocer's | Newsagent's | Chapel |

2.12 Word square: London

(For instructions see Unit 1 page 10.) Can you find the place names in the word square? When you have found them all, look at the six unused letters, and see if you can work out the name of a famous London station.

```
G  A  L  L  E  R  Y  S  C  P  C
N  P  S  Q  U  A  R  E  A  S  R
I  E  I  E  A  S  T  R  T  A  O
R  S  D  C  M  H  K  P  H  I  S
A  Y  T  I  C  A  U  E  E  N  S
H  W  O  R  R  A  H  N  D  T  T
C  S  A  C  A  T  D  T  R  P  E
T  E  B  U  T  N  O  I  A  A  P
A  O  T  S  E  W  D  N  L  U  N
T  G  I  B  E  N  D  E  N  L  E
E  L  B  R  A  M  O  H  O  S  Y
```

Big Ben (*2 places*)*
City
Charing Cross
　(*2 places*)
East End (*2 places*)
Harrow
Hyde Park (*2 places*)
Marble Arch
　(*2 places*)
Piccadilly Circus
　(*2 places*)

Saint Paul's Cathedral
　(*2 places*)
Serpentine
Soho Square (*2 places*)
Stepney
Strand
Tate Gallery (*2 places*)
Thames
Tower
Tube
West End

Additional question: which of these names should be written and said with **the**?

(2 places) means that the two parts of the name appear in two different places in the square. We have done *Big Ben* as an example.

Unit 3   Quantifiers and distributives

3.1

Put **all**, **each**, **every**, **several**, **a lot of**, **none** or **few** in the spaces in this passage. In some cases, more than one word will fit.

There was once a very serious rabbit. He was not handsome or clever but he worked hard and saved _____ his money. The beautiful lady rabbit who lived near him was a widow, and she had _____ admirers, but he knew that _____ of them was as rich as he was.

The widow had _____ children, so _____ time he visited her, he brought a different present for _____ child.

One day, a handsome stranger came to town. Soon, _____ female rabbit was in love with him.

3.2

Substitute **little**, **a little**, **few** or **a few** for the words underlined in these sentences.

1 There are <u>several</u> things we have to talk about.
2 A lot of food was prepared, but <u>hardly any</u> of it was eaten.
3 <u>Hardly any</u> people managed to attend the concert.
4 Would you like <u>some</u> more cake?
5 There are <u>not many</u> people who can be trusted any more.
6 I have <u>practically no</u> reason to be grateful to her.
7 There are still <u>some</u> people who can be trusted.
8 How would you like to spend <u>two or three</u> days in the country?
9 I think there is still a <u>drop</u> of wine left.
10 He is not an expert, but he knows <u>something</u> about cars.
11 A lot of people have tried, but <u>almost none</u> of them has succeeded.
12 There is <u>not much</u> you can do to help.

3.3

Only one of the expressions given in brackets will fit in the sentence. Rewrite each sentence with the correct form inserted.

1 Could you come and see me _____ tomorrow? (sometimes/some time)
2 I looked at the eggs: _____ was broken. (every one/everyone)
3 You can have another cake: pick _____ you like. (any one/anyone)
4 One other person can go with you: pick _____ you like. (any one/anyone)
5 Has _____ got a copy of the minutes? (every one/everyone)
6 This problem has gone on too long; we must solve it _____ soon. (some time/sometimes)
7 I wrote to all my friends, but _____ of them replied. (not one/no-one)
8 She _____ pops round to see us on Saturdays. (some time/sometimes)
9 Has _____ seen my jacket? (any one/anyone)
10 We had a singsong, but not _____ joined in. (every one/everyone)
11 Give me a magazine to read; _____ will do. (any one/anyone)
12 _____ I wonder why you married me. (some time/sometimes)

3.4

In the sentence *I wrote some letters*, the word *some* is pronounced [səm], i.e., unstressed. In the sentence *I have read some of your essays*, the word *some* is pronounced [sʌm]. Say these sentences aloud, decide which way *some* is pronounced in each sentence and tick the right box.

	[səm]	[sʌm]
1 I need some money right away.	☐	☐
2 There's some man outside asking to see you.	☐	☐
3 Have you got any money? I need some right away.	☐	☐

	[səm]	[sʌm]
4 There is something that I must tell you.	☐	☐
5 Put some more coal on the fire.	☐	☐
6 He knows some funny stories.	☐	☐
7 Then he told us some story about being the son of a duke!	☐	☐
8 Then he told us some stories about his life in Africa.	☐	☐
9 Some students learn more quickly than others.	☐	☐
10 I met some friends of yours last night.	☐	☐
11 Some of them would like to see you again.	☐	☐
12 They put on some music and started to dance.	☐	☐

3.5 (See table below.)

Consider each of these sentences and decide whether **some** or **any** will fit. Mark a 1 in the appropriate column. Sometimes both words will fit. For example, in Sentence 9, the usual question is *Don't you like any of this music?* The question *Don't you like some of this music?* is a question with a special purpose (it expects the answer yes). If this happens, mark the usual question 1 and the special purpose question 2.

In a few of these sentences, you could leave out both **some** and **any** without any important change of meaning. For example, Sentence 2 could read *I need more paper.* Which other sentences would also be acceptable without **some** or **any**?

		Some	Any	
1	There is hardly			milk left.
2	I need			more paper.
3	Would you like			more tea?
4	Have you got			change?
5	Please have			more cake.
6	She replied without			hesitation.
7	He had made hardly			mistakes.
8	There must be			music you like!
9	Don't you like	2	1	of this music?
10	I couldn't get you			cigarettes.
11	Nobody lives there			more.
12	I must go. I have			work to do.
13	I rarely get			letters nowadays.
14	Don't leave under			circumstances.
15	Shouldn't you do			revision for your test?
16	Anna bought			books for her brother.
17	It will not make			difference to me.
18	Will it make			difference to you?

3.6

Complete these sentences by adding **some** *or* **any** to form the compounds **something/ anything, somebody/anybody, somewhere/ anywhere**, or the adverbials **some time/any time**.

1 'Where have you been?' 'I haven't been _____where.'
2 Your face looks familiar. Haven't I seen you _____where before?
3 There is _____thing I do not understand about this report.
4 '_____thing you can do, I can do better.' (*Song title*)
5 Perhaps we should meet again _____ time.
6 I cannot see _____body today. I am far too busy.
7 _____body has been smoking in here. I can still smell it.
8 I have looked for my glasses but I cannot find them _____where.
9 She left abruptly without telling _____body where she was going.
10 They must be _____where! They cannot have disappeared completely.
11 Pop in and see us _____time you are passing.
12 I have had hardly _____thing to eat since Sunday.
13 You look as if you are about to say _____thing unpleasant.
14 We never seem to go _____where interesting these days.
15 I don't like the look of this disco. Can't we go _____where else?
16 You can have _____thing you like as long as it is not too expensive.
17 I wish there were _____thing I could do to help.
18 Can I tell you _____thing? I think you are very pretty.

3.7

Use these base sentences **I like these objects**
                           I like them
to make positive sentences with **both** or **all** about:

a two objects
   1 I like _____ these objects.
   2 I like _____ them.
b several objects
   3 I like _____ these objects.
   4 I like _____ them.

Now make up negative sentences using the base sentences and the words **not . . . either** or **not . . . any** about:

a two objects
   5 I do not like _____ these objects.
   6 I do not like _____ them.
b several objects
   7 I do not like _____ these objects.
   8 I do not like _____ them.

Now, rewrite sentences 5 and 6 using **neither** in place of **not . . . either**; and rewrite sentences 7 and 8 using **none** in place of **not . . . any**. How do these sentences with **neither** and **none** differ in emphasis from the original sentences with **not . . . either** and **not . . . any**?

3.8

Substitute the word in brackets for the word underlined, and make any changes to the sentence which are necessary. We have done the first one.

1 I do not take as many <u>pills</u> as I used to. (medicine)
   I do not take as much medicine as I used to.
2 You should try to eat less <u>bread.</u> (potatoes)
3 There is not much <u>work</u> for young people nowadays. (jobs)
4 Too much <u>time</u> is wasted on unimportant things. (hours)
5 How many <u>five-pound notes</u> are there in the cashbox? (money)
6 I need a few more <u>minutes.</u> (time)
7 We are having far fewer <u>problems</u> with the new computer. (trouble)
8 Much of <u>what</u> you say makes sense to me. (the things)
9 There is very little <u>nightlife</u> in this place. (nightclubs)
10 We own a large number of <u>houses</u> around here. (property)

11 We could do with a little more <u>information</u>. (facts)
12 There has been a great deal of <u>discussion</u> about it. (meetings)
13 A large number of <u>items</u> are missing.* (material)
14 We are no longer getting many <u>reports</u> from abroad. (news)
15 There are very few <u>chairs</u> in the room. (furniture)
16 He has had plenty of <u>opportunities</u> to get married. (chance)
17 We were just having a bit of <u>fun.</u> (laughs)
18 Anna sends you lots of <u>kisses.</u> (love)

*Strictly correct would be *A large number of items is missing.*

3.9

Choose the correct alternative for each sentence. Only one alternative is correct for each particular situation described by the sentence.

1 Are these | either / both | your children?

2 I watched | all / the whole / the whole of | *Gone with the Wind* from start to finish.

3 Tell | all / everyone | that Willy is here.

4 I have told you | the whole / everything | I know.

5 I have two daughters and a son. | All / Both | my children go to school, but | none / neither | of them likes it very much.

6 Don't keep staring at her | all / all the | time.

7 | All / Everything | I need now is a place to sleep.

8 The children | each one / each | received a different present.

9 'I'll give you £20.00 for it?' 'Is that | all / the whole / everything | you can afford?'

10 I can only afford to buy two; they cost £5.00 | each one / each | .

11 I have two sons. | All / Both | of them go to school, but | none / neither | of them likes it.

12 Why don't you take | all / all of / the whole | them if you like them?

13 You can take one of these dresses back: I do not need | both / any / either | of them.

14 She can recite | all / the whole / the whole of | *Endymion* from memory.

15 You can take | either / both | road; they | either / all / both | lead to the town centre.

16 He was so hungry that he ate | a whole / all a | chicken.

17   You can have the red one or the blue one,

but you cannot have | either / each / both | .

18   Tell me | all the / the whole / all | story, just as it
happened.

3.10
Substitute an expression with **every** for the
words underlined in these sentences, and make
any other necessary changes.
1   He gave <u>them each</u> a hundred pounds.
2   He goes to London on <u>alternate Thursdays</u>.
3   I get angry <u>whenever</u> I think of it.
4   <u>You</u> are <u>all</u> invited.
5   I see her <u>daily</u>.
6   <u>All</u> members of staff were interviewed.
7   He gave <u>all</u> he had to the poor.
8   <u>All</u> the passengers were given a free meal.
9   A B C Ⓓ E F G Ⓗ I J K Ⓛ M N O Ⓟ . . . We
have circled the <u>fourth letter, the eighth
letter, the twelfth letter, and so on</u>.

3.11
What is the difference in meaning between these
pairs of sentences? One way to show the
difference is to describe the different situations
in which each sentence might be said; e.g. in
Question 1 you might ask (i) when you expected
the answer 'yes'. You might ask (ii) if you just
wanted to be given the information.
1   i) Did he give you some money?
     ii) Did he give you any money?
2   i) Nobody can tell you exactly what
         happened.
     ii) Anybody can tell you exactly what
         happened.
3   i) I have spent the whole morning tidying
         up the office.
     ii) I have spent all morning tidying up the
         office.
4   i) Has anybody borrowed my calculator?
     ii) Has somebody borrowed my
         calculator?
5   i) I could see you some time tomorrow if
         you are free.
     ii) I could see you any time tomorrow if
         you are free.
6   i) I do not know anything about politics.
     ii) I know nothing about politics.
7   i) Some woman phoned but she did not
         leave a message.
     ii) A woman phoned but she did not leave
         a message.
8   i) I'd like some books by Burgess. (*some*
         pronounced [səm])
     ii) I like some books by Burgess. (*some*
         pronounced [sʌm])
9   i) I have read every one of his novels.
     ii) I have read all his novels.
10 i) He spoke to all the children.
     ii) He spoke to each child.
11 i) A lot of people do not know that.
     ii) Not many people know that.
12 i) Everybody knows how to make an
         omelette.
     ii) Anybody knows how to make an
         omelette.

Just for fun

3.12 Definitions
Sentences 1–10 are well-known sayings,
proverbs or quotations. They are followed by
ten definitions or explanations, labelled 'A' to
'J'. Can you match the sentences with the
definitions or explanations?

Sentences
1   'Come up and see me some time!'
2   'You can have any colour you like as long
     as it's black.'
3   There is no smoke without fire.
4   Every cloud has a silver lining.
5   All that glitters is not gold.
6   'You can fool some of the people all of the
     time. You can fool all of the people some of
     the time. But you cannot fool all of the
     people all of the time.'
7   'Anyone for tennis?'
8   No news is good news.
9   Take each day as it comes.
10 'From each according to his ability; to each
     according to his need.'

Definitions/Explanations

A   A proverb which warns you that things are not always as good as they seem.

B   A saying which advises you not to worry about the future beyond tomorrow.

C   Said by Henry Ford, who was the first to mass-produce a motor-car.

D   A line from a play set in a country house with weekend guests.

E   Said by Abraham Lincoln to defend the system of representative government.

F   An invitation given by a famous actress, Mae West, in a film.

G   A phrase from the Communist Manifesto describing the Socialist system.

H   A proverb which says that all rumours have some truth in them.

I   A saying which suggests that everything is all right unless you hear to the contrary.

J   A proverb which predicts that there is good in the worst situations.

Unit 4 Adjectives

4.1

Make adjectives from these nouns using the suffixes -y, ly, ish, -like or ful. Take care with the spelling.

1	hunger	7	truth	13	youth
2	coward	8	father	14	prince
3	noise	9	life	15	plenty
4	child	10	fun	16	filth
5	child	11	snob	17	boy
6	fool	12	leisure	18	skill

4.2

Complete the table on the right. The examples show that in some cases you can form only a -ful or only a -less adjective.

4.3

Using the suffixes -ish, -ly, -y, -like, -ful or -less, make adjectives from the words in column A which have the meaning given in column B.

Examples	-ful	-less
colour- youth- hair-	colourful youthful —	colourless — hairless
1 use-		
2 wonder-		
3 hope-		
4 shame-		
5 thought-		
6 beauti-		
7 help-		
8 forget-		
9 sense-		
10 success-		
11 reck-		
12 aw-		
13 harm-		
14 ruth-		
15 truth-		
16 play-		
17 price-		
18 fright-		

Adjective

	A	*Word*	B	*Meaning*
1	red	more or less red		
2	day	happening every day		
3	silver	looking or shining like silver		
4	worth	of little or no value		
5	business	serious and professional		
6	grease	or covered in grease		
7	home	cosy; welcoming		
8	breath	out of breath		
9	power	very strong		
10	plenty	which there is a lot of		
11	elder	rather old (a politer word than *old*)		
12	life	looking as if it were real		
13	peace	quiet; without disturbance or noise		
14	old	more or less old (getting old)		

A	Word	B	Meaning		Adjective
15	care		who does not take care		_____
16	winter		cold; not warm or friendly		_____
17	nose		wanting to know what is not your business		_____
18	hand		useful; easy to reach or obtain		_____

4.4

Can you match the everyday nouns (of Germanic origin) in group A with the corresponding adjectives (of Latin origin) in group B? For example, the word **sun** has a corresponding Latin adjective **solar** in addition to the simple adjective *sunny*.

Group A: brother, woman, friend, god, fun, year, mother, man, cat, dog, mind, brain, sight, touch, hand, house, earth, east.

Group B: maternal, canine, terrestrial, fraternal, manual, mental, divine, feline, oriental, cerebral, feminine, masculine, annual, amicable, visual, comic(al), tactile, domestic.

4.5

There is usually a difference in meaning and use between the simple adjectives and the adjectives of Latin/Greek origin (see Section 4.4). We talk about a *sunny day* but about *solar energy*. Choose the adjective which best fits the meaning of these sentences.

1 Animals which are active during the hours of darkness are called | nightly / nocturnal | animals.

2 Animals which are active during the day are called | diurnal / daily | animals.

3 There is now a | walking / pedestrian | precinct in the | town / urban | centre.

4 | Country / Rural | people often find it difficult to adjust to | an urban / a town | environment.

5 Mr Green is a | tooth / dental | surgeon.

6 This food is not | salty / saline | enough for my taste.

7 | Salty / Saline | solutions are prepared in the laboratories.

8 Harvard has a world-famous | law / legal | school.

9 Every citizen has a | lawful / legal | right to protect himself against attack.

10 Many of Escher's paintings make use of | eye / optical | illusions.

11 The police were able to call on several | eye / optical | witnesses to give evidence.

12 | Home / Domestic | murders account for one in five of all murders in the UK.

13 There is a difference between calendar months and | moon / lunar | months.

14 For | mouth / oral | hygiene you should use | a mouth / an oral | wash as well as | tooth / dental | paste.

15 It was a fine $\begin{vmatrix} \text{starry} \\ \text{stellar} \end{vmatrix}$ night, with a severe $\begin{vmatrix} \text{ground} \\ \text{terrestrial} \end{vmatrix}$ frost.

16 The US has launched a probe into deep $\begin{vmatrix} \text{starry} \\ \text{stellar} \end{vmatrix}$ space.

17 Because he was so young, he went before the $\begin{vmatrix} \text{child} \\ \text{juvenile} \end{vmatrix}$ court, and was later interviewed by $\begin{vmatrix} \text{a senior} \\ \text{an elder} \end{vmatrix}$ police officer.

18 He trained as a $\begin{vmatrix} \text{sea} \\ \text{marine} \end{vmatrix}$ engineer at the Academy of $\begin{vmatrix} \text{Sea} \\ \text{Maritime} \end{vmatrix}$ Studies.

4.6
a Make adjectives from these verbs using the suffix **-able**. Take care with the spelling.

1	predict	10	value
2	believe	11	vary
3	change	12	work
4	deny	13	obtain
5	despise	14	cure
6	recognize	15	advise
7	regret	16	translate
8	rely	17	forget
9	transfer	18	describe

b Form the negative of the adjectives by adding the prefix **un-** or **in-**. (Numbers 3, 5 and 7 do not have a negative form. The negative of 9 is more usually *non-transferable* or *not transferable*.

Examples: replaceable irreplaceable
        repeatable unrepeatable

4.7
a Add the suffix **-able** or **ible** to the following stems:

1	adapt-	7	debat-
2	contempt-	8	feas-
3	respect-	9	memor-
4	vi-	10	avoid-
5	terr-	11	hospit-
6	irrit-	12	elig-

13	respons-	16	prob-
14	fall-	17	desir-
15	cap-	18	flex-

b Form the negative of numbers 10 to 18 by adding the prefix **un-** or **in-** (remember that **in-** changes to **il, im-** or **ir-** in some cases).

4.8
a Form adjectives ending in **-ive** from the following verbs:

1	destroy	10	progress
2	exceed	11	produce
3	extend	12	persuade
4	respond	13	attract
5	deceive	14	receive
6	impel	15	represent
7	explode	16	permit
8	possess	17	repeat
9	repel	18	retain

b Use adjectives 10–18 in these sentences:
1 He can talk you into doing what he wants you to do. He is a very _____ talker.
2 All the men try to talk to her: she is a very _____ woman.
3 He is ready to listen to what other people have to say. He is _____ to new ideas.
4 'One man, one vote' is the basis of _____ government.
5 Many songs have the same words sung over and over. I find them rather _____
6 He forgets nothing. He has a very _____ memory.
7 The conservative group want to keep things as they are, and the _____ group want to change everything.
8 She wrote eight novels in five years. It was her most _____ period.
9 'The _____ society' describes a society which is very tolerant of people's private behaviour and morals.

c Use adjectives 1–9 in these sentences:
10 The students were all eager to answer his questions. He found them most _____ .
11 She often does things on the spur of the moment, without thinking of the consequences. She is a rather _____ girl.
12 He is much nicer than he looks. His appearance is _____.

13   The ugly green-eyed monster in the film was really _____.

14   War might break out between the two countries at any moment. It is a highly _____ situation.

15   The bill came to £150.00 for two people. We thought this was _____.

16   Criticism which is _____ discourages people.

17   They will have to make _____ alterations in order to increase the size and the capacity of the factory.

18   A _____ mother is one who treats her children more like her personal property than as human beings.

4.9

a Here are 12 adjectives in -ate. Can you match nine of them to the definitions given below?
   adequate, affectionate, appropriate, corporate, deliberate, delicate, elaborate, illiterate, obstinate, private, proportionate, temperate.

1   describes someone who cannot read or write
2   friendly, loving and eager to show it
3   enough, but no more than enough
4   opposite of public
5   not accidental, done on purpose
6   describes a mild climate without extremes
7   done carefully, with great attention to detail
8   suitable, fitting the situation
9   of a person, not strong; of a thing, easily broken

b Add -ary or -ory to these stems, and then match the resulting adjectives to the definitions.

Stems:

compuls-	imagin-	satisfact-
contempor-	introduct-	station-
element-	necess-	tempor-

Definitions:

10   not moving; standing still
11   not permanent; for the present
12   simple; opposite of advanced
13   living/happening at the same time as something or someone else

14   not real; which does not actually exist
15   good enough; which comes up to the required standard
16   describes something which you must do; not optional
17   describes, for example, the first sentences in a book or speech
18   describes something which you cannot do without

4.10 Which ending?

a Add -ent or -ant to these stems to form adjectives.

1	magnific-	10	sil-
2	indec-	11	viol-
3	import-	12	curr-
4	hesit-	13	immigr-
5	suffici-	14	toler-
6	dec-	15	perman-
7	pregn-	16	consist-
8	afflu-	17	rec-
9	indign-	18	migr-

b Add -ic or -ical to these stems to form adjectives.

1	realist-	10	antibiot-
2	techn-	11	publ-
3	alphabet-	12	atom-
4	biolog-	13	med-
5	fantast-	14	scientif-
6	romant-	15	clin-
7	pract-	16	mathemat-
8	specif-	17	automat-
9	crit-	18	rad-

c Add -ous, -ious, -eous or -uous to these stems to form adjectives.

1	ambit-	10	jeal-
2	danger-	11	court-
3	ambig-	12	superstit-
4	obv-	13	virt-
5	miscellan-	14	enorm-
6	ridicul-	15	spontan-
7	var-	16	ard-
8	stren-	17	simultan-
9	outrag-	18	tremend-

4.11

a Similar words, different meaning

1 **true/truthful**
   i) This play is based on a _____ story.
   ii) I believe her: I think she is a _____ person.

2 **childish/childlike**
   i) You cannot have everything you want: don't be so _____.
   ii) She has a _____ quality, a sort of innocence, which I like.

3 **young/youthful**
   i) Our teacher is full of _____ enthusiasm for her subject.
   ii) Enjoy yourself while you are still _____.

4 **uneatable/inedible**
   i) This meat is so tough that I find it _____.
   ii) Some of the _____ varieties of fungus are poisonous.

5 **unreadable/illegible**
   i) The inscription was _____, but I recognized it as Latin.
   ii) *War and Peace* may be a good novel, but I find it _____.

6 **historic/historical**
   i) 'Ladies and gentlemen, this is a _____ moment: the first manned landing on another planet!'
   ii) The library contains a copy of *Magna Carta* and other _____ documents.

7 **economic/economical**
   i) The country is experiencing a time of great _____ difficulty.
   ii) This soap is very _____: you only need to use a little of it at a time.

8 **electric/electrical**
   i) I see you have an _____ cooker; I prefer gas.
   ii) The battery gave off a sudden _____ discharge.

9 **sensible/sensitive**
   i) John will be all right on his own; he is a very _____ boy.
   ii) Don't criticize her too harshly: she is very _____.

b Same word, different meaning
Say how they differ in meaning.

1 **old**
   i) She is an old friend of ours.
   ii) He is an old man.

2 **hard**
   i) He is a hard worker.
   ii) Do you think this is a hard exercise?

3 **new**
   i) Have you met the new neighbours?
   ii) I like your new dress.

4 **heavy**
   i) He is a heavy smoker.
   ii) What a heavy parcel!

5 **certain**
   i) I am certain that this book used to belong to me.
   ii) There is a certain Mr Smith whom I would like you to meet.

6 **present**
   i) The present Foreign Secretary is better than the last one.
   ii) Is everybody present?

7 **concerned**
   i) Why do you have such a concerned expression on your face?
   ii) I wish to speak to the people concerned.

8 **proper**
   i) This is not the proper time to talk about money.
   ii) I mean the town proper, excluding the suburbs.

9 **involved**
   i) I do not want to hear a long involved explanation.
   ii) The police took statements from everyone involved in the accident.

4.12
Complete the unfinished words in these sentences either with **-ing** or with **-ed** according to the meaning of the sentence.
1 I find these figures very disturb_____.
2 It is surpris_____ how many people cannot swim.

3 We showed them our holiday slides. They said nothing but I think they found them quite interest_____.

4 The children seemed to be thrill_____ with their presents.

5 He looked bor_____ but he assured me he was having a good time.

6 He had a satisf_____ expression on his face. He was obviously pleas_____ with himself.

7 I went to the sauna for a really relax_____ massage. Afterwards, I felt very relax_____.

8 I have never been so embarrass_____ in my life – I had forgotten my notes!

9 That is a very tir_____ job: no wonder you look so exhaust_____.

10 He kept us entertain_____ with excit_____ stories about his African adventures.

11 I find penguins the most fascinat_____ animals in the zoo.

12 Do you get many disappoint_____ customers, or are most people satisf_____ with your service?

4.13

A field which is fifty acres in extent is a *fifty-acre field*. Make similar compound adjectives from the following:

1 a programme which lasts half an hour
   a _____ programme

2 a drive which takes five hours
   a _____ drive

3 a lorry which can carry 15 tons
   a _____ lorry

4 a flight which lasts 3½ hours
   a _____ flight

5 a ruler which measures up to twelve inches
   a _____ ruler

6 an engine with a capacity of 3½ litres
   a _____ engine

7 a child which is five years old
   a _____ child

8 a man whose height is six feet
   a _____ man

9 a walk which covers eight miles
   a _____ walk

10 a tank with a capacity of 16 gallons
   a _____ tank

11 a 300mm telephoto lens
   a _____ telephoto lens

12 a **** hotel
   a _____ hotel

A castle which was built in the fourteenth century is a *fourteenth-century castle*. Make similar compound adjectives with the following:

13 a student who is in his second year.
   a _____ student

14 a flat on the third floor
   a _____ flat

15 a computer which is of the second generation
   a _____ computer

16 a decision made at the last minute
   a _____ decision

17 an excellent meal
   a _____-class meal

18 a very poor production
   a _____-rate production

4.14
Complete the table.

He is from	He is a(n)	He speaks
1 Hungary	Hungarian	Hungarian
2 Saudi Arabia		
3 Denmark		
4 Poland		
5 England		
6 Spain		
7 Holland		
8 Turkey		
9 Portugal		
10 Japan		
11 Norway		
12 USSR		
13 Czechoslovakia		
14 China		
15 Finland		
16 Israel		
17 Greece		
18 Thailand		

4.15
Put the following into the correct order:
1 English / lovely / several / old   tables
2 pretty / French / young / a lot of   girls
3 dining-room / Regency / few / valuable / last / these   chairs
4 first / really important / Impressionist / his / three   paintings
5 dark blue / best / silk / my / all   shirts
6 young / many / German   factory workers
7 marble-topped / old-fashioned / these / oval / all   wash stands
8 wildlife / Mike's / all / black and white / latest / photographs
9 cotton / a few / plain* / hand-woven / carefully-chosen   dresses
10 non-stick / brand-new / a number of / French-made   frying pans
11 really important / the first / national / government-sponsored survey
12 one-month / last / his / exhausting / European   tour

*(Note: regard *plain* as a colour category)

4.16
Form the comparative and superlative of these adjectives. They all take -(e)r and -(e)st, except for numbers 9 and 23. Pay attention to any spelling changes which are necessary.

1	tiny	13	grey	25	soon
2	handsome	14	late	26	thin
3	lively	15	quiet	27	calm
4	dry	16	polite	28	healthy
5	pleasant	17	clever	29	true
6	simple	18	big	30	wide
7	mellow	19	fat	31	early
8	good	20	wide	32	narrow
9	bad	21	foggy	33	free
10	far	22	able	34	rare
11	sad	23	ill	35	flat
12	heavy	24	common	36	pretty

4.17
Make up sentences on the pattern A > B.

       big

For example A > B becomes A is bigger than B.

No.	A	adj	B
1	Anna	old >	Louise.
2	Girls	clever >	boys.
3	The sun	bright >	the moon.
4	Northerners	friendly >	southerners.
5	Rome	beautiful >	Milan.
6	Cats	intelligent >	dogs.
7	Dior dresses	elegant >	Balmain's.
8	Men	sensible >	women.
9	The English	witty >	the Americans.
10	Some people	honest >	others.
11	Physics	hard >	chemistry.
12	Boys	sensitive >	girls.

(*Note:* you may not agree with the opinions given in this exercise or the next one!)

4.18
Make up sentences using these four patterns:

$\left\{\begin{array}{l} A = B \longrightarrow A \text{ is as } \textbf{adj} \text{ as } B. \\ A > B \longrightarrow A \text{ is more } \textbf{adj} \text{ than } B. \\ \qquad\qquad (or \underline{\qquad} er than) \end{array}\right.$

$\left\{\begin{array}{l} A \neq B \longrightarrow A \text{ is not as/so } \textbf{adj} \text{ as } B. \\ A < B \longrightarrow A \text{ is less } \textbf{adj} \text{ than } B. \end{array}\right.$

No.	A	adj	B
1	English	easy >	Japanese.
2	Japanese	difficult >	English.
3	Japanese	easy ≠	English.
4	Health	important >	money.
5	A change	good =	rest.

		common	
6	Blackbirds	>	eagles.

		welcome	
7	You	=	flowers in May.

		interesting	
8	Programmes	<	they used to be.

		bad	
9	Thirst	>	hunger.

		good	
10	Half a loaf	>	no loaf at all.

		good	
11	Things	≠	they used to be.

		healthy	
12	Jogging	>	smoking.

		harmful	
13	Cigarettes	<	cigars.

		far away	
14	Pluto	>	Mars.

		distant	
15	Pluto	>	Mars.

		distant	
16	Mars	<	Pluto.

		ill	
17	She	>	she was yesterday.

		noisy	
18	The towns	>	the villages.

4.19

Put the adjectives in brackets into the form which best suits the meaning of the sentence.

1 That is (incredible) story I have ever heard!
2 It is not always (bright) students who do well in tests.
3 Terylene shirts are harder-wearing, but cotton shirts are much (comfortable).
4 Which is (deep), Lake Garda or Lake Iseo?
5 She is much (self-confident) than she used to be.
6 (tall) man in Manresa is a basketball player.
7 I like both of them, but I think Michael is (easy) to talk to.
8 Most people are (well off) than their parents were.
9 She has a lot to be thankful for – (sad) thing of all is that she does not realize it.
10 I want to rent a car – (powerful) one you have.
11 You look a lot (well) than you did last time I saw you.

12 There is nothing (irritating) than locking yourself out of your own house.
13 Both roads lead to the city centre, but the left-hand one is probably a bit (short) and (direct).
14 As I get (old), I notice that the policemen seem to be getting (young)!
15 Nothing could be (fine) than to be in Carolina. (*song title*)
16 'Is Cambridge (old) university in Britain?' 'No, Oxford is about 50 years (old).'
17 If you were (tidy) and (well-organized) than you are, you would not keep losing things.
18 The boys in our school are much (good-looking) and a lot (good) at football than the boys in other schools in the town.

Just for fun

4.20 'Muddle-headed and boggle-eyed'
Here are *fourteen* compound adjectives, and definitions for *ten* of them. Can you match the definitions and ten of the adjectives?

blue-eyed, bow-legged, broad-minded, broad-shouldered, cross-eyed, flat-footed, good-natured, knock-kneed, left-handed, narrow-minded, open-hearted, round-shouldered, short-tempered, thick-skinned.

Definitions

1 describes someone who gets angry very easily
2 describes the result of too much horseriding
3 describes a very tolerant person
4 describes an intolerant person
5 we call the boss's favourite 'the boss's _____ boy'
6 describes a person with a pleasant, generous character
7 describes a person who is not at all sensitive to other people's feelings
8 Ten per cent of the population are this: you notice it when they write, for example.
9 describes your appearance if you try to look at the tip of your own nose!
10 describes, for example, a boxer's physique (body)

Unit 5 Pronouns

5.1
Rewrite this passage, putting in suitable pronouns and possessive adjectives. (Note: the duck is female and the frog is male.)

One summer's day, a duck decided to go to the river for a picnic. _____ took a lot of food with _____, and was really looking forward to eating _____. _____ sat down on the river bank, and spread the food out in front of _____.

'_____'re not going to eat all that food _____, are _____?' said a small voice. _____ looked up and saw a frog sitting at the water's edge.

'Please give _____ some of _____,' pleaded the frog, wiping a tear from _____ eyes.

She gave _____ a sandwich. To _____ surprise, _____ did not eat _____, but simply put _____ on the ground beside _____.

'Won't _____ give _____ something else? After all, my need is greater than _____.'

Bit by bit, the duck handed over most of _____ food. Soon, the frog had a huge pile of food in front of _____. With an effort _____ picked _____ all up and started to swim across the river. But the food was so heavy that the frog and _____ load sank like a stone and the duck never saw _____ of _____ again.

Moral: When _____ is hard to say 'no', say 'no'.

5.2
Give short answers to these questions. Use the pronoun I and take care with the verb form.

Example

	⊕	⊖
'Who wants a drink?'	—	

Answer: 'I do.'

Who wants a drink?'		—

Answer: 'I don't.'

		⊕	⊖
1	Who did that?	—	
2	Who is coming with me?	—	
3	Who likes macaroni?		—
4	Who put my coat on the floor?		—
5	Who's been sitting in my chair?	—	
6	Who can spell 'receive'?	—	
7	Who will go and fetch me a paper?		—
8	Who has got a red pen?		—
9	Who wants to go to the pictures?	—	
10	Who broke this window?		—

11	Who would like to go for a walk?	—	
12	Who made the cakes?	—	
13	Who doesn't like cabbage?		—
14	Who could swim a hundred metres underwater?	—	
15	Who knows how to work the record player?	—	
16	Who made all this mess?		—
17	Who has not finished yet?		—
18	Who has to do all the work? (2 answers)	—	

Repeat the exercise using the pronouns **he** or **she** instead of **I**.
Repeat the exercise using the pronoun **they**.

5.3
a Complete these sentences using the impersonal pronoun **it**.
e.g. (snow), so we stayed in
Answer: It was snowing (or *It had been snowing*) so we stayed in.

1   (so cold) that the river froze over.
2   (rain) when I left the house.
3   If (rain) we will stay in. (*2 possibilities*)
4   (warm) today – you do not need an overcoat.
5   You cannot take good photographs when (cloudy).
6   Do you think   (freeze) at the moment?
7   I do not like to go sailing when   (too windy).
8   (very late)   – I must go now.
9   (three miles) to the nearest petrol station, and I had to walk all the way.

b Now, complete these sentences using the pattern THERE + IS / WAS
e.g. I do not understand / *one thing*.
Answer: There is one thing I do not understand.

10   *some people* / are waiting to see you
11   *very little* / was / left to eat
12   I cannot do / *much* / about it
13   *some letters* / are here / for you
14   *a bit of cheese* / is / in the refrigerator
15   *a lovely smell* / is / in here

16   I should like / *nothing better* / than to stay here with you
17   I want / to tell you / *something*
18   *nothing* / is / broken

5.4
The statement *X is important* becomes *It is important to/that X*
when X is a long phrase or group of words.
Make up sentences on the pattern IT IS ADJECTIVE TO/(THAT) X from the information given:

	X	*Adjective*
1	speak another language fluently	difficult
2	everyone should keep quiet about it	important
3	believe he was once a school principal	hard
4	everything should be finished on time	vital
5	do a full-time job and run a home	not easy
6	just sit and watch other people	interesting
7	nobody else noticed the mistake	curious
8	he failed his examination	incredible to me
9	be able to speak other languages	unnecessary for you
10	to leave while it is still light	better

11 you and I should not be
    seen together   better
12 learn that everyone
    passed the test   pleasing
13 read every page   not necessary
                                 for you
14 you did not notice
    anything wrong   surprising
15 repeat the course   not worthwhile
                                 for you
16 you should say that   funny
17 know the name of every   impossible for
    pupil   him
18 work overtime   essential for me

5.5

Make up sentences using each of the adjectives in column C in turn, with a suitable completion from column F. You have a free choice of verbs from column B and some choice of pronoun from column E. Take care to choose the correct preposition from column D.

e.g. 1 *kind*. You could make up the sentence, *It was kind of him to say that.*

Note that you can use more than one of the phrases in column F with the same adjective if you want to – *as long as your sentence makes sense.*

Note also that both prepositions in Column D may be correct but the meaning is different.

A	B	C	D	E	F
It	is is not was must be could be cannot be would be would have been	1 kind 2 wrong 3 good 4 hard 5 easy 6 annoying 7 nice 8 interesting 9 clever 10 not good 11 useful 12 stupid	for of	me you him her us	to join the society to say that to help us like this to find out what was going on to bring up four children on your own to have to miss all the fun not to keep a copy of the letter to have been invited to the party to be on your own so much to hide the truth from you to come to the meeting to believe he had taken the money

5.6

In English, it is possible to make general statements using the pronouns **we, you, they** in an impersonal sense. In each of these sentences, put the pronoun **we (us, our), you (your)** or **they (them, their)**. Choose the word which best suits the meaning of the sentence.

1 '_____ can never find a taxi when _____ need one.'
2 'I see _____ have invented a bomb which will kill people without damaging property. What will _____ think of next?'
3 '_____'ll kill us all with these dangerous weapons _____ are inventing!'

4 '_____ must not grumble, I suppose. _____'ve had a pretty good year.'
5 '_____ never know who _____'ll bump into when _____ go out.'
6 'It says in the paper that _____'ve had a lot of rain in the West Country. I'm glad I'm not there!'
7 'Enjoy _____selves while _____ can: _____ cannot take the money with _____ when _____ die.'
8 '_____ say _____ are going to have a hard winter.'
9 'Do you think _____ might let _____ have a party if _____ promise not to make a noise?'

10 'Fellow-students, _____ can only persuade the authorities to give in to _____ demands if _____ remain united. Let _____ stand together!'

11 '_____ can lead a horse to water, but _____ cannot make him drink.'

12 'It says in the paper that _____ are thinking of putting up the price of petrol again.'

5.7

Replace the underlined noun with a pronoun, and make any other changes which are necessary. Take care with the prepositions **to** and **for**.

e.g. Give John a <u>present</u>
   Answer: Give *it* to John.
   Give <u>John</u> a present
   Answer: Give *it* to *him*.

1 Hand <u>John</u> his glasses.
2 Hand John <u>his glasses</u>.
3 Teach <u>the children</u> the alphabet.
4 Teach the children <u>the alphabet</u>.
5 Buy <u>Mary</u> the flowers.
6 Buy Mary <u>the flowers</u>.
7 Buy <u>Mary</u> <u>the flowers</u>.

8 Get <u>Father</u> the paper.
9 Get Father <u>the paper</u>.
10 Fetch <u>Anna</u> her briefcase.
11 Fetch Anna <u>her briefcase</u>.
12 Tell <u>the students</u> the truth.
13 Tell <u>the students</u> the truth.
14 Send George <u>the money</u>.
15 Send <u>George</u> the money.
16 Tell everyone <u>the news</u>.
17 Bring me <u>your work</u>.
18 Show <u>the boss</u> <u>the accounts</u>.

5.8

a How many meaningful sentences can you make from the elements in the three columns? (The sentence *There is an elephant in your ear* is grammatically correct, but not *meaningful*.)

b If you read straight across, you can make meaningful sentences
e.g. 1 They told me a strange story.
In each case, make the noun or pronoun in column 2 the subject of the sentence to form sentences using the pattern I WAS GIVEN A PRIZE.
e.g. They told me a strange story. *becomes*
    I was told a strange story.

1	They told	me	a strange story.
2	They gave	him	a fortnight's holiday.
3	They will teach	you	how to defend yourself.
4	They handed	every contestant	a sealed envelope.
5	They have awarded	John	first prize.
6	They promised	us	a pay increase.
7	They will ask	you	a number of questions.
8	They have not told	the people	the truth.
9	They have offered	us	another flat.
10	They will show	you	how to meditate.
11	They have found	her	a job.
12	They are not telling	us	anything.

5.9

Put the appropriate possessive adjective (**my,
your, his, her, our** or **their**) or the definite article
(**the**) into these sentences.

1   She sat in front of the mirror, running
_____ fingers through _____ hair.

2   'Do you want to put _____ coat on?' 'No,
I'll just put it round _____ shoulders.'

3   I felt somebody tap me on _____
shoulder, and then grab my arm.

4   I felt somebody tap _____ shoulder, and
then grab me by _____ arm.

5   He had _____ hat pulled well down over
_____ eyes, and _____ hands were
thrust deep into _____ pockets.

6   She turned up _____ collar of _____
coat to protect _____ neck from the cold
wind.

7   He was severely bruised about _____
legs, but _____ face was unmarked.

8   He shook me warmly by _____ hand and
put _____ arm round _____ shoulders.

9   Before you go to bed, make sure you wash
_____ face, brush _____ teeth and put
_____ clothes away neatly.

10   'Let me take you by _____ hand, and lead
you through the streets of London' (*line
from a popular song.*)

11   'Close _____ eyes, hold out _____
hand, and see what the good Lord has
brought you!' (*said when you want to give
a child a surprise present*)

12   'We were stabbed in _____ back' means
'we were betrayed by our own people'.

13   They lay on _____ backs and closed
_____ eyes.

14   If you do not want to hear it, put _____
fingers in _____ ears.

15   You look a mess! Tuck _____ blouse into
_____ skirt and straighten _____
shoulders.

16   I looked him straight in _____ eye and
told him to take _____ shirt off.

17   The police grabbed him by _____ scruff
of _____ neck, and put handcuffs on
_____ wrists.

18   '_____ shoe's untied, but I don't care,
I'm not figurin' on goin' nowhere*
I'd have to wash and to comb _____ hair,

And that's just wasted effort.' (*old folk
song*)

*In correct English, this should be, of course, *anywhere*.

5.10

In these sentences, choose the alternative that
fits.

1   Don't tell me your problems. I've got
enough problems of | me / mine / my own |.

2   Who is that man? Is he a friend of | you / your / yours |?

3   Come and sit beside | me / myself / mine |.

4   It belongs to an old friend | of my father's / from my father / of my father |.

5   She prefers to live by | her own / herself / her |.

6   She prefers to live on | herself / hers / her own |.

7   A friend of | my father / my father's | is a painter. He
painted this portrait of | mine / me / my own | when I
was only sixteen.

8   Is that car | your / yours | or is it | of your wife / your wife / your wife's |?

9   He has | his / an / the | own business.

10   What I would really like is a car of | the / one's / my |
own.

11 If a letter starts 'Dear Sir', it should finish with the words | You / 'Yours faithfully' / Your |.

12 Louisa's work is much tidier than | mine / me / my | or | of Anna / Anna / Anna's |.

5.11

In these sentences, choose the alternative that fits.

1 Don't do everything for | him / himself |, he must learn to do things for | him / himself |.

2 Please | you / yourself |. It is entirely up to | you / yourself |.

3 They are in love – they only have eyes for | themselves / each other |.

4 I'll see you both next year. Look after | you / yourselves |.

5 They are very fond of | themselves / each other |.

6 He is very conceited. He had a very high opinion of | him / himself |.

7 We had no difficulty in making | ourselves / us | understood.

8 She gave Michael the apple and kept the orange for | her / herself |.

9 The solicitor wrote a letter to John and | I / me / myself | in which he asked us if we could settle the matter between | us / ourselves |.

10 They had only five pounds between | them / themselves |, so they bought some food and shared it equally between | them / each other / themselves |.

11 He is old enough to | dress himself / get dressed | now.

12 I will join you as soon as I have | had a wash / washed myself | and | got dressed / dressed myself |.

13 As for | me / myself |, I prefer to let people make up | their own / each other's / one another's | minds.

14 Look after the pennies and the pounds will look after | them / each other / themselves |. (Proverb)

15 Everyone should ask | himself / oneself / themselves | if they are doing enough.

16 Put | you / yourself | in my position. Would you blame | you / yourself | if you were | I / me / myself |?

17 They seem to get on with | each other / themselves | very well.

18 We meet | us / ourselves / Ø | every day.

5.12
Give a suitable reply to the following questions
using ———self/ves.
e.g. 'Did someone wash your hair for you?' 'No,
I _____
Answer: 'No, I washed it myself.'

1   Did your mother make that for you?
    No, I _____
2   Did one of Mr Smith's employees give you
    that?
    No, Mr Smith _____
3   Was this violin made by one of
    Stradivarius's pupils?
    No, it _____
4   The students had a dance in the college. Did
    the teaching staff organize it?
    No, the students _____
5   What did you think of the film *Close
    Encounters*?
    I thought the film _____ boring, but I
    liked the music.

6   What do you think of 'The Police' (pop
    group)?
    I _____, but my friends think they are
    great.
7   Did you teach Anna to play the guitar?
    No, she _____
8   Who actually writes the Queen's speech?
    I don't think she _____
9   Do you want someone to go with you to the
    doctor's?
    No, I can _____
10 Will you do this exercise for me?
    No, do _____
11 Did the local police call in the CID to
    investigate the crime?
    No, they _____
12 Do you still wash and dress him?
    No, he is old enough to _____

5.13
Join these sentences with the relative pronouns
who, which or **whose**. If **who** or **which** can be
left out, leave them out.

1	I like people	speak their minds.
2	There is something	I do not understand about this.
3	She only eats vegetables	have been organically grown.
4	There are not many films	I really enjoy.
5	He is the sort of man	ideas make people really angry.
6	We are looking for someone	can help us in the shop.
7	What do you think of boys	wear make-up?
8	I recently met an author	books are all about witchcraft.
9	Only learn the words	are worth learning.
10	He is the man	everyone is talking about.
11	Is this the guitar	you bought in Spain?
12	There is a prejudice against people	speak with a strong accent.
13	Draw a triangle	sides measure 3, 4 and 5 cm.
14	Do you know anyone	birthday is in June?
15	I need a watch	has a built-in alarm.
16	Was it John	told you that?
17	I work for a company	turnover exceeds £5m. per annum.
18	The clothes	she wears are really strange.

5.14

Join the subject in column 1 to the expression in column 2 using the relative pronoun **who(m)**. If the pronoun can be left out, leave it out.

1	2
1 The man	invented the ball point pen.
2 The girl	he wants to marry.
3 People	go jogging.
4 The woman	interviewed you.
5 The policeman	won the medal for bravery.
6 The women	you talked to.
7 A man	I once met.
8 The couple	live next door.
9 Everyone	is involved.
10 The boy	you saw.
11 All the people	would like to meet you.
12 All the people	you would like to meet.

5.15

a Each of the numbered questions or statements below is followed by its response. Complete the responses with the interrogative pronouns **which?** or **what?** (In one or two cases either pronoun is possible.)

1 Could I speak to Mr Smith?
   _____ Mr Smith do you want?
2 Give me the money.
   _____ money?
3 Could I have my books back please?
   _____ are your books?
4 I'm going to buy some books.
   _____ books do you need to buy?
5 Put one of those logs on the fire.
   _____ one?
6 Where did you put the photos?
   _____ photos?
7 Anna and Louisa are nice girls.
   _____ class are they in?
8 My son is nearly seventeen.
   _____ subjects is he taking?
9 I fly either Swissair or British Airways.
   _____ airline do you prefer?

b Ask these questions with **which?** or **what?** In one or two cases either pronoun is possible.

10 _____ kind of films do you like?
11 I don't know _____ dress to wear tonight.
12 _____ of these sets do you recommend?
13 _____ buses go to the town centre?
14 _____ is your favourite food?
15 _____ food do you like best of all?
16 _____ food do you prefer, French or Italian?
17 I'd like to get a job, but I do not know _____ job suits me best.
18 A teacher soon gets to know _____ children are really interested in English, and _____ ones are not interested in the least.

5.16

a Complete these sentences with one of the words **some, any, no, body, thing, where + else**.

1 We always go to *La Lupa*. Can't we go _____ for a change?
2 'Did you give it to Anna?' 'No, I gave it to _____.'
3 'Is that all you need?' 'No, I want _____ as well.'
4 'Have you got what you need?' 'Yes, thanks, I don't need _____.'
5 'Why does Louisa always go around with Anna?' 'Because she doesn't know _____.'
6 'Why do you always come here?' 'Because there's _____ to go.'
7 'Why does she always wear the same dress?' 'Perhaps it is because she hasn't got _____ to wear.'
8 If you don't want it, I will give it to _____.
9 'Why do you always have your hair cut at Tony's?' '_____ cuts it as well as he does.'

b Complete these sentences with one of the possessive forms **some, any, no, every, + /body's** or **body else's** according to the meaning of the sentence.

10 He took _____ by mistake.
11 It wasn't _____ fault. It was just an accident.

12 She knows _____ secrets.
13 It's _____ business what I do in my private life.
14 Soon, _____ patience was exhausted.
15 _____ washing powder can give the same whiteness as DIZZ.
16 Why does _____ garden always look tidier than mine?
17 It was _____ fault. I am the one to blame.
18 Because his own bike had a flat tyre, he simply took _____ .

Just for fun

5.17 How mysterious!
How many pronouns (including the possessive adjectives) can you make from the letters of **how mysterious**? For example, the letters **m** and **y** form the word **my**, the letters **h** and **e** form the word **he**.

Score:
22–26 words   Brilliant!
15–21 words   Very good
10–14 words   Good
less than 10   We advise you to read Chapter 5 of *Cassell's Students' English Grammar*.

5.18 Watch yourself!
Can you form 12 reflexive verbs by matching these 12 verbs to the definitions given below?

Verbs
ask, behave, blame, enjoy, give, help, kill, let, make, please, pull, take

1   commit suicide
    _____ yourself
2   have a good time
    _____ yourself
3   feel guilty
    _____ yourself
4   wonder
    _____ yourself
5   take as much as you want
    _____ yourself
6   do only what you want to do
    _____ yourself
7   believe in your own importance
    _____ yourself seriously
8   behave as if you were in your own home
    _____ yourself at home
9   surrender (e.g., to the police)
    _____ yourself up
10 make an effort to regain your self-control
    _____ yourself together
11 relax
    _____ yourself go
12 do what you should do/not do anything wrong
    _____ yourself

Unit 6   Prepositions

6.1

Rewrite this passage putting in suitable prepositions.

Farmer Jones was very lonely and very bored. He lived _____ himself _____ an old house _____ the edge _____ the village and rarely talked _____ anyone. The villagers thought that he ought to have a pet _____ company, but the only pet they could find was a dog _____ only one ear.

When the farmer saw it, he shouted 'Get _____ _____ my house.' The dog, _____ his surprise, responded _____ doing exactly the opposite. It wagged its tail and went _____ the house.

The farmer stared _____ the funny dog _____ a while and then said finally 'Ah well, you might as well stay, I suppose. Come and sit _____ _____ me.'

The dog wagged its tail, but walked _____ _____ the man, and went to sit _____ the other side _____ the room.

'Sit on the chair,' said the farmer. The one-eared dog promptly sat _____ it.

The farmer took the dog outside and pointed up the road: the dog immediately turned round and went _____ the road!

'Why do you always do the opposite _____ what I tell you to do?' he asked. The dog just looked up _____ him _____ his head _____ one side, and his solitary ear sticking up _____ a radio aerial.

6.2 Opposites

Can you complete the table by giving the simple or compound preposition which is opposite in meaning to the one in the table? We have done the first one to help you.

1	up	down
2	above	
3	in	
4		under
5		outside
6		in front of
7	on top of	
8		from
9	towards	
10	with	
11	on to	
12		after
13		to (the hour)
14	including	
15	into	
16	near (to)	
17	like	
18		against (opposing)

6.3

Can you label the diagrams? Each letter stands for one of the prepositions listed underneath. (Note: the arrows go to, from, through or past the circle.)

1

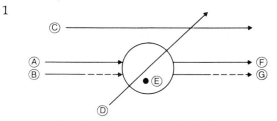

away from, from, in, past, through, to, towards

2

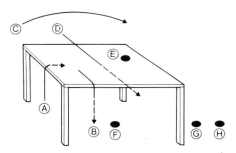

across, near, next to, off, on to, on, over, under

3

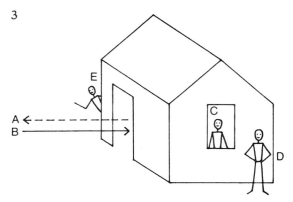

behind, in front of, inside, into, out of

4

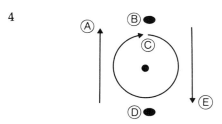

above, below, down, round, up

6.4

Which of the prepositions commonly form expressions with the words on the right? We have done one of them to help you.

a

above below on over under	
1 *above below*	sea level
2	the horizon
3	freezing point
4	the table
5	16 (years of age)
6	suspicion
7	protest
8	£200.00
9	the ground

b

at by during in on	
10	night
11	the night
12	(the) summer
13	seven o'clock
14	September
15	Monday
16	Mondays
17	7th October
18	the interval

6.5

Use some of the expressions from exercise 6.4 to complete these sentences. We have done number 4 to help you.

1 The sun rose . . .
2 La Paz is 12 400 feet . . .
3 The temperature seldom drops . . .
4 The dog sleeps **under the table.**
5 Children . . . are not admitted.
6 The police now know what happened: I am no longer . . .
7 All right, I'll sign it, but only . . .
8 It is quite a bargain: you should get it for . . .
9 He fell over and lay . . .
10 I usually stay in . . .
11 Where were you . . . of the accident?
12 We spend a lot of time on the beach . . .
13 See you . . .
14 The damage was done some time . . .
15 I should have finished . . . the latest.
16 She always used to do the washing . . .
17 I am having lunch with Elizabeth . . .
18 We stayed in our seats . . .

6.6

Which of the prepositions on the left form commonly-used expressions with the words on the right? (More than one may be possible.)

a

at on in	
1	present
2	time
3	times
4	my birthday
5	holiday
6	the time
7	the past
8	frequent intervals
9	future
10	this occasion
11	one time
12	recent years

b

for since	
13	the middle of last year
14	a number of years
15	she got married
16	ages
17	several hours
18	the last six months

c

during	while	
19		the interval
20		the children are in bed
21		the summer
22		the sun is shining
23		we have time
24		the present crisis

6.7

Use some of the expressions from Exercise 6.6 to complete these sentences.

(The numbers of the sentences are the same in exercises 6.6 and 6.7

e.g. 1 He is away + ____ present = 1 He is away at present)

1　He is away . . . .
2　You are only just . . . .
3　I get very lonely . . . .
4　What did you do . . . .
5　They have gone . . . .
6　It seemed like a good idea . . . .
7　We often used to have fights . . . .
8　They still meet . . . .
9　Look where you're going . . . .
10　I'll let you off . . . .
11　He used to be quite a good swimmer . . . .
12　I haven't seen much of them . . . .
13　He hasn't been here . . . .
14　They have been married . . . .
15　She has not worked . . . .
16　I haven't seen her . . . .
17　The discussion went on . . . .
18　We have been without electricity . . . .
19　We went for a coffee . . . .
20　We always watch TV . . . .
21　Where did you stay . . . ?
22　Shall we go to the beach . . . ?
23　Let's enjoy ourselves . . . .
24　Everyone must economize . . . .

6.8

Choose the correct preposition.

a　**at　in　to.**
1　How long has she been _____ hospital?
2　Will he be sent _____ prison?
3　Which university are you _____?
4　He's busy. He is _____ class _____ the moment.

5　Why don't you come _____ church with us?
6　I am _____ work until 5.30 most days.
7　I'll meet you _____ the airport.
8　One day a stranger came _____ town.
9　The ship was _____ sea for ten days.
10　You are _____ serious trouble.
11　How do the children get _____ school in the morning?
12　He'll end up _____ prison if he's not careful!

b　**by　until**
13　It will be ready _____ Thursday.
14　You will have to wait _____ Thursday.
15　We ought to be there _____ nine thirty.
16　_____ the time you receive this letter I shall be back in Italy.
17　They worked _____ ten and then went home.
18　It should have arrived _____ now.

c　**at　to**
Note: In one or two cases, you could use either **at** or **to**. Choose the one which fits the meaning of the sentence better.

1　It is rude to point _____ people.
2　'Catch!' she shouted, throwing the ball _____ him.
3　I need help. I look _____ you to support me.
4　Why are you shouting _____ me? What have I done wrong?
5　'Which ones do you want?' she said. I pointed _____ the biggest.
6　What are you laughing _____?
7　I waved _____ her, but she stayed where she was.
8　He stared _____ the object for a long time without speaking.
9　We shouted _____ Simon to come and join us.
10　The boys were throwing stones _____ an unfortunate cat.
11　I cannot get _____ the money: it is locked away in the safe.
12　I'm trying to get _____ Dorchester, but the road is blocked.

6.9
Choose the correct preposition.

a   by   with

1   Someone shot the deer _____ a high velocity rifle.
2   She was delighted _____ her present.
3   We got it clean _____ soaking it in soapy water.
4   I was reassured _____ his calm manner.
5   All the children went down _____ measles.
6   The blankets had all been chewed _____ mice.
7   He tried to open the tin _____ a knife.
8   We were amused _____ the way he kept repeating himself.
9   The cat was run over _____ a car.

b   of   from   by

10   Are you afraid _____ mice?
11   No, but I have a great fear _____ spiders.
12   Is this a picture _____ Degas?
13   No, it is one _____ Renoir's early paintings.

14   I bought a record _____ a symphony _____ Bruckner _____ a shop in Dorchester.
15   This is a rare stamp _____ my father's collection.
16   *If* is the title _____ a poem _____ Rudyard Kipling. It is one _____ Anna's favourites.
17   Everyone knows Mimi's song _____ the opera *La Bohème* _____ Puccini.
18   Lloyd George was an old friend _____ my father's.

6.10
In some of these sentences, you could use **about** or **on**. In others, only one of these prepositions is suitable. In the columns, mark the one you think is correct or more suitable with 1. If you think that the other word would also fit, but is less suited to the meaning of the sentence, mark the second word with a 2. We have done number 3 to help you.

	on	about	
1 Professor Hawkes gave a lecture			the Visigoths.
2 We had a nice little chat			the work he was doing.
3 Have you any good books	1	2	wildlife photography?
4 He taught a great deal			the English language.
5 She wrote an essay			'Freedom of Speech'.
6 She wrote us a long letter			her stay in Cannes.
7 He addressed the meeting			the subject of unions.
8 He told the children a story			duck and a frog.
9 My father could talk			any subject you like.
10 They had an interesting discussion			astrology and so on.
11 There will be a discussion tonight			Women and Society.
12 Could I have a word with you			a rather personal matter?

6.11

How many meaningful sentences can you make up from the three columns? (For each sentence you make up, try to describe – in English! – the situation in which it might have been said.)

	A		B		C
A	I want to see you	1	about	a)	a very serious matter.
		2	besides		
B	He came to see us	3	but	b)	the terrible road conditions.
		4	despite		
C	She seems to know everyone	5	except	c)	Christopher and his family.
		6	with		
D	You cannot leave	7	without	d)	those documents.
		8	concerning		
E	Everything must be recorded	9	including	e)	what was said at the meeting.

6.12

Which phrases in column **B** can complete the phrases in column **A**?

	A		B
1	She used to		
2	Do you want to	a)	live alone.
3	She is used to		
4	I need to		
5	I am looking forward to	b)	living alone.
6	Do you object to		
7	We expect to		
8	I am resigned to	c)	leave home.
9	Will you be able to		
10	You don't need to		
11	He talked her into	d)	leaving home.
12	He persuaded her to		

6.13

How many meaningful sentences can you make from this table?

1	I am			a)	getting up early.
2	I would never	A	resort to	b)	telling lies.
3	He isn't	B	confine ourselves to	c)	working in an office.
4	You'll soon get	C	object to	d)	driving on the left.
5	We should	D	accustomed to	e)	warning him not to do it again.
6	I definitely	E	looking forward to	f)	being told what to do.
7	She is	F	resign yourselves to	g)	listening to criticism.
8	We are really	G	used to	h)	going to Spain.
9	You'll have to			i)	taking a holiday at home.

6.14

From the table in Exercise 6.13, find a suitable reply to each of these statements of questions.

1 Surely you don't need to tell them the truth, do you?
'I would . . .

2 Why are you never late for work?
'Because I . . .

3 I'm really worried about taking my car to England.
'Don't worry. You'll . . .

4 Do you think we ought to expel him from (ask him to leave) the club?
'No, we should . . .

5 Why don't you do what you're told?
'Because I definitely . . .

6 We cannot afford a holiday abroad this year.
'In that case, you'll have to . . .

7 Are you feeling excited about your holiday?
'Yes, we are really . . .

8 Why is he always so miserable in the morning?
'Perhaps it is because he isn't . . .

9 How does she feel about her new job?
'I don't think she is . . .

6.15

Replace the underlined words by the preposition (or prepositional phrase) in brackets, and make any other changes which are necessary,

including supplying a part of the verb **to be** in some cases.
e.g. I have absolutely <u>no idea how to</u> solve mathematical problems. (hopeless)
Answer: I *am hopeless at* sol*ving* mathematical problems.

a

1   I <u>cannot type very well.</u> (no good)
2   I <u>think that I might</u> make mistakes. (afraid)
3   He <u>says he might</u> join the debating society. (interested)
4   She left <u>but she did not</u> say goodbye first. (without)
5   He <u>doesn't want to</u> work in an office <u>any more.</u> (tired)
6   Switch off the lights, <u>then you can</u> leave. (before)
7   They had a crash <u>because they</u> drove too fast. (through)
8   He is <u>one of the people who</u> runs the youth club. (involved)
9   She went on her own, <u>and did not</u> wait for the others. (instead)
10 I <u>regularly</u> get up while it is still dark. (accustomed)
11 She <u>does not always</u> remember people's names. (bad)
12 We can only improve <u>if we</u> work harder. (by)

b Rewrite these sentences beginning with the words given underneath each sentence.
e.g. It was very kind of you to invite us.
I'm grateful to you . . . .
Answer: I'm grateful to you *for inviting us*

13 I am glad that you phoned.
    Thank . . . .
14 They persuaded him not to go.
    He was discouraged . . .
15 They made it impossible for me to address the meeting.
    They prevented . . . .
16 The police said that he had driven without due care and attention.
    The police accused . . . .
17 He is trying to decide whether to change jobs.
    He is thinking . . . .

18 Do everything you can to get good grades in your examinations.
    Concentrate . . . .
19 Everybody was very pleased that Jeremy had passed his driving test.
    Everybody congratulated . . . .
20 The suspicion was that they had cheated.
    They were suspected . . . .
21 She would not have the courage to ask a man to dance with her.
    She would not dream . . . .
22 'Live a day at a time' – that is my philosophy.
    I believe . . . .
23 It will be a pleasure for me to visit you next summer.
    I'm looking forward . . . .
24 He often says how much he would like to emigrate to Australia.
    He talks a lot . . . .

6.16
Choose the preposition from column **B** which goes with the adjective in column **A**.

a	A	B	
1	different		what I had expected
2	fit	from	one more season
3	contrary		what people believe
4	ashamed		himself
5	aware	for	the possibilities
6	absent		work
7	new		this kind of situation
8	bound	to	Liverpool
9	capable		doing much better
10	grateful		everything you have done for us
11	not averse	of	earning a few pounds extra
12	conscious		what other people think of you

b	A	B	
13	late		school
14	jealous	from	his sister's success
15	due		the bad weather
16	separate		the rest of the money
17	ready	for	anything
18	fond		his nephews
19	proud		their student's results
20	allergic	to	scented soap
21	responsible		everyone's safety
22	safe		harm
23	sick	of	being told what to do
24	similar		the one we had at home

6.17

Choose the preposition in column **B** which goes with the verb in column **A**.

	A	**B**	
1	We rely		your discretion.
2	I borrowed some money	**about**	the bank.
3	Some young people rebel		authority.
4	How do you account	**against**	the difference?
5	Common salt consists	**for**	chlorine and sodium.
6	It appeals		my sense of humour.
7	I must apologize	**from**	being so late.
8	We have decided to abstain	**of**	voting.
9	Everyone in the world longs		peace.
10	Why did you get rid	**on**	your old car?
11	It doesn't amount		very much.
12	They asked me about	**to**	the accident.
		B	

b	**A**	**about**	rheumatism.
13	He suffers		how good you are.
14	It depends		his habit of coming late?
15	Has he been cured	**against**	
16	I can hardly wait		the summer to come!
17	Joe belongs	**for**	a number of societies.
18	Will you pay		the taxi?
19	It is time to ask	**from**	a pay increase.
20	Can one insure	**of**	being struck by lightning?
21	It is silly to worry		growing old.
22	This soup tastes	**on**	iodine.
23	He has just recovered		a serious illness.
24	In despair, I turned	**to**	the church for help.

6.18

How many meaningful sentences can you make from the following tables? (Remember: 'I ate a piano for breakfast' is grammatical, but not meaningful!)

a

1	Fresh air is			you.
2	My uncle is	good	for	me.
3	I am	bad	to	mathematics.
4	Too much smoking is		at	remembering names.
5	Most people are			

b

6	His face is	familiar	to	me.
7	Don't get	annoyed	with	the results.
8	He was very	angry	about	himself.
				the way things turned out.

c

9	She is very	sensitive	to	people's feelings.
10	He said he was	sorry	about	her failure.
			for	what other people had said.
				her.

6.19

Replace the words underlined with a compound preposition formed from the word in brackets, and make any other necessary changes.

1. All those <u>who think that we should</u> go on strike, raise your hands. (favour)
2. <u>If you believe what it says in the papers,</u> we are in for a crisis. (according)
3. <u>Speaking as a representative</u> of the committee, I should like to thank you all for what you have done. (behalf)
4. <u>Taking into consideration</u> the number of absences, I have decided that nobody will get a certificate! (view)
5. <u>Even though there was</u> deep snow everywhere, he decided to go out. (spite)
6. Everyone on the staff <u>with the exception of</u> Simon liked the idea. (apart)
7. We dealt with all the prepositions which express relationships <u>but we excluded</u> those which refer to time and space. (other)
8. <u>Having decided not to</u> wait for the others, he went on ahead. (instead)
9. <u>They were not only kind enough to</u> visit her in hospital, but they also looked after her bungalow for her. (addition)
10. Tonight's play has been cancelled; <u>this is because there has been</u> a lack of interest. (owing)
11. The fire in the oil well was put out, <u>and in order to achieve this they used</u> explosives. (means)
12. <u>If a fire should break out,</u> sound the alarm. (case)

Unit 7   Verb forms

7.1
Rewrite this passage, putting the verbs in brackets into a suitable form. In some cases no change is needed, and in others more than one form might fit the sense of the sentence.

The farmer (stare) down at the dog. He simply (can) not (understand) such peculiar behaviour.
   'Perhaps it (be) because the poor thing (have) only one ear,' he (think) to himself. Anyway, he (begin) to spend all his spare time (train) the dog, until eventually it (do) everything he (order) – as long as he (say) the opposite of what he (want).
   A horse, which (watch) these strange events, finally (ask) the dog 'Why (do) you always do the opposite of what he (tell) you to (do)? Is it because you (have) only one ear?'
   'Of course not,' (reply) the dog. 'I (start) to (do) it because I (not/think) he (be) interested in an ordinary dog, do you?' And, indeed, the farmer (be) no longer lonely or bored: he now (have) very interesting company.

Moral: There (be) nothing peculiar about (be) peculiar.

Note: The exercises which follow are mainly concerned with the *form* of verbs. The *use* and *meaning* of these forms are dealt with in Units 8, 9 and 10.

7.2
How many grammatical combinations can you make from the tables, i.e., by adding **it** to an item from column **A** + an item from column **B**. Example: IT + CAN + MOVE forms the grammatically correct combination *it can move.*

a

		A		B
It	1	is		a) move.
	2	was		b) moving.
	3	will be		c) moved.
	4	can		

b

It	1	has		a) move.
	2	has been		b) moving.
	3	will		c) moved.
	4	should be		

c

It	1	Ø		a) move.
	2	ought to		b) moves.
	3	doesn't		c) moved.
	4	didn't		

Note: in this and other exercises, the symbol Ø represents the empty category, i.e., there is nothing in this space. For example, IT + Ø + MOVED = it moved.

7.3
Instructions as for Exercise 7.2

a

		A	B
He	1	had	a) talk.
	2	had been	b) talking.
	3	would	c) talked.
	4	would have	
	5	would have been	

b

I	1	Ø	a) go.
	2	must	b) goes.
	3	must be	c) going.
	4	had to	d) went.

c

A She	1	Ø	a) work.
B They	2	don't	b) works.
	3	won't	c) working.
	4	won't be	d) worked.

7.4
Instructions as for Exercise 7.2

a

	1	Does		a) work?
	2	Did	she	b) works?
	3	Has		c) working?
	4	Is		d) worked?

b

	1	Haven't		a) Ø	A see		
	2	Didn't	you	b) be	B seeing	him?
	3	Won't		c) been	C seen		
	4	Had					

c

	1	Ø	a)	been able to	
I	2	haven't	b)	be able to	do it.
	3	won't	c)	had to	
	4	wouldn't have	d)	have had to	

7.5
Instructions as for Exercise 7.2

a

	1	is	a)	Ø	
It	2	was	b)	be	done.
	3	has	c)	being	
	4	had	d)	been	

b

	1	must	a)	Ø	
It	2	must have	b)	be	done.
	3	could	c)	being	
	4	could have	d)	been	

c

	1	would not	a)	move .
They	2	cannot	b)	be moved .
	3	have not	c)	moved .
	4	did not need to	d)	been moved .

7.6
Rephrase the complete sentences beginning with the word(s) given underneath each sentence. (i.e., from **active** to **passive** or vice versa). Take care to keep the correct **tense**. We have done the first sentences to help you.

a
1 They announced a delay.
  A delay was announced.
2 They have announced a delay.
  A delay . . .
3 Somebody wants you on the phone.
  You . . .
4 They make these cars in Japan.
  These cars . . .
5 They are building a new factory here.
  A new factory . . .
6 We could not move it.
  It . . .
7 Has somebody fed the dog?
  Has the dog . . .
8 Is someone picking you up tonight?
  Are you . . .
9 You must keep the money in the safe.
  The money . . .

b
10 My car has been stolen.
   Someone has stolen my car.
11 My car was stolen last year.
   Last year, thieves . . .
12 The car will have to be sold.
   I . . .
13 He is being watched very closely.
   The police . . .
14 No special skills are needed to operate this machine.
   You . . .
15 It is said that money cannot buy happiness.
   They . . .
16 I wasn't fooled by his story.
   His story . . .
17 He could not be persuaded to leave.
   Nobody . . .
18 I was told to wait outside.
   The secretary . . .

7.7
a Use **can/could** or a part of **be able to** in these sentences. In some cases, more than one form may fit the meaning of the sentence.
1 I _____ not see you tonight.
2 I will not _____ see you tonight.
3 Has he _____ get any more information?
4 I'm sorry I _____ not phone you earlier.
5 You ought to _____ catch the 4.41 if you hurry.
6 It would help me a lot if you _____ give me a lift.
7 If you are short of money, I might _____ lend you a few pounds.
8 You _____ not be working very hard if you _____ afford to go out every night.
9 It was awful to be in the same room without _____ talk to you.

b Use **must(n't)** or a part of **have to** in these sentences. In some cases, more than one form will fit.
10 Anna's very busy: she _____ write three essays this week.
11 You _____ be more careful in future.
12 Listen carefully. I don't want to _____ tell you twice.
13 I _____ wait for an hour for the bus yesterday morning.

14   There _____ have been at least 10 000 people there.

15   I wish I could just take the car without _____ ask permission every time.

16   We're very lucky, I suppose. We _____ grumble.

17   I might _____ go to London next Thursday.

18   This is the second time I _____ warn you about overspending.

7.8

Add **-s** or **-es** to these verbs (make any other necessary changes of spelling) and then enter them into the correct column according to the pronunciation of the ending. For example, add **-s** to **sit** to make **sits**, which is entered in column 1 because it is pronounced [sɪts].

	[s]	[z]	[ɪz]
1 go			
2 help			
3 say			
4 watch			
5 operate			
6 laugh			
7 emphasize			
8 belong			
9 like			
10 reply			
11 worry			
12 fix			
13 halve			
14 amuse			
15 climb			
16 fly			
17 judge			
18 bathe			

7.9

Add **-ed** or **-d** to these verbs (with any other necessary changes of spelling) and then enter them into the correct column according to the pronunciation of the ending. For example, **-ed** is added to **lift** which goes in column 3 because it is pronounced [lɪftɪd].

a		[t]	[d]	[ɪd]
1	like			
2	live			
3	want			
4	refuse			
5	laugh			
6	persuade			
7	try			
8	play			
9	reach			
10	offer			
11	benefit			
12	land			
13	photograph			
14	separate			
15	panic			
16	realize			
17	explode			
18	vanish			

b				
1	house			
2	fix			
3	decide			
4	search			
5	rub			
6	remind			
7	slip			
8	remember			
9	allow			
10	picnic			
11	profit			
12	insist			
13	worry			
14	giggle			
15	occur			
16	develop			
17	fit			
18	prefer			

7.10 Irregular verbs
Complete the table.

1	hear		
2		bound	
3			ridden
4	set		
5		fell	
6			found

7	become		
8		tore	
9		slid	
10	catch		
11		ate	
12	shut		
13	feed		
14		sought	
15			hurt
16	bite		
17		sold	
18			broken
19	spread		
20		lay	
21	lay		
22		drove	
23	deal		
24			drunk
25	beat		
26	show		
27		stuck	
28			led
29	strike		
30			flown
31		lost	
32			shaken
33	meet		
34	forbid		
35	mean		
36			cost

7.11

Replace the underlined words by the verb in brackets, making any necessary changes (e.g. of pronoun or tense).

1 They gave us false information. (mislead)
2 The word 'accommodation' is often written down incorrectly. (misspell)
3 If you think I would do such a thing, you are wrong! (mistake)
4 I don't know where I have put my calculator. (mislay)
5 The weatherman said that there would be more snow. (forecast)
6 We could not have known beforehand how much money we would need. (foresee)
7 Nostrodamus predicted that the French Revolution would take place. (foretell)
8 The council dealt with people's objections and the scheme went ahead. (overcome)
9 I was close enough to be aware of what they were saying. (overhear)

10 The car which went past us when we were driving on the motorway must have been doing at least a hundred miles an hour. (overtake)
11 I wanted the central heating to come on earlier so I made an alteration to the time switch. (reset)
12 Because of engine trouble, the Finnish team could no longer stay in the race. (withdraw)
13 The authorities decided not to make public the facts about the disaster. (withhold)
14 The soldiers were subjected to a hard training programme. (undergo)
15 Martin agreed that it would be his responsibility to provide the slides for Mike's lecture. (undertake)
16 This place has rats everywhere! (overrun)
17 She was a brilliant skater: her performance was much better than everyone else's. (outshine)
18 The Cathedral in Chartres has been destroyed and put back up again several times during its history. (rebuild)

7.12

Make these sentences *negative*, using the short form _____n't wherever possible. Make any other necessary changes.
e.g. He is going somewhere interesting.
Negative: He *isn't* going *any*where interesting.

1 There are some apples in the pantry.
2 She likes spaghetti bolognese.
3 I know something about it.
4 He is being examined this week.
5 I am used to being left alone.
6 Has the dog had something to eat?
7 They can go by car.
8 You must do some really hard physical work.
9 The concert will finish at ten o'clock.
10 Will you need to take some warm clothes with you?
11 Shall I see you again?
12 He would have done it without payment.
13 Has your car been serviced recently?
14 She put something in her handbag.
15 We were very happy with the arrangements.
16 You ought to have said something to him.

17 I have been feeling particularly well lately.
18 He used to be a heavy smoker.

7.13

a A mother could ask a young man three different questions about his love for her daughter depending on her (the mother's) attitude:

Mother wants to know:
'Do you love her?'   Symbol ⑦
Mother thinks so:
'You love her, don't you?'   Symbol ⊕
Mother doesn't think so:
'You don't love her, do you?'   Symbol ⊖

Ask the three different types of question, ?, + and − about the actions on the left. We have done the first one to help you.

	⑦	⊕	⊖
1 can swim	can you swim ?	You can swim, can't you ?	You can't swim, can you?
2 know the answer			
3 have answered his letter			
4 are coming with us			
5 like my book			
6 went to the bank			
7 have got enough money			
8 will be able to come			
9 have been drinking			

b Politely contradict these questions or statements using **do/does/did**.
e.g.: 'Why didn't you finish it?'
Reaction: 'But I *did* finish it!'

1 I'm sorry you don't want to go out with me.
2 I am surprised that your wife doesn't drive.
3 Why don't you practise?
4 It's a pity Sarah doesn't like mathematics.
5 Why didn't you tell me it was your birthday?
6 I know you don't really love me.
7 It's a shame your brother doesn't like card games.
8 I expect they've cut off your phone because you didn't pay the bill.
9 You would play much better if your practised.

7.14

Which of these verbs on the right end only in **-ise** and which can end in either **-ise** or **-ize**? We have done the first two to help you.

		-ise	-ize
1	adv-	advise	
2	apolog-	apologise	apologize
3	compr-		
4	modern-		
5	organ-		
6	rev-		
7	exerc-		
8	prom-		
9	general-		
10	dev-		
11	public-		
12	special-		
13	improv-		
14	econom-		
15	surpr-		
16	util-		
17	advert-		
18	critic-		
19	patron-		
20	superv-		
21	legal-		
22	maxim-		
23	disgu-		
24	visual-		
25	comprom-		
26	recogn-		
27	desp-		
28	final-		
29	telev-		
30	emphas-		

7.15

a The ending **-ate** may be pronounced [eɪt] or [ət] depending on the way the word is used. How is the ending pronounced in each of these sentences?

	[eɪt]	[ət]
1 I estimate we will be there by 6.		
2 She made an appropriate reply.		
3 The design proved to be too elaborate.		
4 Please moderate your language.		
5 Don't let the meeting degenerate into a row.		
6 It was a deliberate attack on the government.		
7 Please give me an estimate for the work.		
8 It is an approximate, not a precise, answer.		
9 There has been a moderate improvement in production.		
10 I always associate this song with Paris.		
11 He knows how to delegate responsibility.		
12 They appointed a man to co-ordinate the work.		

b Here are 13 verbs in **-ate**. Can you find the definitions for nine of them?

Verbs
segregate, evaluate, interrogate, simulate, collaborate, indicate, concentrate, demonstrate, stimulate, aggravate, assassinate, compensate, tolerate

Definitions
1 make the situation/things worse or more serious
2 kill a public figure for political reasons
3 put up with/accept other people's habits, opinions, etc.
4 think hard, to focus your mind on
5 keep groups of people apart, usually for racial or political reasons
6 excite someone, to make them want to do something
7 point out or to refer to something
8 try to decide what a plan, an idea, etc., is worth
9 prove something, to show how something works or why it is worth buying

7.16

a Form verbs from the stems by adding **-ize** or **-ify**.
More difficult: in the third column, put in nouns associated with or derived from the verb in column 1 or column 2.
We have done the first one to help you.

	-ize	-ify	Associated nouns
1 quant-		quantify	quantity
2 computer-			
3 electr-			
4 minim-			
5 styl-			
6 person-			
7 personal-			
8 liqu-			
9 divers-			
10 idol-			
11 solid-			
12 liquid-			
13 moral-			
14 fals-			
15 indemn-			
16 test-			
17 intens-			
18 mobil			

b Here are 13 verbs in **-ify**. Rephrase the following sentences using nine of those verbs (or words derived from them).
Verbs
certify, clarify, classify, exemplify, identify, justify, magnify, modify, mystify, notify, qualify, ratify, specify.
1 Can you say which man is the one who attacked you?
Can you _____ him?
2 I have no idea how he does that trick.
I am completely _____ .
3 He has not had the right training to do that work.
He is not _____ for that work.
4 She tried to defend what she had done.
She tried to _____ her actions.
5 These binoculars bring things eight times closer.
These binoculars have a _____ of 8x.
6 You will be told officially when your new flat is ready.
You will be _____ when it is ready.
7 It is not easy to sort the books into categories.
It is not easy to _____ them.
8 They have made some alterations to the engine to make it more efficient.
They have _____ the engine.
9 He offered additional information to make the situation clearer.
He _____ the situation.

7.17
a *Prefixes:* **re-, over-, under-, un-, mis-**
Add one of the above prefixes to the verb in brackets and replace the words underlined, making any other necessary changes.
1 I do not like food which has been <u>warmed up a second time.</u> (heat)
2 We have been <u>asked to pay too much</u> for this wine. (charge)
3 This steak is <u>too rare</u> in my opinion. (cook)
4 He <u>took everything out of</u> his suitcase. (pack)
5 I <u>was wrong in my estimate</u> of the cost of our holiday. (calculate)
6 The army <u>forcibly removed</u> the elected government. (throw)
7 He <u>gave back</u> the money he had borrowed. (pay)

8 I'm sorry I'm late: <u>I did not wake up at my usual time.</u> (sleep)
9 <u>I got a false impression of</u> his intentions. (interpret)

b *Prefixes* **re-, over-, un-, dis-, co-, out-.**
Add one of the above prefixes to the verb in brackets to complete the sentences, making any other necessary changes.
10 She _____ her coat and took it off. (button)
11 They have _____ the electricity supply because we have not paid the bill. (connect)
12 There are too many errors in your essay. It will have to be _____ . (write)
13 If they are to avoid war, the superpowers must learn to _____ . (exist)
14 John is such a big boy now: he has _____ all his clothes. (grow)
15 He _____ the knot instead of cutting the string. (tie)
16 The plane tried to land but _____ the runway. (shoot)
17 The arguments in favour of trying to reach base camp _____ the risks, so we set off at once. (weigh)
18 We could not find the dog anywhere. It had completely _____ ! (appear)

Just for fun

7.18 A matter of com-position!
How many verbs can you make from the prefixes in column 1 and the roots in column 2?

Prefixes		Verbal roots
ad-	(as-, at-)	-duce
con-	(com-	-fer
de-		-form
dis-	(dif-)	-fuse
ex-	(e-)	-ject
in-	(im-)	-mit
ob-	(of-, op-)	-pose
per-		-press
pre-		-scribe
pro-		-sent
re-		-serve
sub-	(suf-, sup-)	-tain
trans-		-tend

Unit 8   Verbs – meaning and uses

8.1

Rewrite this passage putting the verbs in brackets into a suitable tense form. In some cases, more than one form will fit the meaning of the sentence.

· The three bears (work) hard and (look) forward to a nice bowl of soup when they got home. What they (not/know) was that, while they were out, a pretty girl called Silverlocks (get) into their cottage. She (try) the soup in each dish, and (drink) up the soup in the smallest one. Then, because she (feel) very tired after her meal, she went into the other room, where there (be) three comfortable chairs. She (try) them all, but (choose) the smallest one to curl up in, because it (have) the softest cushions.

She was still there, fast asleep, when the three bears (come) back.

The bears (notice) at once that someone (be) in.

'Who (drink) my soup?' (shout) the big and the middle-sized bears at the same time.

'Someone (drink) up *all* my soup!' (squeak) the small bear.

Then they (go) into the next room, where the comfortable chairs (be).

'Who (sit) in my chair?' (say) the two bigger bears simultaneously.

The small bear (look) down at his chair, which (be) in the darkest corner of the room. He (say) nothing, but (wait) patiently for the other two bears to go away.

Moral: Two's company; four's a crowd.

8.2

Here are some questions and answers. You can work out from the nature of the answer which verb form is needed in the question. For example: the answer 'Yes, I thought it was very good.' fits the question 'Did you like the film?' rather than the question 'Do you like the film?'

1   'Where | do you come / are you coming | from?'
'I was born in Switzerland, but we moved to South Africa when I was three'.

2 | 'Do they get / 'Are they getting | more rain in northern than in southern Europe?'
'I believe the rainfall is much heavier in northern Europe.'

3 | 'Do you learn / 'Are you learning | to play the guitar?'
'Oh no, a friend of mine left that guitar here.'

4   'What | do you do / are you doing | for a living?
'I'm a chartered accountant.'

5   'Why | do you measure / are you measuring | that?'
'To see if it will fit in my kitchen.'

6   'How much | do you weigh / are you weighing | ?'
'About 170 pounds.'

7   'Why | does everybody get / is everybody getting | so angry?'
'They have just heard that the factory is going to close down.'

8   'How | do you make / are you making | a date and nut loaf?'
'I'll give you the recipe if you like.'

9   'What | do you do / are you doing | with that electric drill?'
'I've got to put up some shelves.'

10 'What time | does the post come / is the post coming | ?'
'About half past eight as a rule.'

11 'Why |does the post arrive / is the post arriving| so late at the moment?'
    'Because of the snow, I expect.'

12 |Does Janet come / Is Janet coming| to the party?'
    'I hope so.'

13 'Why |don't you work / aren't you working|?'
    'It's my teabreak!'

14 |Does Janet come / Is Janet coming| to your lectures?'
    'Sometimes.'

15 'What |do you get / are you getting| when you |add / are adding| magnesium to water?'
    'A very bright flash of light!'

16 'How many Christmas cards |do you send / are you sending| this year?'
    'I've decided not to send any.'

17 'How much petrol |does the tank hold / is the tank holding|?'
    'About 60 litres, I think.'

18 |Do you play / Are you playing| tennis this week?'
    'No, unfortunately. I've got to revise for my exams.'

8.3

a How many meaningful sentences can you make combining elements from each column or list?

i) 1 Are you coming to the dance
    2 Everybody is going to the dance
    3 We go swimming
    4 We are going swimming
    5 I play football

    a) tonight(?)
    b) every Saturday(?)
    c) on Saturday(?)
    d) most Thursday evenings(?)

ii)
1 He   a) always   A complains.
2 He is   b) seldom   B complaining.
            c) forever
            d) still

iii)
1 She   a) never   A gave me presents.
2 She was   b) always   B giving me presents.
            c) constantly

b Test the sentences you have made from the columns by describing a situation in which each one could be used.
e.g. There is a dance at school this evening. You ask a friend:
'Are you coming to the dance tonight?'

8.4

The verbs in brackets are verbs which usually occur in the present simple. They can, however, be used in the continuous form when they have another meaning, or when you want to emphasize the continuous or temporary nature of the action. Complete the sentences using the correct form.

1   i) I must stay in because I _____ a parcel.
    ii) I _____ you are tired after your walk.   (expect)

2   i) They may not accept my plan but at least they _____ .
    ii) Most people _____ him to be the best guitarist in America.   (consider)

3   i) I _____ the price of petrol has gone up again.
    ii) When _____ you _____ John again?   (see)

4   i) This jug _____ one litre exactly.
    ii) They _____ a meeting to discuss the matter.   (hold)

5   i) What _____ you _____ about?
    ii) What _____ you _____ about the new timetable?   (think)

6 i) He _____ the wine to see
      if it is all right.
   ii) This soup _____ funny.   (taste)
      What is it made of?

7 i) Don't let me down: I
      _____ on you!
   ii) Love? It _____ what you   (depend)
      mean by 'love'.

8 i) There's something wrong
      with my eyes: I _____
      double.
   ii) I _____ much better   (see)
      with glasses than without.

9 i) 'Was that a knock at the
      door?' 'I don't think so.
      You must _____ things.'
   ii) He isn't really deaf: he   (hear)
      _____ every word you
      say.

10 i) We'll discuss it when we
      _____ more time.
   ii) We _____ a lovely time,   (have)
      we wish you were here
      with us.

11 i) In the expression $e = mc^2$,
      the letter e _____ for
      energy.
   ii) How many Social   (stand)
      Democrats _____ for
      Parliament in this
      election?

12 i) The rule about uniforms
      _____ not _____ to
      older children.
   ii) How many universities   (apply)
      _____ you _____ to?

13 i) I _____ for a promotion,
      but I'll be lucky to get one.
   ii) I _____ you are not in a   (hope)
      hurry.

14 i) _____ you _____ fun?   (have)
   ii) _____ you _____
      change for a pound?

15 i) How much _____ it
      _____ to insure a car in
      England?
   ii) I shall have to give up   (cost)
      smoking: it _____ a
      fortune!

16 i) I _____ it is going to
      rain.
   ii) I _____ of going to   (think)
      Canada next spring.

17 i) He _____ to be very ill.
   ii) He _____ in *Aida* at   (appear)
      Covent Garden.

18 i) 'I've lost my handbag.'
      'What _____ it _____
      like?'
   ii) I _____ for a place to   (look)
      live.

8.5
Join the phrases in columns 1 and 2 to make as
many meaningful sentences as possible.

a

	1	2
1	He went there	a) a week ago.
2	He has been there	b) for a week.
		c) since Easter.

b

3	What did you do	e) last night?
4	What have you done	f) today?
5	Have you been	g) lately?
	working hard	h) this morning?
6	Did you work hard	

c

7	What were you doing	i) when the teacher
8	What did you do	came into the room?
9	What have you done	j) before you joined ICI?
		k) since I last saw you?

8.6
Use sentences which you have made from the
tables in Exercise 8.5 to answer these questions.
Sections a, b and c in this exercise correspond to
sections a, b and c in Exercise 8.5.

a

10	'How long did he go for?'	'He . . .'
11	'Is he still there?'	'Yes, he . . .'
12	'When did he go there?'	'He . .'
13	'How long has he been there?'	'He . . . *or* . . .'

In **b** and **c**, we give you answers to some of the questions which you can make from tables **b** and **c** in exercise 8.5. Match these answers to some of the questions.

b

14   'I stayed in.'
15   'Four tests!'
16   'Yes, I have.'
17   'No, we didn't.'

c

18   'Talking and making a noise.'
19   'We stood up.'
20   'I was working in Saudi Arabia.'
21   'I worked for Pirelli.'

8.7

b These charts give information about the lives of three people, Joe, Bill and Stephanie. Use the information to complete the sentences which follow. Use the verbs in brackets and pay attention to the tense which is needed.

8.7

a Which expressions go with the word **since** and which go with **for**?

Since	For	
		1 you left.
		2 I got married.
		3 a long time.
		4 several months.
		5 1982.
		6 the last time we met.
		7 a year.
		8 a fortnight ago.
		9 twelve months.
		10 April.
		11 ages.
		12 last summer.
		13 years.
		14 a fortnight.
		15 Easter.
		16 the whole summer.
		17 yesterday.
		18 a few seconds.

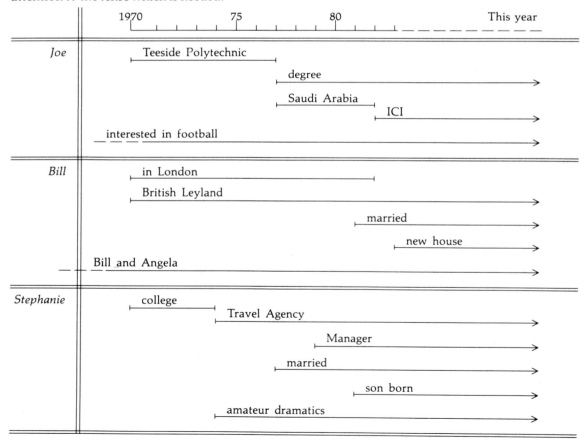

About Joe

(*Note:* _____ = **verb** needed; .... = **since/for** needed)

1 Joe _____ Teeside Polytechnic .... seven years. (study)
2 He _____ his BSc degree in 1977. (get)
3 After leaving Teeside, he _____ in Saudi Arabia .... five years. (work)
4 He _____ a science graduate .... 1977. (be)
5 He _____ Saudi in 1982, and _____ for ICI .... then (leave, work)
6 He _____ interested in football .... many years, but (be) he _____ football .... he was at school. (not/play)

(In the next two sections x is the number of years between the start of the action and the year in which you, the student, are doing this exercise)

About Bill

7 Bill _____ in London .... 12 years.
8 He _____ at British Leyland .... 1970.
9 He (always/have) the same job, and he (never/think) about changing.
10 He _____ married in 1981, i.e. he _____ married .... x years.
11 They _____ a new house x years ago.
12 Bill's wife is called Angela. They (meet) while they _____ at school: they _____ each other .... over 15 years.

About Stephanie

Ask questions about her. We have given the answers to help you.

Question	Answer	*Verb in question*
13 When _____ college?	1970–74	(be)
14 How long _____ travel agency?	x years	(work)
15 When _____ travel agency?	In 1974	(join)
16 How long _____ manager?	x years	(be)
17 How many children _____ since she got married?	Only one	(have)
18 When _____ interested in amateur dramatics?	After leaving college	(become)

8.8

How many phrases in column 2 can complete each of the phrases in column 1?

a	1	2
1	I used to play a lot of football	a) for six years.
2	I played a lot of football	b) when I was younger.
3	I haven't played much football	c) since I left school.
4	I didn't play much football	d) in the last few years.

b		
5	I haven't had anything to eat	e) up to that moment
6	I hadn't spoken	f) already.
7	I've had a lot to eat	g) yet.
8	I had waited	h) until then.

c Choose suitable sentences from **a** and **b** to complete these sentences:

9 _____, so I think I'll make myself a sandwich.
10 _____, but I still like to watch a good game.
11 _____, but I finally decided to say something.
12 _____, but I gave it up when I left school.
13 _____; I couldn't eat another thing!
14 _____ to hear what he had to say.
15 _____; I was far too busy studying for my exams.

8.9

Can you match each phrase in column 1 with a suitable phrase from column 2? Use each phrase only once.

a	1	2
1	I wanted to talk to Frances but	a) she left.
2	You cannot talk to Frances because	b) she was leaving.
3	I managed to catch Frances just as	c) she had already left.
4	I managed to catch Frances just before	d) she has already left.

b		
5	He has been working in the garden	e) — his hands were always dirty.
6	He had been working in the garden	f) — his hands are still dirty.

| 7 | He used to work a lot in the garden | g) | — his hands are always dirty. |
| 8 | He works a lot in the garden | h) | — his hands were still dirty. |

c

9	She has been in bed	i)	at 10 o'clock.
10	She always used to go to bed	j)	before she has had something to drink.
11	She was just going to bed	k)	since 10 o'clock.
12	She never goes to bed	l)	when the phone suddenly rang.

Of the 12 sentences you have made from **a**, **b** and **c**, which six sentences would fit the following?

13 _____, but now she stays up until midnight.

14 _____, so his wife told him to wash them.

15 _____. Never mind, I'll talk to her tomorrow.

16 _____. Please don't wake her up.

17 _____, so I left a message on her desk.

18 _____. He could never get them really clean.

8.10

a Replace each of these sentences with a sentence using the verb **let**. We have provided some words to help you.

1 I suggest that we go.　　_____, _____ we?

2 I should like to see that.　　_____ look.

3 She must not see what you are doing.　　_____

4 They can leave when they have finished.　　_____

5 They cannot leave until they have finished.　　_____

6 Why don't we have a party?　　_____, _____ we?

7 Give the bones to the dog.　　_____ have _____

8 Remind me to take the files with me.　　_____ forget to _____

9 I'll do that for you!　　_____

b **Do** is used with verbs to form a kind of imperative which expresses a request, an invitation, a suggestion, etc. Add sentences with **do** to each of the following, based on the words given in brackets.
e.g. 'You still look hungry.' (more sandwiches)
Answer: 'You still look hungry. Do have some more sandwiches.'

10 You room is a mess! (tidy)

11 There are a lot of schools along this road. (drive)

12 Let's keep in touch. (phone/any time)

13 Look at all the mistakes you have made. (careful in future)

14 I'm sure your boyfriend would enjoy himself. (bring/party)

15 I'm longing to see what you have written. (look)

16 You really ought to see a doctor. (appointment)

17 We'd love to hear about your interview. (what happened)

18 I think your car is in a very dangerous condition. (seen to)

8.11

In the sentence *A gave B a present* we are mainly telling you something about A. In the sentence *B was given a present*, we are more interested in B. Using the words in the table, answer the following pairs of questions with either an *A gave B a present* or *B was given* type of sentence according to the way the question is phrased. (Also, take care with tenses.)

Example
award/first prize
　'How did he get on in the competition?'
'He . . .
= He was awarded first prize.
　'What did the judges think of him?' They . . .
= They awarded him first prize.

1	give / day off
2	ask / to make a statement
3	tell / the truth
4	promise / an increase
5	show / the girl's photo
6	give us / our new timetables

7	hand / a note
8	send / a letter
9	teach / a new song
10	offer / another job
11	show / how to make an omelette
12	tell / to wait outside

1   i)   'What happened? Why aren't the children at school?' 'They . . .

    ii)   'How have you rewarded the children for being so good?' 'We . . .

2   i)   'What happened? What did the police say?' 'They . . .

    ii)   'What happened to you at the police station?' 'I . . .

3   i)   'How did you learn about things like politics?' 'My parents (always) . . .

    ii)   'Were you able to find out what you wanted to know?' 'Yes, I . . . always . . .

4   i)   'Are you getting more money next year?' 'Well, we . . .

    ii)   'What has the boss said about our pay?' 'He . . .

5   i)   'How will people know about the girl?' 'Everybody . . .

    ii)   'What will the police do to find the girl?' 'They . . .

6   i)   'What's happening? What is the teacher doing?' 'She . . .

    ii)   'What is happening on Wednesday?' 'We are . . .

7   i)   'How did Joe contact you if you were in a meeting?' 'My secretary . . .

    ii)   'How did you find out that the chairman had arrived?' 'I . . .

8   i)   'How will I hear about my examination results?' 'You . . .

    ii)   'Will the school let me know about my results?' 'Don't worry, someone . . .

9   i)   'What did you do at school today?' 'We . . .

    ii)   'What did the teacher do with you at school today?' 'She . . .

10   i)   'I heard you had lost your job. Has anything happened since?' 'Yes, I . . .

    ii)   'I thought your firm had made you redundant.' 'No, in fact they . . .

11   i)   'What did you learn in the cookery class?' 'We . . .

    ii)   'What did your cookery teacher do with you today?' 'He . . .

12   i)   'What did the receptionist say to you?' 'She . . .

    ii)   'Why aren't you inside?' 'We . . .

8.12

a These passages are written in the passive voice. Make them a little easier to understand by writing them in the active, starting with the word *You* . . .

i) Report of a chemical experiment
Avogadro's law can be used to give information about the equations for reactions involving gases. The reaction between NH_3 and HCl can be investigated by connecting two syringes. The tap between the syringes is opened and one gas is pushed into the other syringe. When the reaction is over, the volume of any remaining gas is measured.

ii) Instructions on how to clean a tape recorder head
Parts which are in contact with the tape should be cleaned from time to time. A soft cloth should be used, and it should be moistened with cleaning spirit. Before cleaning, the tape recorder should be disconnected from the mains, and the batteries should be removed.

b Here are some typical notices which you might see in any English town. What do they mean? (Use a complete sentence for each one. We have given you some words to help you).

1   ENGLISH SPOKEN
    All our staff_____

2   BOOKS BOUGHT AND SOLD
    We _____

3   KEYS CUT
    You can _____

4   CHEQUES NOT ACCEPTED WITHOUT A BANK CARD
    We _____ unless_____

5   HELP NEEDED
    We _____ someone to _____

6 DOGS NOT ALLOWED IN THE SHOP
   You _____ (bring) _____

c Here are some typical newspaper headlines. Use full sentences to say what they mean (Pay attention to tenses)

7 VILLAGES CUT OFF IN STORMS
   'The recent storms_____

8 SENIOR OFFICIAL ASSASSINATED
   'An unknown gunman _____

9 MAN HELD FOR QUESTIONING IN MURDER CASE
   'The police _____

10 'HOSTAGES TO BE FREED SOON'
   'The kidnappers _____

11 PETROL TO BE RATIONED?
   'Is it true that _____?

12 RAILWAYS: STRIKE DECLARED OFFICIAL
   'The Rail Union _____

8.13

a *Leonardo da Vinci designed a submarine* is a statement of *fact*
Leonardo da Vinci is reputed to have designed a submarine is an expression of opinion.
Change these statements of fact into expressions of belief, opinion, etc. using the verbs in brackets. Take care with tenses, and with the transformation of *can* in questions 8 and 9.

1 Girls mature earlier than boys. (say)
2 Charles Dickens had a hard childhood. (believe)
3 White rhinos are getting scarcer. (report)
4 Northerners are friendlier than southerners. (suppose)
5 Girls help their mothers in the house. (expect)
6 The Chinese discovered gunpowder. (know)
7 Mohammed Ali was the greatest boxer of all time. (acknowledge)
8 Women can stand pain better than men. (say)
9 Man can go for weeks without sleep. (say)

b Reply to the questions by making up sentences based on the words in brackets. Use the pattern shown in the example.
e.g. 'Why is this car in the museum?'
Answer: 'Because it was the first one to be made'
        (*or* ... 'one of the first ...')

10 'Why is this stamp so valuable?'
   'It ... (first/print)
11 'Do you know what is happening?'
   'Me? I'm always ... (last/tell)
12 'Did you go to the party?'
   'No, but ... (like/invite)
13 'Are you going to the party?'
   'Well, I ... (like/invite)
14 'What is special about this conference?'
   'It ... (first/hold abroad)
15 'Do you want to come with us?'
   'Of course. I ... (not want/leave out)
16 'Can I have one of these cakes?'
   'No, they ... (not eat/yet)
17 'Can we open our parcels now?'
   'No, they ... (not open/Christmas)
18 'Can I have something to eat, nurse?'
   'The doctor said you ... (not give/till tomorrow)

Unit 9 The future

9.1

Put the verbs in brackets into the tense which fits the meaning of the sentence. This exercise is a general revision of tenses, so take care. In some cases more than one verb form may be suitable.

A cat and a tortoise were having an argument.

'I (be) very fast, and you (be) very slow,' (say) the cat.

'All right,' (reply) the tortoise, 'we (have) a competition.'

'I (win)', (say) the cat at once.

'We (see),' (reply) the tortoise, (smile) to himself. 'I (bet) you that I (can) travel 100 metres in the same time as you.'

The cat (agree), sure that he (can) travel much faster than any tortoise. They (shake) hands, and the tortoise (lead) the cat to the top of a tall tower. You see, the tortoise (learn) about the law of gravity at school. One day, his teacher (speak) about gravity.

'What (that/mean)?' the tortoise (ask). He was not usually curious about things, but gravity (sound) to him like something a tortoise (can) make use of.

'It (mean),' (say) the teacher, 'that two bodies of different mass (fall) at the same speed, and (reach) the ground at the same time.'

The cat (look) down anxiously at the ground far below them. 'What (we/do)?' he (ask) in a small voice.

'We (jump) when I (count) three. 1 – 2 – 3, go!'

They (jump) and, thanks to the law of gravity, they (fall) together and (hit) the ground at exactly the same moment. The cat (land) on his feet, but the tortoise (land) on his back, (break) his shell and most of his bones. He (be) in hospital for a long time afterwards.

Moral: Gravity is strictly for cats.

9.2

a Above each pair of sentences there are two expressions. Put the expressions into the sentences, one for each, according to the meaning of each sentence.

1 *won't you / don't you*
   i)   Why _____ talk to me? What have I done wrong?
   ii) I'm afraid that Mr Smith is busy. Why _____ speak to Mr Jones instead?

2 *will you do / will you be doing*
   i)   I hear you are having a garden party this afternoon. What _____ if it rains?
   ii) What _____ at exactly 10.15 tonight?

3 *won't / wants to*
   i)   He _____ talk to you because he is rather shy.
   ii) He _____ talk to you but he is rather shy.

4 *I will go / I want to go*
   i)   Everyone else is busy so _____
   ii) Joe says he is going alone, but _____ too.

5 *I get / I'll get*
   i)   She is not feeling very well so _____ the papers for her.
   ii) Every morning _____ the papers for her.

6 *He won't work / He doesn't work*
   i)   _____ because he is lazy.
   ii) _____ because he is disabled.

7 *I'll come / I'm coming*
   i)   _____ with you if you like.
   ii) _____ whether you like it or not.

8   *won't go / won't be going*
   i)   I'm very busy so I _____ to her party.
   ii) I don't like her and I _____ to her party.

9   *will / won't*
   i)   _____ they come with us? We have a spare seat.
   ii) _____ they come with us? We would love to have them.

b In the following sentences, choose the form in brackets which you think best fits the meaning of the sentence. In 10–14, only one alternative is possible. In 15–18 more than one might fit: in these cases, choose the forms which are more likely to be used.

10   What _____ after school today? (do you do / are you doing)
11   What _____ tonight? (do you do / are you doing)
12   'If things get worse, I might lose my job.' 'What _____ do then?' (will you do / are you doing)
13   *You are saying goodbye to some people going on holiday. You ask:* 'Where _____ this time tomorrow?' (will you be / are you)
14   *You also ask:* 'What _____ this time tomorrow?' (are you doing / will you be doing)
15   I have heard that you _____ married on Saturday. Is it true? (get / are getting / will get)
16   I've got two tickets for the match on Saturday, _____ with me? (Are you coming / Will you come)
17   I believe the new restaurant _____ next week. (will open / will be opening)
18   We all want to know how you got on in the test. Why _____ us? (won't you tell / aren't you telling)

9.3

a How many expressions can you make from the elements in the columns? The symbol Ø means that no word is needed (i.e., the empty category).

She/He	1	Ø	a)	leave.
	2	is to	b)	leaves.
	3	will	c)	leaving.
	4	will be		

Use some of the expressions you find to complete these sentences. Choose the expression which best fits the meaning of the sentence.

1   'Here are his orders: he _____ leave for Spain at once.'
2   A fast train _____ for King's Cross every 20 minutes.
3   'Is it true that she _____ to get married?'
4   'Will you be here much longer?' 'No, I _____ in about five minutes' time.'
5   'Tell her to switch off all the lights before she _____.'
6   'I'm sure he _____ the TV on if you ask him to.'

b Make expressions from the elements in these columns. Then complete the sentences underneath.

We	1	'll	a)	Ø	A	drive
They	2	'll have	b)	be	B	driving
			c)	been	C	driven

7   'There isn't a train to Leicester.' 'O.K., we _____ instead.'
8   By the end of the rally, they _____ 2000 miles.
9   'If everything goes according to plan, we _____ through York at nine o'clock.'
10   'By 9.00 we _____ for five hours, so I suggest we take a break at 10.00.'
11   They _____ if they have to.
12   'By the end of the Motor Show, I expect we _____ every make of car in the exhibition!'

9.4

Which forms can be used in these sentences:

1   By the time you | receive / will receive / will have received | this letter, I | am / will be | in Thailand.

2 When you | are / will be | ready, I | start / will start | the engine.

3 As soon as I | hear / will hear / will have heard | something, I | will let / let | you know.

4 They | do not / will not | get in touch with you unless you | ask / are asking / will ask | them to do so.

5 | Do / Will | you do something for me before you | go / will go / are going | ?

6 If anyone | is calling / calls / will call | , tell them I | am / will be | back in half an hour.

7 I | don't / won't | start until everyone | is arriving / will arrive / has arrived | .

8 The race | is beginning / will begin | as soon as the signal | is given / will be given | .

9 Unless you | hear / will hear | to the contrary, you should assume that the meeting | takes place / will take place | as planned.

10 Before you | go / will go / are going | , | do / will | you do me a favour?

11 Please stop before you | get / will get / are getting | into trouble.

12 If you | don't / won't | want that sandwich, I | eat / will eat / will be eating | it.

13 If we | don't hurry / won't hurry / aren't hurrying | , the concert | is / will be / has been | over before we | get / will get | there!

14 | Will / Do | you please stay in your seats until the plane | is coming / will have come / has come | to a complete standstill.

15 Please stay in your seats while the plane | is still moving / still moves / will still move | .

16 They | don't / won't | go back to work until they | are given / will be given | a 12 per cent pay rise.

17 They | deliver / will deliver | the goods as soon as they | are able / will have been able / have been able | to clear customs.

18 I | do / will | not do anything until I | have had / will have / am having | a chance to talk to the foreman.

9.5

Each pair of sentences can be completed using a verb from the list at the top of the exercise. In each pair, one of the sentences would sound better with **going to** and the other would sound better with **will**.

Verbs

buy, do, eat, lend, marry, pull down, start, take, tell

1 i) This road is in a terrible condition.
       When _____ they _____ something
       about it?
   ii) This road is in a terrible condition. I
       suppose they _____ something about
       it sooner or later.

2 i) He _____ (not) _____ cakes: he
       says they are fattening.
   ii) _____ (not) _____ those cakes,
       _____ you? They are very fattening!

3 i) 'That bridge looks very unsafe.' 'Yes,
       they _____'
   ii) 'That bridge looks very unsafe.' 'I expect
       they _____ one of these days.'

4 i) 'Get a calculator of your own. I _____
       (not) _____ you mine.'
   ii) '_____ you _____ your calculator?
       I've left mine at home.'

5 i) 'Where have you been?' 'I _____ (not)
       _____ unless you promise to keep it to
       yourself.'
   ii) 'Where have you been?' 'I _____ (not)
       _____ you!'

6 i) '_____ (be) _____ Susan?' 'No, I
       think he wants to stay single.'
   ii) 'Do you think he _____ Susan?'

7 i) 'I shall have to walk to work. The car
       _____ (not) _____.'
   ii) 'We're wasting our time. It _____
       (not) _____: there's something wrong
       with the motor itself.'

8 i) 'I _____ a new car!'
   ii) 'How am I going to get to work every
       day? I know, I _____ a car!'

9 i) 'I _____ an umbrella with me.' 'Why?'
       'It might rain.'
   ii) 'I _____ an umbrella in case it rains.'

9.6

a Replace the words underlined in the first
sentence by an expression using WILL (NOT) BE
(. . . ING). Write the full forms, but if you do the
exercise orally, use the short forms (-**'ll** and
won't).

1 He's in his office.
   He _____ at this time of day.
2 He's having his lunch.
   He _____ about now.
3 I expect to see her on Friday.
   I _____ her on Friday.
4 I don't think he's back yet.
   He _____ back yet.
5 He is sure to be at the funeral.
   He _____ (come) _____ to the funeral,
   I'm sure.
6 We are expecting them to arrive at any
   moment.
   They _____ at any moment.
7 You must be very hungry after so much
   exercise.
   You _____ (feel) _____ after so much
   exercise.
8 I suppose you want something to eat.
   You _____ something to eat.
9 Everyone else is going to the dance tonight.
   What about you?
   Will _____ to the dance tonight?

b Replace the words underlined with an
expression using **will** or **won't**.

10 He refuses to eat.
   He _____
11 I cannot get the car to start.
   The car _____
12 I should like to invite you to come to the
   theatre tonight.
   _____ to the theatre tonight?
13 I really wish you would agree to come with
   us!
   _____ you _____ with us?
14 I am happy to make the beds if you are
   willing to do the washing up.
   I _____ if you _____.
15 No wonder he is overweight. He persists in
   eating between meals.
   No wonder he is overweight. He _____
   between meals!
16 I have a pen which does not write.
   My pen _____
17 I very much want you to come home, Bill
   Bailey.
   _____ you _____? (*title of an old song*)

18 <u>You cannot persuade her to</u> listen to
    anyone.
    She _____ to anyone.

9.7

Complete these sentences using expressions with
WILL (NOT) + ABLE TO, NEED TO or HAVE TO. (In
most cases, either **have to** or **need to** will fit).
The words in brackets will help you.

1   If I cannot go by car, _____. (train)
2   If I can borrow the book from the library, I
    _____. (buy one)
3   If it is raining tomorrow, we _____.
    (picnic)
4   If the buses aren't running, you _____.
    (taxi)
5   Once you get a job, you _____. (a car of
    your own)
6   If you intend to go to Poland, you _____.
    (apply for a visa)
7   We have seats right at the back of the
    theatre: we _____. (hear a thing)
8   It's a long way to Edinburgh: you _____.
    (set off early)
9   My passport expires next month: I _____.
    (new one)
10 My car has broken down: I _____.
    (borrow someone else's)
11 'I'm taking my car to Spain.' 'You _____
    an international driving licence before you
    go.' (get)
12 It is an X film (Adults only). The children
    _____. (get in)
13 'Why don't you get some glasses?'
    'I _____ first.' (eyes tested)
14 'I'm sorry, but I _____ tomorrow. I have
    to go to London.' (see)
15 All the lines are engaged. I _____ later.
    (try)
16 'They say they are going to get married.'
    'But _____ first?' (parents' permission)
17 If you practise, you _____ (soon)
    _____ as well as Segovia!' (play)
18 'I'm going to spend the weekend with my
    mother.'
    'You _____ you are coming.' (let her
    know)

9.8

Match each expression in column **A** with a
question tag from column **B**.

A	B
1 You won't forget,	a) aren't they?
2 Our train leaves from platform 3,	b) shall we?
3 The students are having a test,	c) aren't you?
4 Joe is leaving soon,	d) won't it?
5 We shan't need visas,	e) won't I?
6 Being married won't make any difference,	f) will you?
7 I'll see you again,	g) won't you?
8 You will be careful,	h) will it?
9 Susan isn't going to marry him,	i) doesn't it?
10 You are about to say something unpleasant,	j) isn't he?
11 It will be all right to park the car here,	k) will they?
12 Your parents won't mind,	l) is she?

Use six of the expressions to complete these
sentences. We have given you the first words of
number 13 to help you.

13 I know why the school is so quiet.
    The students are having a test.

14 Mountaineering is a dangerous sport.
    _____, _____?

15 I don't think this is a restricted area.
    _____, _____?

16 'It's very late. Why don't you spend the
    night here?' _____, _____?

17 The party is on Friday, and you are invited.
    _____, _____?

18 I think he is a horrible person _____,
    _____?

Just for fun

9.9 Seeing the light!
Study the circuit, and then deal with the problems we have set you.

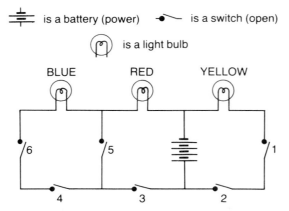

≐ is a battery (power)   ⊸ is a switch (open)

is a light bulb

1   Which light(s) come on when you close switches 1 and 2?
2   Which light(s) come on when you close switches 3 and 5?

3   Which light(s) come on when you close switches 3, 4 and 6?

Now, for the 'fun'! complete these sentences. Pay attention to changes of verb form, conjunction, etc.
e.g. The yellow light will come on if you close switches 1 and 2.

1   _____ switches 3 and 5.
2   Both _____ and _____ switches 3, 4 and 6.
3   _____ switches 1, 2, 3 and 5.
4   All the lights _____
5   If you want _____, you will have to close switches 3 and 5.
6   If _____ would _____ switches 1, 2, 3, 4 and 6.

e.g. The yellow light will not come on unless you close switches 1 and 2.
7   The red light _____
8   _____ if you didn't _____ 3 and 5.
9   Neither _____ nor _____ 3, 4 and 6.

Unit 10 Modals

10.1
Put the verbs in brackets into the form which best fits the meaning of the sentence.

There was once a hippopotamus who (be) a mathematical genius. He (can/do) any calculation in his head, and he always (get) the right answer. One day, he (lie) in his mudhole, (hum) to himself and (work) out π to 300 decimal places, when he (feel) a terrible pain behind the eyes.

'It (must/be) all this calculating that (give) me such a headache,' he (think), 'I really (ought/go) and have my eyes (test).'

To tell you the truth, the hippo (be) very short-sighted, but he (refuse) to (admit) it, even to himself. The optician (give) him a strong pair of glasses, and (say) (because he (not/want) to (hurt) the hippo's feelings):

'You (not/need) to (wear) them all the time, but I (think) you (wear) your glasses whenever you (feel) like (do) any sums in your head.'

'The hippo (catch) sight of himself in the mirror, and (think) how intelligent he (look) in his glasses, so he (keep) them on, stopping (admire) himself in every pool as he (walk) back to his mudhole. On the way he (spot) a notice nailed to a tree. Thanks to his wonderful new glasses, he (can/make) out what (write) on it. It (say), quite simply '2 + 2 = 5'!

10.2
a Use **can/cannot** or **could/could not** in these sentences (In some cases, either is possible.) In how many cases could you use a part of **be able to** instead, without any important change of meaning?

1 _____ you tell me the time, please?
2 No more for me thanks. I _____ eat another thing.
3 Who is that outside? It _____ be the postman – he has already been here.

4 _____ I go round to Stuart's house tonight?
5 Mr Brent is busy this morning, but he _____ see you this afternoon.
6 If the window had not been open, I _____ have got in.
7 It _____ be 10 o'clock already! I had no idea it was so late.
8 I told him that he _____ leave whenever he wanted to.
9 I'll get a car of my own as soon as I _____ drive.

b Complete these sentences beginning with the word in brackets and using a suitable part of **be able to**.
e.g.
I _____ finish it by Friday. (should)

Answer: I should be able to finish it by Friday.

10 I can't come round tonight but I _____ phone you. (might)
11 Interpreters _____ translate without thinking. (have to)
12 _____ type, what else can you do? (apart/from)
13 It is _____ do shorthand. (useful)
14 She has tried very hard but so far she _____ find a job. (hasn't)
15 To become a lifesaver, you _____ swim. (need)
16 I'm not sure whether I _____ finish on time. (shall)
17 I _____ speak Italian quite fluently. (used)
18 My brother is an invalid. He hates _____ do things for himself. (not)

10.3
a How many grammatical combinations can you make from the elements in column A and column B?

	A		B
1	will		
2	might	a)	have to
3	used	b)	to have to
4	would	c)	having to
5	would have	d)	had to
6	has		
7	without		

b Use suitable combinations from the last exercise **a** to complete these sentences.

1 I hope it will not be necessary, but I _____ borrow some money from you.
2 When we were children, we _____ get up at five every morning.
3 One thing is certain: I _____ walk home if you hadn't come along.
4 Joe's wife is away. It is the first time he _____ look after himself.
5 He was in a hurry, but the receptionist told him that he _____ wait his turn.
6 John isn't here: he _____ go to Egypt again.
7 You _____ speak up, I can hardly hear you.
8 I _____ spend the night at Stuart's house: it depends when the party finishes.
9 I wish you would put your things away _____ be reminded every time.

10.4
a Use **mustn't** or **doesn't/don't have to** according to the meaning of the sentence:

1 You _____ come with us if you don't want to.
2 The children can look at the stamp collection, but they _____ touch anything.
3 You _____ be surprised if she suddenly bursts out crying.
4 He _____ go to school tomorrow: it is his half-term (a holiday).
5 You _____ leave the building without asking permission first.
6 I know they are only dancing, but they _____ make so much noise, surely?
7 I'm sure I _____ tell you what she is like. You know her as well as I do.

8 Some fungi are edible, but there are others which _____ be eaten under any circumstances.
9 'You _____ be mad to work here, but it helps!' (*sign in an office*)

b Use **didn't have to** or **not allowed to** according to the meaning of the sentence:
10 I had enough money, so I _____ borrow after all.
11 The film was an X (Adults only), so the children _____ see it.
12 They sent the money immediately: I _____ remind them.
13 There was a 'Men Only' room which women _____ go in.
14 The students _____ use dictionaries during the test.
15 The afternoon programme was optional: you _____ attend lessons unless your teacher specifically recommended it.
16 I _____ go up to London: they came down here instead.
17 For reasons of safety, there were parts of the plant which we _____ visit.
18 There was only a short queue so we _____ wait long.

10.5
a Which sentences in column **A** go with the question tags in column **B**?

	A		B
1	We don't have to fill in a form,	a)	haven't we?
2	We have to do every question,	b)	don't we?
3	We need to pass a test,	c)	must we?
4	We've got to pay it all back,	d)	haven't we? (or don't we?)
5	We must tell them everything,	e)	do we?
6	We mustn't say that,	f)	mustn't we?
7	They didn't need to be so rude,	g)	aren't they?
8	They had to leave early,	h)	won't they?
9	They won't have to wait very long,	i)	didn't they?

10 They have had to
    make a lot of changes,
11 They are having to
    sell the business,
12 They will have to get
    rid of the stock,

j) did they?

k) haven't they?

l) will they?

b To which of the 'coloured' questions from **a** would the following be suitable short answers?

13 Yes, you do. (3 possibilities)
14 No, you mustn't
15 Yes, you have. (2 possibilities)
16 Yes, they did.
17 Yes, they have.
18 Yes, they will. (2 possibilities)

10.6

a Complete these sentences using the appropriate form of verb in brackets and the expressions **must** or **can't**.

1 You aren't serious, are you? You (joke)!
2 It (be) Simon. I'm sure it was really Joe who did it.
3 'How old do you think she is?' 'Oh, she (be) in her late fifties I would think.'
4 'How old do you think she is?' 'Oh, she (be) more than thirty at the most.'
5 The fight was terrible. It (last) more than two hours.
6 I knew it wasn't true. She (lie).
7 I heard about the fight. It (be) a very unpleasant experience for you.
8 I heard about the fight. It (be) a very nice experience for you.
9 Did you see that car that went by? It (travel) at 100 mph!

b Comment on each of these situations using the appropriate form of words in brackets and **didn't need to** or **needn't have**:

10 Anna was just about to ask Chris for some money when she realised she had enough in her purse already.
    She had enough, so _____. (ask)

11 Anna borrowed some money from Chris. Later she realised that she had had enough in her purse anyway.
    She _____ after all. (borrow)

12 I told him the whole story. He wasn't the least bit interested.
    I _____. (bother to tell)
13 I started to tell him the story, but he stopped me because he had already heard it.
    I _____. (tell)
14 She mislaid the manuscript, which meant that she had to type it all out again. Later she found the original manuscript in a drawer.
    She _____ after all.
15 She mislaid the manuscript but fortunately someone found it again before she had actually started to retype it.
    Fortunately, she _____. (retype)
16 Joe's wife asked him to do the washing-up while she was out. He not only did the washing-up, but the rest of the housework as well. When she returned, she said:
    'You _____.' (do all the housework)
17 I decided to take my car to France. I asked the AA if I should get an international driving licence. They said it wasn't necessary.
    'I _____ an international licence for France. (get)
18 I also took out an insurance which cost me £75.00. A friend of mine got an identical insurance for only £25.00.
    'I _____. (pay so much)

10.7

a There is something wrong in each of the following situations on the left. Using the words given on the right and an expression with **should**, say what the situation should be:

1 think   There _____ a dot over the third letter.

2 french bread   The word *french* _____ written _____ capital letter.

3   GREEN
    AMBER   The RED _____ top, and
    RED   the GREEN _____ bottom.

4 'come in' he   The word *come* _____
   said.   capital letter, and there _____ a comma after *in*.

5 A well   _____ hyphen (-)
   educated man   between _____.

6 'Gentlemen   The word *ladies* _____
   and ladies'   before _____.

7 (60) CAR   The car _____ (not)
                   _____ travelling at
                   85mph.

8 NO SMOKING   The woman _____

9 thankyou   The words _____ (not)
                   _____ joined. They
                   _____ as two words.

b Comment on these situations, using
expressions with **should**. In some cases, more
than one form will fit. (You can complete the last
four sentences as you please.)

10 He was driving in a built-up area at 60 mph.
    He was stopped by the police and taken to
    court.
    He _____ (not) _____ so fast.

11 Today is a normal school day. Mohammed
    is absent without any reason.
    He _____ in school.

12 Why are you sitting at that desk. It is
    Arthur's desk. not yours.
    You _____ there.

13 Look, there's Mohammed walking down
    the road.
    _____ he _____ at school today?

14 She looks really ill.
    She _____ a doctor right away.

15 My socks are full of holes!
    You _____ them!

16 I feel very very tired.
    You _____ so _____

17 Joe and his wife are always fighting.
    They _____

18 I feel terrible this morning!
    It's your own fault. You _____ last night!

10.8

a Which of the words in the right hand column
will fit in the sentences on the left? (More than
one might fit.)

1 _____ I ask you something?	may
2 I _____ go out this evening: I haven't decided yet.	can
	might
3 You _____ usually get a table without booking.	could
4 You _____ find driving on the left a little strange at first.	
5 Ask her: she _____ be able to help you.	
6 He says you _____ go out if you want to.	
7 I _____ be young, but I'm not stupid.	
8 You _____ never tell when you will need one.	
9 He _____ play really well when he wants to.	

b

10 I _____ be able to come round tonight.	may not
11 He _____ want to come with us.	cannot
12 There _____ be many people who believe that.	
13 Do it now: you _____ have time later.	
14 Don't smoke so much: it _____ be good for you.	
15 Don't shout at her: it _____ have been her fault.	
16 He _____ have don it: he wasn't even in England at the time.	
17 I don't know anyone called Pye. He _____ even be a student at this college.	
18 The dog _____ be feeling well – he won't eat anything.	

10.9

a How many grammatically correct
combinations can you make from the table?

1	If I am not too busy,	a) may		
		b) might		
2	If I were not so busy, I	c) can	go round to
		d) could	see Martin.
		e) will	
		f) would	

b How many elements from each column can be combined to make sentences which are *both grammatically correct and meaningful?*

1 If I have enough money,	a) I might buy a new car next year.
2 If you were not so busy,	b) you could come with us.
3 If I had enough money,	c) I would buy a new car.
4 If you are free,	d) I want you to come as well.
5 If my father lent me the car,	e) I could take you with me.
6 If my father lends me the car,	

c Use some of the combinations from **b** to rephrase these sentences.

1 I cannot take you with me unless my father lends me the car.
   If _____
2 There is only one way I could take you with me.
   If _____ lent _____
3 I shan't buy a new car: I simply haven't got the money.
   If I _____
4 I'm saving up to get a new car. I hope I shall have enough!
   If I _____
5 I'm going out with Chris and Mary tonight. I'd like you to come with us.
   If _____ free, _____
6 It is a pity you are so busy.
   If _____ , _____

10.10

a How many grammatically correct combinations can you make from the table?

I	1 might	a go	if I had	A time	
	2 would	b have gone,		B had time	
	3 could				

b In the four situations which follow, express an opinion about what went wrong.
Use the pattern X WOULD (NOT). IF Y HAD (NOT)...
Make any necessary changes (e.g. *too long* to *so long* in no. 2).

Example:
The answer to no. 1 is:
The soup wouldn't be tasteless if enough salt had been added during the cooking.

What is wrong	Theory about what went wrong

First situation: You are having a meal

1	The soup is tasteless.	Not enough salt was added during the cooking.
2	The meat is dry.	It was under the grill for too long.
3	The vegetables are soggy.	Too much water was used.

Second situation: Your car has just been serviced

4	The engine is noisy.	It wasn't properly serviced.
5	It runs badly.	They didn't change the oil.
6	It won't start properly.	They forgot to set the timing.

Third situation: Your children are not speaking to each other

7	Claire is angry with Julian.	He borrowed her radio without asking.
8	Julian is angry with Claire.	She didn't give him anything for his birthday.
9	She is very upset.	He was rude to her friend Jacky.

Fourth situation: Your friend has a cold which has lasted three weeks!

10	She (still) has a cold after three weeks.	She didn't go to the doctor's in the first place.
11	She is ill.	She ignored your advice.
12	She has a very sore throat.	She has continued to smoke.

10.11

Use the same situations as in exercise 10.10 **b**, but notice that the situations are in the past.

Situation 1: You had a meal the other day.
A number of things were wrong.
1 The soup was tasteless.
2 The meat was dry.
3 The vegetables were soggy.

Situation 2: Your car gave you a lot of problems a couple of weeks ago, just after it had been serviced.
4   The engine was noisy.
5   It ran badly.
6   It wouldn't start properly.

Situation 3: Last week, Claire and Julian had a quarrel, and refused to speak to each other.
7   Claire was angry with Julian.
8   Julian was angry with Claire.
9   She was very upset.

Situation 4: Last summer a friend of yours caught a cold which lasted for over three weeks.
10 She still had the cold after three weeks.
11 She was ill.
12 She had a very sore throat.

10.12

a   Complete these sentences as you wish, but use suitable expressions with **(not) be able to**, **(not) have to** or **(not) need to**. The words in brackets may help you if you are not sure how to complete the sentences.

Action	*Possible, probable or certain result*
1 If cigarettes become too expensive, people _____.	(give up)
2 If the price of petrol continues to rise, we _____.	(smaller cars)
3 Once spaceships are as common as aeroplanes, people _____.	(the other planets)
4 If the countryside continues to disappear, we _____.	(more nature reserves)
5 If they build a tunnel under the Channel, we _____.	(to France more easily)
6 Once we can produce solar energy cheaply, we _____.	(depend on oil)
7 Unless we create more jobs, young people _____.	(find work)
8 When the oil runs out, we _____.	(other kinds of fuel)
9 If rail fares go on rising, _____.	(afford to go by train)

b   In sentences 10–18, you are free to complete the sentences as you wish (we have given prompts in brackets for 10–13). Use suitable expressions with **(not) be able to**, **(not) have to** or **(not) need to**.

10 If we all spoke the same language, everyone _____.	(communicate)
11 If there were no television, we _____.	(make our own amusements)
12 If you wanted to buy a big house in Hollywood, you _____.	(earn a lot of money)
13 If people didn't have cars, they _____.	(walk)

14 If I were President for one month, I _____.
15 If I had been born a girl/boy, _____.
16 If each person in the country gave me £50.00 _____.
17 If they closed all the schools, _____.
18 If the country were governed by women, men _____.

10.13

Explain the difference in meaning or emphasis between the sentences in each pair. (One way to describe the difference is to describe the situations in which each might be used.)

1   i)   The window was open and a thief could get in.
    ii) The window was open and a thief was able to get in.
2   i)   Can you do something for me?
    ii) Could you do something for me?
3   i)   The train should be here by now.
    ii) The train should be here any minute now.
4   i)   They should have finished by now.
    ii) They ought to have finished by now.

5 i) You mustn't go out.
   ii) You don't have to go out.
6 i) I must get my uniform cleaned.
   ii) I have to get my uniform cleaned.
7 i) I may come round to see you later.
   ii) I might come round to see you later.
8 i) You can do it now (it is all right with me).
   ii) You can do it now (you don't need any more lessons).
9 i) You must wait here until you are called.
   ii) You are to wait here until you are called.
10 i) I can't leave the house at the moment.
   ii) I am not allowed to leave the house at the moment.
11 i) You must let the boss see what you have done.
   ii) You will have to let the boss see what you have done.
12 i) You needn't write out all the sentences in full.
   ii) You don't need to write out all the sentences in full.

Just for fun

10.14

a In the following situations, the first sentence describes what I actually did. Complete the following sentences to say what I could have done instead.

Table 1

red + blue = purple   red + yellow = orange
blue + yellow = green (more blue = dark green; less blue = light green)

I mixed *red* and *blue*, and got *purple*

1 If I had mixed red and yellow, _____ orange.
2 If _____ green.
3 If _____ used _____ more blue, _____ .
4 If _____ light green.

Table 2

12 × 3 = 36   (multiply 12 by 3)
12 ÷ 3 = 4   (divide 12 by 3)
12 + 3 = 15   (add 3 to 12)
12 − 3 = 9   (subtract 3 from 12)

I multiplied 12 by 3. The answer was 36.

5 If _____ , _____ 4 .
6 If _____ to _____ , _____ .
7 If _____ from _____ , _____ .
8 If _____ by itself, _____ 144 .

Table 3

	Tea	Coffee	Chocolate
with milk	1	3	5
without milk	2	4	6
with sugar	A	A	A
without sugar	B	B	B

I wanted tea without milk or sugar, so I pressed 2 and B

9 If _____ black coffee with sugar, I _____ .
10 If _____ chocolate with milk and sugar, _____ .
11 _____ , _____ 1 and A.
12 _____ , _____ 4 and B.

b Look at Table 1, and complete these:
13 You will only get purple if _____ .
14 If you _____ , you would get green.
15 If _____ more yellow, _____ get a lighter shade of green.
16 You should get orange if _____ .

Look at Table 2 and complete these:
The answer to 12 × 3 is 36.
If you then added another 12, the answer would be 48.
17 _____ divided 48 by _____ , _____ 3.
18 _____ 3 by itself, _____ 9.
19 _____ , _____ 81.
20 _____ your age from 81, _____ (?)

Look at Table 3, and complete these:
You would press 1 if you wanted milk in your tea
21 _____ A unless _____ drink.
22 _____ A with 3 unless _____ .
23 If you didn't press A, _____ drink.
24 You _____ (not) _____ got chocolate without milk or sugar if _____ .

Unit 11   Phrasal verbs

11.1

Put the verbs in brackets into the correct form, and supply the particles (adverb or preposition) which are missing from the spaces marked _____ _____

The hippo (look) _____ the notice board once again. 2 + 2 = 5??? He (scratch) his head and (begin) to mutter _____ himself 'That can't be right. There (must/be) some mistake.'

He (sit) _____ and (try) _____ (work) _____ for himself how 2 + 2 (can) possibly (make) 5. He (think) too _____ the person who (write) the expression _____ _____ the board. Somebody (write) it, and they (must/have) a good reason for (do) so. There must be something in it. Finally, he (get) very angry, (tear) the notice _____ , and (take) it with him. He (put) it _____ the ground and (continue) (stare) _____ it for days on end, no longer (bother) (eat) or (drink). 2 + 2 = 5???

He (take) _____ his glasses to (wipe) _____ some mud. Immediately the board and the crazy expression (become) a blur – he (can) no longer see the figures; nor could he (make) _____ the plus or equal signs. Suddenly he (begin) (feel) much better, as if a big weight (lift) _____ his shoulders. He smiled, rolled _____ in the mud, and (begin) (sing). He no longer (have) a problem. After that he (give) _____ maths, and (take) _____ singing instead.

Moral: If you (want) (see) things really clearly, take your glasses _____

11.2

How many verbs in the vertical column can be combined with the particles in the horizontal row (i.e., adverbs or prepositions) to form phrasal (including prepositional) verbs?

	out	on	up	to	across	off
carry						
catch						
come						
get						
hold						
work						

11.3

a   Use some of the combinations from 11.2 with the verbs **catch, carry** and **come** to complete these sentences (make any necessary tense changes).

1   How much does the bill _____ _____ ?
2   _____ _____ , we're going to be late!
3   You go ahead. I'll _____ _____ with you later.
4   When will the first issue of the new magazine _____ _____ ?
5   We were stuck until Joy _____ _____ with a good idea.
6   Miniskirts are silly. I was surprised that they _____ _____ .
7   Don't stop. Please _____ _____ with what you were doing.
8   I _____ _____ some old love letters when I was clearing out the desk.
9   If you _____ _____ your orders exactly, everything will be all right.

b   Use some of the combinations from 11.2 using **get, hold** and **work** to complete these sentences.

10   I can't _____ _____ sums in my head. I need a calculator.
11   What time do you usually _____ _____ in the morning?
12   She has _____ _____ very well: she is now manager of the agency.
13   The mail has been _____ _____ by the rail strike.

14 She boarded the bus at Charing Cross, and _____ _____ at Oxford Circus. (*two possibilities*)

15 Some teachers know their subject, but have difficulty in _____ it _____ to their students.

16 Let's go for a walk to _____ _____ an appetite for lunch.

17 _____ _____ tightly! If you let go, you might fall.

18 Close your eyes and _____ _____ your hand, and see what I have got for you.

11.4

How many phrasal verbs can you make by combining the verbs and the particles in the matrix?

	away	across	down	in	off	up
break						
cut						
give						
keep						
fall						
see						

11.5

a Use some of the combinations from 11.4 with the verbs **break, cut** and **fall** to complete these sentences. Make any necessary tense changes.

1 The Union _____ _____ negotiations when the management refused to increase their offer.

2 I don't want to give up smoking completely, but I am trying to _____ _____.

3 She _____ _____ and cried when she heard the sad news.

4 It is very rude to _____ _____ when people are talking.

5 Business has _____ _____ a lot lately: turnover is down 15 per cent on last year.

6 The meeting _____ _____ after three hours and everyone went for a drink.

7 This new proposal completely _____ _____ our original planning.

8 My children are forever _____ _____ and hurting themselves.

9 Operator, we've been _____ _____. Could you reconnect me, please.

b Use some of the combinations from 11.4 with **give, keep** and **see** to complete these sentences.

10 After failing several times to get a job, he just _____ _____ trying.

11 We try to _____ _____ with our neighbours in everything they do. The trouble is that they are richer than we are!

12 The old man told me to _____ _____ from his daughter, but I just had to see her again.

13 Will you come to the airport to _____ me _____ ?

14 Even though he was tortured, the prisoner refused to _____ _____ to their demands.

15 He doesn't want any money for his paintings: he is actually _____ them _____ !

16 I think she is horrible: I don't know what her boyfriend _____ _____ her.

17 The notice said '_____ _____ THE GRASS,' but everyone ignored it and walked across the lawn to get to the gate.

18 The gas _____ _____ a most unpleasant smell, so we opened all the windows.

11.6 Up and down

In the left hand column we give you a definition of a **phrasal verb** with **up** or **down**, and in the right hand column a simple phrase or sentence in which the verb might be used. Match these verbs with their definitions and the particles **up** or **down**.

break, bring, come, cut do, get give, hold, lie look, make, pull, put, set, take (2), turn (2)

Definition	Example of use
1 stop doing	_____ *up* staying out late at night
2 start or adopt	_____ *up* a hobby
3 delay or interrupt	_____ *up* the meeting
4 come to a stop	A car _____ ed *up*.
5 arrive unexpectedly	He usually _____ s *up* when you least expect him.

6   repair   _____ ing *up* old cars

7   invent   _____ *up* stories about yourself

8   introduce a subject   _____ *up* the matter at the right time

9   organize/create   _____ *up* a new organization

10   reduce   _____ *down* the number of cigarettes you smoke

11   remove   _____ *down* the curtains to wash them

12   refuse   _____ *down* an offer, or a proposal of marriage

13   stop functioning   Machines _____ *down* when they are not looked after.

14   dismount   It's not easy to _____ *down* off a camel.

15   reduce   Prices only _____ *down* during sales.

16   despise   _____ *down* on people who are not as lucky as you

17   let go of   Too exciting a book to _____ *down*

18   recline   If you are tired, go and _____ *down*.

11.7   In and out

Instructions as for Exercise 11.6. Verbs:

break, call, come, die, drop, fill, fit, give, live, make, pass, put, stand (2), try, turn (2), watch

1   complete   I hate _____ ing *in* forms.

2   visit casually   _____ *in* and see us sometime.

3   enter illegally   _____ *in* and steal money and jewels.

4   substitute   I'm _____ ing *in* for a sick colleague.

5   go to bed   It's late: I think I'll _____ *in*.

6   enter   Please _____ *in*!

7   ask for help   The local police had to _____ *in* Scotland Yard.

8   be convenient   _____ *in* with our plans.

9   be resident   The students _____ *in*.

10   test   _____ *out* a new idea

11   perish   species which have _____ d *out*

12   distribute   _____ *out* the leaflets after the meeting

13   issue/publish   _____ *out* a new magazine

14   be careful   _____ *out*! You nearly knocked me over!

15   discern   _____ *out* the letters in the semi-darkness

16   faint   _____ *out* in the heat

17   be prominent   Real genius always _____ s *out* above the rest of us.

18   finally become   It's _____ ed *out* nice again, hasn't it? (*this is a very common observation about the weather*)

11.8

a   The expressions in the left hand column contain phrasal verbs with **up**. They are followed by one of the prepositions **to, on, with** or **for** (In some cases, there are two possibilities, for which we have given two expressions). Can you supply the missing prepositions?

	to	on	with	for
1 build up _____ a climax				
2 catch up _____ the news				
catch up _____ the car in front				
3 check up _____ his background				
4 come up _____ another idea				
5 face up _____ the truth				
6 get up _____ mischief				
7 keep up _____ the neighbours				
8 live up _____ your reputation				
9 look up _____ a man you admire				
10 make up _____ lost time				
11 put up _____ difficulties				
12 stand up _____ a bully				
stand up _____ what you believe in				

b Phrasal verbs with **down** and **in**. Can you supply the missing prepositions?

	to	on	with	for
1 come down _____ details				
come down _____ influenza				
2 settle down _____ married life				
3 cut down _____ the amount you eat				
4 get down _____ business				
5 go down _____ yellow fever				
6 look down _____ poor people				
7 burst in _____ a meeting				
8 put in _____ a pay rise				
9 drop in _____ some friends				
10 go in _____ sport				
11 join in _____ the rest of them				
12 keep in _____ the boss				

11.9

a Here are twelve phrasal verbs having the pattern VERB + ADVERB + PREPOSITION. Can you use *nine* of them in the sentences?

Verbs
be up to, boil down to, cash in on, do away with, fall back on, fall behind with, go back on, get away with, keep on at, look back on, look forward to, run out of

1 Now we have got a computer, we can _____ the old filing system.

2 He's lost his job and he is _____ with his mortgage repayments.

3 He's trying to avoid paying tax, but he won't _____ it.

4 In her autobiography, she _____ her life in India.

5 We've booked a holiday in Spain, and we're _____ it very much.

6 I've _____ sugar; I must go and get some more.

7 What on earth have you _____ ? You're as white as a sheet.

8 He promised to do it, but now he wants to _____ his word.

9 If the new scheme fails, we can always _____ the old one.

b   Come and go
Put a suitable form of **come** or **go** into the following sentences:

10 After all, what it _____ down to is this: we need more money.

11 I don't agree with the plan entirely, but I'll _____ along with it.

12 As soon as you try to do anything, you _____ up against regulations.

13 He's applied to emigrate to Canada, but I don't think he'll _____ through with it.

14 We are against higher taxes, and our party has _____ out against them.

15 She promised to help, but later _____ back on her word.

16 At first he would not admit it, then he _____ out with the truth.

17 The council seems to have _____ in for a lot of criticism lately.

18 Please _____ on with what you were saying.

11.10

a   Put the pronoun **it** in the correct place in these sentences:

			A		B	
1	I haven't time to look at your work now. I'll	*look*		*through*		later.
2	He knows his subject but he can't always	*put*		*across*		.
3	Don't decide right away. Take your time to	*think*		*over*		.
4	I don't know what is wrong with this. I've	*gone*		*over*		several times.
5	If you are not sure of the meaning of a word,	*look*		*up*		.
6	'Serendipity' is a strange word. I only	*came*		*across*		recently.
7	Don't decide right away. Take your time to	*think*		*about*		.
8	He's upset now about his friend's death, but he will	*get*		*over*		.
9	Here's the file. Check the man's identity, then	*hand*		*over*		.

b   The words in brackets fit into the sentences. Put them in the place which sounds most natural. If they will fit in both columns, mark your preference with 1 and 2.

10   John started to laugh, which *gave* | | *away* | | at once. (the game)

11   Be sure to *put* | | *away* | | before you go. (everything)

12   The old lady *gave* | | *away* | | to a cats' home. (all her money)

13   Be sure to *put* | | *away* | | . (what you don't need)

14   At the end of his speech, he told a joke which *brought* | | *down* | | . (the house)

15   Can you *put* | | *up* | | for a couple of nights? (John and Mary)

16   It will soon be time to *put* | | *up* | | . (next year's calendar)

17   I've decided to *take* | | *out* | | (a year's subscription to Punch)

18   I'd like time to *think* | | *over* | | (things)

11.11

Use the pronoun **it** to refer to the object given in the left hand column and insert the pronoun in the phrasal verb in the correct place. We have done one of them to help you.

a problem a bridge	1	{ *talk* _____ over _____ { *walk* _____ over _____
your money an insult	2	{ *live* _____ off _____ { *laugh* _____ off _____
a house a form	3	{ *live* _____ in *it* _____ { *fill it* _____ in
a trumpet an old house	4	{ *blow* _____ down _____ { *pull* _____ down _____
a problem a handball	5	{ *talk* _____ about _____ { *throw* _____ about _____
a tree a tyre	6	{ *climb* _____ up _____ { *pump* _____ up _____
a door an old trunk	7	{ *look* _____ behind _____ { *leave* _____ behind _____
a bed a light	8	{ *lie* _____ on _____ { *switch* _____ on _____
your money the garden wall	9	{ *hand* _____ over _____ { *look* _____ over _____

a river
an idea
10 { get _____ across _____
{ get _____ across _____

a moral
code
money for
your old age
11 { live _____ by _____
{ put _____ by _____

a lie
a difficult
project
12 { see _____ through _____
{ see _____ through _____

the staircase
the matter
13 { walk _____ up _____
{ bring _____ up _____

a difficulty
the
manifesto
14 { get _____ round _____
{ hand _____ round _____

a tree
an object in
water
15 { stand _____ under _____
{ hold _____ under _____

11.12
The same phrasal (including prepositional) verb, but with different meanings, will fit each pair of sentences. Can you find a verb for each pair of sentences? You will need combinations of the following verbs and particles:

Verbs: bring, get, go, look, put, stand, take, turn,

Particles: across, away, back, down, for, off, on, out, up

1	{ Don't let the fire { Every Friday, they	_____ _____	for a meal together.	
2	{ I would like to { Rob a bank? You'll never	_____ _____	before 5 o'clock if possible. with it!	
3	{ A few years ago, we { He went outside and	_____ _____	on people with regional accents. the road to see if the postman was there.	
4	{ We tried to { I can't seem to	_____ _____	the road, but there were too many cars. to her how important she is to me.	
5	{ Why don't you { He's a mimic who can	_____ _____	your overcoat? any person he meets.	
6	{ You will never { The police told the crowd to	_____ _____	the money that you lent him. in order to let the cars go by.	
7	{ Don't forget to { I was really	_____ _____	all the lights before you go. by her unkind remarks.	
8	{ We had to { The council	_____ _____	a side street to avoid the traffic jam. our proposal for a public enquiry.	
9	{ I've always wanted to { Your story interests me. Do	_____ _____	the stage. with it.	
10	{ It was the second time he had { After his wife died, he	_____ _____	the subject. the children on his own.	
11	{ Mr Jenkins has agreed to { Don't be rude. I won't	_____ _____	Parliament as a Liberal candidate. any more.	
12	{ The meeting has been { It looked nice, but I was	_____ _____	until a later date. by the funny smell.	

11.13

a   Can you match 12 of these 15 phrasal verbs with the definitions?

Verbs	*Definitions*
1 brush up	a) fall asleep
2 butt in	b) interrupt
3 clear off	c) wait or stand in a place without any purpose
4 doze off	
5 end up	d) refresh your knowledge
6 explain away	
7 hang about	e) leave suddenly
8 patch up	f) stop talking
9 show off	g) separate
10 shut up	h) make a mistake
11 slip up	i) criticize, shout at
12 split up	j) draw attention to yourself in a vain or boastful way
13 tell off	
14 wear off	
15 wind up	k) try to persuade someone that nothing really happened
	l) repair the damage done by a fight or quarrel

b   Now, use *all fifteen* verbs in these sentences, taking care with word order, and making any necessary changes of tense.

1   I was so tired that I just _____ _____.

2   He started by disliking her and _____ _____ by marrying her!

3   'Can I _____ _____ there? I think you are wrong.' *(said in a conversation)*

4   Why is that man _____ _____ outside our house? Do you think he's a burglar?

5   I've forgotten most of my Portuguese. I must _____ it _____ again.

6   She decided to _____ _____ the company, sell her house and retire to Mallorca.

7   The door salesman was very persistent, but I told him to _____ _____.

8   Everybody was talking at once, but they _____ _____ when the chairman came in.

9   John and Mary _____ _____ several months ago, but I think they will soon be back together again.

10   I paid more than I needed to for my car insurance. I _____ _____ by not asking for a discount.

11   The children were very noisy, so they were _____ _____ for misbehaving.

12   As the effects of the anaesthetic _____ _____, she began to come round.

13   He liked to _____ _____ by riding his bicycle without holding the handlebars.

14   It was not going to be easy to _____ _____ the lipstick which his wife had found on his collar!

15   John and Mary _____ _____ their quarrel and became friends again.

Just for fun

11.14   'to be or not to be'

There are a number of idioms (fixed expressions) having the pattern PART OF TO BE + PARTICLE. Can you match these idioms with the definitions?

Group 1 *Idioms*	*Definitions (or explanations)*
1 It's all over.	a) We have finished. (or our relationship has)
2 They're off!	b) He is coming soon.
3 It's off.	c) I am very tired.
4 I'm all in.	d) It is finished.
5 We're through.	e) What is wrong?
6 He's away.	f) The race has started.
7 He'll be along soon.	g) It is mislaid, but not lost.
8 It's around here somewhere.	h) He is in another place, town, etc.
9 What's up?	i) It is not fresh (of meat, fish, etc.)

Group 2

10 What's on?

j) What is the subject (of the story, film, etc.)?

11 What's it about?

k) What (strange thing) is he talking about?

12 He's out.

l) What is his town (country) of origin?

13 He's back.

m) He has returned.

14 What is he up to?

n) What is the purpose of it?

15 Where is he from?

o) What programme (film, etc.) are they showing?

16 What is it for?

p) I am completely in favour.

17 I'm all for it.

q) He is not at home, in his office, etc.

18 What's he on about?

r) What (strange) thing is he doing?

Unit 12 Adverbials

12.1

The adverbials at the head of each paragraph belong in the spaces marked _____*. Can you fit the adverbials into the sentences?

*Note that the adverbial to be entered in the space marked _____ may consist of more than one word (e.g. *too hard*)

1 *deeply, frankly, just the same, in love*
_____ , I do not expect you to believe this story of how a cobra and a boa constrictor fell _____ _____ , but I will tell it to you _____ .

2 *By chance, during the rainy season, from a storm, generally, immediately, one afternoon*
They met _____ _____ _____ when they were sheltering _____ , and they were _____ attracted to each other. (You see, *snakes* like snakes, even if *people* do not like snakes).

3 *even, greatly, naturally, never, seriously, soon*
The cobra _____ admired the boa's muscular body, and the boa declared that he had _____ seen anything so beautiful as the cobra's head markings. _____ they _____ fell in love, and _____ began to talk _____ of marriage.

4 *anxiously, equally, so easily, too tightly*
But there was a big problem which could not be _____ resolved.
'If you hold me _____ , you might kill me,' said the cobra _____ .
'And if you kiss me, you might bite me and poison me,' retorted the boa, _____ worried.

5 *anyway, passionately, sensibly, though, too hard, very*
_____ , they promised to be _____ careful, and to behave _____ . It was no good, _____ . The first time they met and

embraced _____ , the boa squeezed _____ and the cobra bit the boa's lip.

6 *even, only, silently, at that moment*
They died before either of them could _____ say a word: _____ their eyes _____ expressed what they were feeling _____ .

Moral: Love is not having time to say you are sorry.

12.2

a Can you match the pictures to the adverbial expressions?

a glove

LOVE

Expressions
a) back to front   d) in and out   g) side by side
b) back to back   e) inside out   h) up and down
c) face to face   f) next door   i) upside down

b Can you match these?

Expressions

j) backwards
k) eastwards and westwards
l) forwards
m) northwards and southwards
n) inwards
o) outwards
p) sideways
q) uphill and downhill
r) upstairs and downstairs

12.3

a   Which of the adverbials in the centre column of the table below will fit the meaning of the 12 sentences? In several cases, more than one will fit.

1 How long will you be		?
2 When will you be	a) **away**	?
3 When will you be going		?
4 The men walk in front; the women walk		.
5 Try not to get too far	b) **back**	with your work.
6 This is the stop where I have to get		.
7 The police told the crowd to stay		.
8 Try to catch up: you're a long way	c) **behind**	the others.
9 The children ran		before I could speak to them.
10 I should like you to stay		after work.
11 The bird was much too far	d) **off**	for me to identify.
12 He went		without saying a word.

12.3

b   Some of the sentences from **a** fit these situations. Which are they?

13 Teacher talking to a pupil who has missed a lot of lessons (*2 possibilities*)
14 Man on a train talking to the other passengers
15 Boss talking to her secretary
16 Wife to her husband as he is about to leave on a business trip (*2 possibilities*)
17 Describing a social custom in a primitive society
18 Something which happened at the scene of an accident (*2 possibilities*)

12.4   Here and there

In each case look at the situation described, and then complete the expression beneath it with either **here** or **there**.

Situations
A and B are two men talking. C is a woman.

1i) A is by the window. He wants B to stand by the door.
     'Stand over _____ !'
ii) A is by the window. He wants B to join him.
     'Stand over _____ !'

2i) A wants the parcel to be put on the desk where he is sitting.
     'Put it down _____ !'
ii) A wants the parcel to be put on the desk on the other side of the office.
     'Put it down _____ !'

3i) A is in his room. He wants B to leave.
     'Get out of _____ !'
ii) A is in his room. He wants B to get out of C's room.
     'Get out of _____ !'

4i) A wants B to go to C's room. He points the way.
     'It's through _____ !'
ii) A is taking B with him to C's room. They are nearly there.
     'It's through _____ !'

5i) C is on the roof. A points her out to B.
'She's up _____ !'

ii) C is with A on the roof. A tells B where she
is.
'She's up _____ !'

6i) A and C are in the office. A wants to know
if her house is far away.
'It's quite near _____ .'

ii) A and C are in the office. A wants to know
if her house is near Highgate Station.
'It's quite near _____ .'

7i) A points to a box in the other desk and tells
B to put something it it.
'Put it in _____ .'

ii) A opens a box and tells B to put something
it it
'Put it in _____ '

8i) A sends B out of the office, but tells him
when to be back.
'Be back _____ by 9.'

ii) A and B are out of the office together. Only
B has to be back.
'Be back _____ by 9.'

9i) B wants to know why C has gone to the
States.
'She's over _____ on business.'

ii) B wants to know why C is in England at this
moment.
'She's over _____ on business.'

12.5

a Put the expressions in the three columns into
their normal (non-emphatic) order. In one or
two cases, more than one order may be suitable.

	A	B	C
1	downhill	the car rolled	towards the village
2	near the fire	come and sit	over here
3	up and down	he paced	in his bedroom
4	off the road	the car skidded	sideways
5	southwards	we continued our journey	into Spain
6	down there	put it	with the others
7	upstairs	she ran	into her bedroom

	A	B	C
8	opposite the cinema	he walked	into the bookshop
9	on the settee	he liked to sit	next to his grandfather

b Same instructions as for **a**. Remember that
more than one order may be suitable in one or
two cases.

	A	B	C
10	the fifth of June	I was born	on Friday
11	in the afternoon	we have a meeting	at 3.30
12	every day	we go to the beach	in summer
13	before meals	take the medicine	three times a day
14	during the week	I'd like to see you	some time
15	for a few minutes	can you stay behind	after school
16	in September	war broke out	1939
17	every Tues. afternoon	classes will be held	during the Spring Term
18	in the month	you should have booked	earlier

12.6

a Match the prepositions in column **A** to the
expressions in column **B** to form adverbial time
expressions:

	A		B
		a)	6 o'clock
1	at	b)	Thursday
		c)	the morning
2	in	d)	night
		e)	the eleventh
3	on	f)	July
		g)	a few minutes' time

b	A		B
		a)	year
1	all	b)	Monday
		c)	May
2	the whole	d)	the following week
		e)	day
3	the whole of	f)	next week
		g)	week

12.7

a In which space in the following sentences would the frequency adverb (on the right) normally go? Remember that these are normal unemphatic statements or questions.

	A	B	C	D	
1 You	can	get	your car	done here.	always
2 He	would	have	been	able to do it.	never
3 I	have	been	told	what to do.	rarely
4 I	go	out	on my own.		hardly ever
5 You	will not	see	Joe	queuing up.	often
6 I	don't	give	interviews	to the press.	normally
7 I	have	wondered	what he does.		often
8 We	used	to meet	for a drink.		sometimes
9 Have	you	been	asked	to attend?	ever

b Respond to each of these statements, orders or questions, using the words given, and putting the frequency adverb in the correct place. Notice that in some cases an emphatic response is needed.

10 Cover your typewriter when you have finished with it!
   I | 1 | do | 2 | ! (**always**)
11 Don't lend money to strangers.
   I | 1 | would | 2 | ! (**often**)
12 Why are you afraid to come ice-skating with us?
   I | 1 | have | 2 | done | 3 | it | 4 | before. (**never**)
13 Don't smoke!
   I | 1 | have | 2 | done | 3 | (**never**)
14 I'm surprised you have never been on a school trip.
   I | 1 | have | 2 | had | 3 | too many other things to do. (**usually**)
15 You ought to change your job, you know.
   I | 1 | have | 2 | wanted | 3 | to. (**often**)
16 Why don't you walk to work?
   I | 1 | used | 2 | to. (**always**)
17 Why don't you go out in the evenings?
   I | 1 | am | 2 | too busy. (**usually**)
18 You say you don't go out because you're too busy.
   I | 1 | am | 2 | too busy! (**usually**)

12.8

a Add **still** or **yet** to these sentences, making any necessary changes.

1 Do you work at Bowmaker's?
2 Have you finished your exams?
3 They will be here when you get back.
4 He hasn't come back. (He'll be here soon.)
5 He hasn't come back! (I wonder what has happened to him?)
6 He won't be back for some time.
7 Are you here? I thought you were leaving.
8 Hasn't the mail arrived?
9 It isn't raining, is it?

b Respond to the statements or questions using the words provided, and adding **still**, **yet** or (**not**)...**any more/any longer**. We have done the first one to help you.

10 Why has she left him?
   Because she doesn't love him **any more**.
11 Is Mr Jones still your accountant?
   No, we _____ employ him.
12 Why do you continue to wear those awful shoes?
   Because I _____ find them very comfortable.
13 Have you ordered my new cooker?
   But you _____ haven't told me which one you want!
14 I see you have got rid of your car.
   Yes, I decided I couldn't afford it _____ .

15 I'm surprised you haven't had your hair done.
    I just haven't got around to it _____ .

16 What are you going to study at university?
    I've been thinking about that question for months, and I _____ haven't decided.

17 I haven't seen you at the bowling alley lately.
    I rarely go there _____

18 When will your next book come out?
    I haven't even finished writing it _____ !

12.9

a Form adverbs in **-ly** from these adjectives:

1	funny	10	private
2	free	11	legal
3	grateful	12	noisy
4	musical	13	ironic
5	sad	14	useless
6	easy	15	useful
7	economic	16	final
8	public	17	political
9	happy	18	gay

b Match the stems in column A to the endings in column B

A		B
1	suit-	
2	horr-	
3	poss-	
4	prob-	a) -ably
5	notice-	
6	comfort-	
7	unbeliev-	
8	reli-	b) -ibly
9	vis-	
10	terr-	
11	respect-	
12	accept-	

12.10

Adverbs of manner are often associated with particular verbs. For example, *run* would go with, say, *quickly* rather than *carefully*; *listen* would go with *attentively* rather than, say, *deeply*. Can you find adverbs in column **A** which suit the verbs in column **B**? (In some cases, you can match more than one verb to the adverbs given in column **B**.

	A	B
a 1	argue	a) carefully
2	behave	b) peacefully
3	breathe	c) forcefully, convincingly
4	eat	d) quickly
5	run	e) fluently, loudly, clearly
6	sleep	f) deeply, heavily
7	speak	g) greedily, voraciously
8	think	h) badly, stupidly
9	whisper	i) softly, quietly
b 10	breathe	j) spontaneously
11	climb	k) sweetly
12	explain	l) deeply
13	feel	m) thoroughly
14	investigate	n) steadily
15	mutter	o) heavily
16	react	p) angrily
17	sing	q) concisely, briefly
18	shine	r) brightly
c 19	cry	s) patiently
20	fight	t) gently
21	leave	u) bravely
22	listen	v) suddenly
23	rain	w) attentively
24	remember	x) distinctly
25	sleep	y) soundly
26	stroke	z) bitterly
27	wait	α) continuously

12.11

Complete these sentences by using a word or a phrase based on the word in brackets.

1 Could you walk a bit _____ , otherwise we'll miss the bus. (fast)

2 He spoke to us _____ . (friendly)

3 She works very _____ . (hard)

4 And she drives very _____ . (fast)

5 He's a good pianist; he also plays the violin quite _____ . (good)

6 If you spoke a little _____ , I might be (slow) able to understand you _____ . (good)

7 He speaks French as _____ as he speaks Italian. (good)

8 Your car runs even _____ than mine does. (bad)

9 He behaved _____ towards us.
(unfriendly)

10 You're playing very _____ Couldn't you
play a bit _____ ? (loud/quiet)

11 Say 'particularly pretty' as _____ as you
can. (quick)

12 Can't you say it any _____ than that?
(quick)

13 Say 'extraordinarily awful' as _____ as
you can. (fast)

14 I can say it _____ than that. (fast)

15 He writes English quite _____ , but he
speaks it very _____ . (good/bad)

16 She sings _____ than anyone I know.
(beautiful)

17 You went too _____ round that bend.
(fast)

18 He spoke to me _____ . (fatherly)

12.12

Put the adverbials which are given underneath
each sentence into the numbered spaces. Put
them in the order which is normal, i.e., which
will give non-emphatic sentences. In one or two
cases, more than one order may be suitable.

1 | 1 | they had been | 2 | waiting | 3 |
patiently/for several hours /outside the
cinema

2 I | 1 | like to get | 2 | | 3 |
by five o'clock/generally/home

3 She | 1 | sleeps | 2 | | 3 |
always/badly/in a strange bed

4 | 1 | he | 2 | spends | 3 | | 4 |
a long time /at his desk /in the evening
/usually

5 She dozed | 1 | | 2 | | 3 |
in her armchair /peacefully /until teatime

6 I would | 1 | go | 2 | | 3 |
by car / never / to work

7 | 1 | she | 2 | cut the bread | 3 |
carefully / into thin slices / with a sharp
knife

8 | 1 | he has | 2 | done | 3 | | 4 |
in history / well / really / this term

9 | 1 | we | 2 | go | 3 | | 4 |
at night / in London / seldom / out

10 I | 1 | used to work | 2 | | 3 |
always / before lunch / much better

11 | 1 | people | 2 | go | 3 | | 4 |
abroad / for their holidays / frequently / in
summer

12 | 1 | we continued to climb | 2 | | 3 |
for hours / steadily / towards the
summit

13 | 1 | I don't | 2 | care | 3 |
frankly / in the least / really

14 | 1 | we | 2 | had to stand | 3 |
| 4 | absolutely still / at our posts / for
the moment / simply

15 | 1 | I | 2 | get a chance to sit | 3 |
and read. / quietly / rarely / unfortunately

16 | 1 | he | 2 | tells me | 3 |
what happens at board meetings. as a
matter of fact / confidentially / quite often

17 | 1 | you can | 2 | blame her for
reacting | 3 |
actually / hardly / violently

18 | 1 | he has | 2 | been | 3 |
| 4 |
abroad / apparently / just / on business

12.13

Rewrite these sentences beginning with the
words given underneath each sentence, making
any necessary changes.

1 You should not go away under any
circumstances.
Under no circumstances ...

2 I have never felt so angry in my whole life.
Never in ...

3 You rarely see so many Russian ships in the
harbour.
Rarely ...

4 She not only plays but she composes as
well.
Not only ...

5 I did not realize until then how much she
wanted to go.
Not until then ...

6 I realized only much later what he was trying to achieve.
Only much...

7 He had scarcely had time to take his coat off when the phone rang.
Scarcely...

8 We had no sooner said yes than they ran upstairs to pack.
No sooner...

9 I have begun to think about politics only recently.
Only recently...

10 I have seldom heard such rubbish.
Seldom...

11 We could not talk freely until the others had left.
Not until...

12 You will be able to extend your visa only in special circumstances.
Only in...

12.14

Can you explain the difference between each pair of sentences? One way to show the difference is to describe the differing situations in which each might be said.

1 i) Only John can speak Arabic really well.
  ii) John can only speak Arabic really well.

2 i) Frankly, I cannot talk to her any more.
  ii) I cannot talk to her frankly any more.

3 i) The post has not come yet.
  ii) The post still has not come.

4 i) In this company, every employee is important.
  ii) Every employee is important in this company.

5 i) They soon decided to leave.
  ii) They decided to leave soon.

6 i) I told you earlier to come round.
  ii) I told you come round earlier.

7 i) Earlier, I wanted John to have it.
  ii) I wanted John to have it earlier.

8 i) In London I only like to eat in expensive restaurants.
  ii) I only like to eat in expensive restaurants in London.

9 i) Often, you won't catch Peter cheating.
  ii) You won't often catch Peter cheating.

10 i) I have never been very interested in politics.
  ii) I never have been very interested in politics.

11 i) I'll see you at nine thirty on Friday.
  ii) I'll see you on Friday at nine thirty.

12 i) Anna carefully put the letters away.
  ii) Anna put the letters away carefully.

Just for fun

12.15 'Quickly and easily'

Can you find the adverbs in the word square? Remember the words may be written backwards or forwards, and they may be vertical, horizontal or diagonal in the diagram!

```
S  E  C  T  E  R  R  I  B  L  Y  L  D
O  N  Y  Y  D  F  A  T  A  L  L  Y  M
C  Y  L  L  U  F  E  S  U  O  T  U  A
E  L  I  H  L  Y  L  D  A  B  S  Y  I
R  T  T  T  F  U  Y  L  E  T  A  L  N
T  L  T  O  A  S  F  R  E  E  L  Y  L
A  O  E  O  I  I  R  I  G  H  T  L  Y
I  C  R  M  R  N  H  L  T  H  I  I  L
N  A  P  S  L  G  L  Y  I  U  R  D  E
L  L  T  D  Y  L  E  N  I  F  A  A  R
Y  L  R  A  E  Y  L  T  C  A  X  E  A
Y  Y  L  W  Y  Y  L  T  H  G  I  R  B
```

The adverbs

badly	finely	readily
barely	firstly	rightly
beautifully	freely	simply
brightly	fully	singly
certainly	lastly	smoothly
duly	lately	terribly
exactly	locally	thinly
fairly	mainly	usefully
fatally	prettily	well

Unit 13   Sentence patterns

13.1

a Put the appropriate *verb of measurement* into the sentences, making any changes necessary.

cost, drop, gain, last, lose, measure, rise, take, weigh

1 It was a long film: it _____ three and a half hours.
2 It was a cheap trip: it only _____ £44.00.
3 It was a big job: it _____ three weeks to finish.
4 The time is 8.00. My watch says 7.55. It has _____ five minutes.
5 The time is 8.00. My watch says 8.05. It has _____ five minutes.
6 That looks heavy. How much does it _____ ?
7 The sun came out and the temperature soon _____ several degrees.
8 It was a cold evening, and the temperature _____ 10 degrees in an hour.
9 The field mouse is quite a small animal: it _____ about 4 cms from nose to tail.

b A similar construction is used with these verbs. Put them into the sentences according to their meaning, making any necessary changes.
contain, cover, do, hold, register, seat, sleep, spend, total

10 This car is very economical: it _____ 45 miles to the gallon. (_____ 18 kilometres to the litre)
11 The petrol tank is small: it only _____ 6 gallons (_____ 25 litres).
12 The bill for maintenance alone _____ £750 000 a year!
13 This cabin cruiser* _____ six people.
14 It is a big farm: it _____ more than 25 000 acres.
15 This equipment measures sound: it can _____ up to 100 000 decibels.
16 I _____ several hours every day just adding up figures.

17 This encyclopaedia _____ over 25 000 references.
18 It is a huge hall: it can _____ 2 500 people.

*a kind of boat which you can live on

13.2

a Can you match each verb in column **A** to an adjective in column **B**?

A		B	
1	come	a)	thin
2	grow	b)	sour
3	turn	c)	young
4	fall	d)	loose
5	wear	e)	true
6	keep	f)	quiet
7	lie	g)	old
8	marry	h)	still
9	break	i)	ill

b Make combinations from the verbs and adjectives and put them into the sentences according to their meaning. Make any necessary changes.

Verbs: go, get, look, make, remain, ring, stand, taste, turn
Adjectives: better, brown, funny, silent, stale, still, sure, tired, true

10 I'm sorry you're ill. I hope you _____ _____ soon.
11 After two or three days, bread will _____ _____ .
12 In autumn, leaves _____ _____ and fall.
13 You _____ _____ Why don't you go to bed?
14 There's something wrong with this soup. It _____ _____ .
15 He was about to speak, but then decided to _____ _____ .
16 _____ _____ ! Don't move!

17 I think everything is secure, but I'll just go and _____ _____ that all the doors are locked.

18 I don't believe him. There is something about his story that does not _____ _____ .

13.3

a Put each verb into the appropriate sentence. Choose either the **base form** (e.g. *do*) or the **present participle** (e.g. *doing*) according to the meaning of the sentence.

Verbs: burn, crawl, cut down, get, move, play, pull, switch on, tap, try, walk.

1 I can feel something _____ up my leg!
2 I saw her _____ the light and _____ into the room.
3 For a while she stood and watched the men _____ trees.
4 He smelt something _____ , so he rang the fire brigade.
5 We could definitely hear someone _____ about downstairs.
6 We listened to the school orchestra _____ the whole of the Jupiter Symphony with hardly a mistake.
7 I felt someone _____ me on the shoulder, but when I turned round, there was no-one there.
8 Look at that poor old lady _____ to cross the road.
9 I watched the man _____ out of his car and _____ out a gun.

b In the following sentences, use a suitable form of **go** together with the appropriate activity verb.

Verbs: cycling, dancing, fishing, hiking, horseriding, sailing, skating, skiing, surfing.

10 'Where is Harry?' 'He _____ but I doubt if he'll catch anything!'
11 '_____ (you) _____ last night?' 'No, I don't like the discos in this place.'
12 'What are you doing at the weekend?' 'We _____ if the boat is ready.'
13 If it had not been raining, we might _____ in the hills above Budapest.

14 'You're wet through! What have you been up to?' 'We _____ .
15 Now that she has her own pony, she _____ every day.
16 If my bicycle were in better condition, I _____ in France this holiday.
17 The ice rink is closed so we won't _____ tomorrow night.
18 If there were more snow, we _____ .

13.4

Choose the alternative which fits the sentence.

1 I shall not waste time | to reply / reply / replying | to his letter.

2 It's high time | we go / we went / to go | .

3 I'd rather | stay / staying / to stay | in tonight.

4 There's no point | to argue / in arguing / you argue | with him.

5 We had to stand up | to get / getting / to getting | a better view of the game.

6 I think we had better | go / going / to go | .

7 I will agree | help / helping / to help | you as long as you behave yourself.

8 Would you care | to have / have / having | a look at my latest effort?

9 It's nearly lunchtime. Why don't we stop | to have / to having / having | a bite to eat?

10 Isn't it about time | you started / you start / starting | taking life seriously?

11 It's no use | you complain / to complain / complaining | – nobody will take any notice of you.

12 I am longing | see / to see / to seeing | you again.

13 He seems | feel / feeling / to be feeling | better today.

14 The car needs | to service / being serviced / servicing | .

15 I daren't | go / to go / going | out after dark.

16 What's the use | to worry / you worry / of worrying | ?

17 If you need anything, please do not hesitate | to ask / asking / ask |

18 Hadn't we better | leave / leaving / to leave | soon?

13.5

In the following sentences, put in the verb in brackets, in either the **to- infinitive form** (to do) or the **gerund form** (doing).

1 I have always tried _____ my best. (do)

2 'My bolognese sauce always seems tasteless.' 'Have you ever tried _____ a little sugar to it?' (add)

3 Where did you get that money from? I don't remember _____ it to you. (give)

4 Did you remember _____ that letter I gave you? (post)

5 Passengers are forbidden _____ to the driver. (talk)

6 I'd love _____ you when I am next in Athens. (meet)

7 There is a regulation which forbids _____ in hospitals. (smoke)

8 Wouldn't you prefer _____ in this evening? (stay)

9 I shall never forget _____ you in Florence when you were with Alan. (meet)

10 Don't forget _____ me a ring as soon as you get back. (give)

11 I cannot help _____ why she never goes out anywhere. (wonder)

12 There was a lot to do. Fortunately, Janet agreed to help _____ the food. (prepare)

13 I don't want to go if it means _____ trains. (chance)

14 I'm sorry, I didn't mean _____ you. (interrupt)

15* 'Won't you stay? There's a good match on TV.' 'No, thanks, I hate _____ football.' (watch)

16* Whenever John comes round, I like _____ something special for him. (cook)

17* 'What do you like best about wintertime?' 'Well, if it has snowed during the night, I like _____ early, (get up) and _____ for a walk in the fresh snow.' (go)

18* 'Do you like _____ people?' (meet) 'Not really. I'm rather a shy person.'

*In sentences 15—18, both forms are possible in theory, but one form is much more likely than the other.

13.6

a There are *two* verbs missing from each sentence. Choose the *first verb* from the list given at the top of the exercise. We leave you to choose the *second one* according to the meaning of the sentence. Make any necessary changes to the form of the verbs.

First verb: fancy, finish, keep, mind, put off, recollect, regret, suggest, try.

1 _____ _____ a man so much younger than herself!

2 If you like tongue-twisters, _____ _____ 'Six Swiss wrist watches.'

3 Are you a student at this school. I don't _____ _____ you here before.

4 I'm sorry to trouble you, but would you _____ _____ me with this suitcase?

5 She is afraid of the dentist, so she always _____ _____ till the last possible moment.

6 I started work when I was 16. Now, I _____ (not) _____ at school.

7 I'll never _____ _____ these papers! There are so many of them!

8 It's very late. I _____ _____ the washing-up until the morning.

9 You will have to _____ _____ her: she has a terrible memory.

b There are *two* verbs missing from each sentence*. Choose one from each list to complete the sentences. Be very careful with verb forms!

First verb: avoid, consider, deny, dislike, enjoy, imagine, miss, practise, resist
Second verb: be able to, emigrate, have to, phone, say, see, talk, tell, travel.

*Each space (_____) represents the missing verb, but remember that the *form* of each verb may consist of more than one part (e.g. *having done*)

10 Can you _____ _____ walk five miles to school every day? That is what we had to do.

11 We like living in the country, but we _____ _____ go to the theatre.

12 He did not _____ _____ her, but he insisted that he did not speak to her.

13 Would you _____ _____ if things got worse in this country?

14 I simply couldn't _____ _____ you to tell you the good news!

15 If you find the sound [h] difficult, _____ _____ 'He hit her on her hairy head with a hard, heavy hammer'.

16 You should try to _____ _____ in the rush hour.

17 I have _____ _____ to you, and I hope we meet again some time.

18 I _____ _____ you what to wear and what to do.

13.7

In the following tables, choose the form in the right hand column which correctly completes the sentence. In one or two cases, both forms may be correct.

a

He			
	1	suggests	
	2	wants	
	3	recommends	a) (that) you wait.
	4	dares	
	5	will tell	
	6	expects	
	7	proposes	b) you to wait.
	8	insists	
	9	prefers	

b

I			
	1	assume	
	2	urge	a) (that) you will wait.
	3	suppose	
	4	expect	
	5	invite	b) you to wait.
	6	must ask	

c

It			
	1	means	
	2	enables	
	3	allows	a) (that) we can do as we please.
	4	forbids	
	5	guarantees	
	6	points out	
	7	permits	b) us to do as we please.
	8	encourages	
	9	ensures	

13.8

a Choose the correct alternative from the central column.

She			
	1	showed	
	2	admitted	
	3	promised	me
	4	complained	(that) Matthew was not responsible.
	5	explained	
	6	taught	
	7	mentioned	to me
	8	warned	
	9	suggested	

b Choose the correct alternative from the central column. The symbol Ø means that no word is required. More than one alternative might fit.

	1	assured		
	2	confessed		
	3	answered	a) Ø	
	4	informed		(that) he
He	5	persuaded	b) me	was not
	6	proved		responsible.
	7	said	c) to me	
	8	told		
	9	claimed		

13.9

a Use the information to make up sentences having the pattern A WARNED, ETC. B TO DO/NOT TO DO SOMETHING. Use the pronouns **he/she** and **him/her/them** where possible. We have done the first one to help you.

1 'Don't be late again!'
   (boss to secretary)   order
   He ordered her not to be late again.

2 'Please wear a tie.'
   (wife to husband)   beg

3 'Do not tell the police anything.'
   (lawyer to client)   advise

4 'Keep away from the Grotto disco.'
   (father to daughters)   warn

5 'Don't talk to strangers.'
   (mother to children)   tell

6 'You cannot go out!'
   (brother to sister)   not allow

7 'Book a table at Luigi's.'
   (girl to boyfriend)   remind

8 'Don't be late.'
   (boy to girlfriend)   ask

9 'Be back by ten thirty.'
   (mother to sons)   expect

b Express the sentences which you have made up in **a** in the passive form. We have done the first one to help you.

1 She...
   She was ordered not to be late again.
2 He...
3 He...
4 They...
5 They...
6 She...
7 He...
8 She...
9 They...

13.10

a Add a suitable form of **let** or **make** to these sentences.

1 Don't _____ me laugh!
2 He punished us by _____ us stay behind after school.
3 As a reward, he _____ us stay up late to watch TV.
4 I did not want to go with them: they _____ me do it.
5 They said I wasn't good enough, but they _____ me try anyway.
6 Try to avoid _____ everyone know what we intend to do.
7 We were _____ to sit still with our arms folded.
8 Stop tickling! You'll _____ me spill my drink.
9 If you are really interested in those books, I'll _____ you borrow them.

b Use the information to make up sentences having the pattern GET SOMEONE TO DO SOMETHING. We have done the first one to help you

	Situation	Solution
1	I've got a broken tape recorder; Tony knows about tape recorders. I...	(have a look)
	I'll get Tony to have a look at it.	
2	The car won't start; Joe is a good mechanic. We...	(see to)
3	Our customer needs this order right away; Mike has got his car here. We...	(deliver)
4	I was too busy to see him; Julia was free. I...	(interview)
5	Mother is ill. What about the housework? The children are at home. She can...	(do)
6	The police knew he had committed the crime; they questioned him. They...	(confess)

7   I haven't time to look at the
    draft; Alan will be here soon.
    I . . .   (go through)
8   The club needed money; Mr
    Smith is rich and generous.
    Perhaps we can . . .   (contribute)

9   This dog needs training. Mrs
    Woodhouse is good at that
    sort of thing.
    Why don't you . . .   (train)

13.11
a   Choose the preposition from the central
column which fits the rest of the sentence.

1 Give your share		John.
2 Buy a drink		the rest of the group.
3 Do a favour	a) **to**	a friend.
4 Reserve a table		me.
5 Leave all your money		your grandchildren.
6 Save a place	b) **for**	Joe.
7 Offer a job		the best applicant.
8 Pass the draft		the technical advisor.
9 Spare something		for the rest of us.

b   Replace the expression (i.e. the noun phrase)
after the preposition by a pronoun, and rewrite
each sentence on the pattern VERB + INDIRECT
OBJECT + DIRECT OBJECT.
e.g. 1   John becomes *him*. *Give him your
share.*

c   Put the three elements into their natural
(usual) order. If more than one order is possible,
choose the more usual alternative. Add the
preposition **to** where necessary.

1   he announced / his resignation / the press
2   she explained / her colleagues / the situation
3   he forgot to mention / his boss / the matter
4   I shall have to report / this / the authorities
5   He teaches / mathematics / young people
6   Don't tell / anything / the others
7   I have promised / a party / the children
8   Would you like to read / the class / a story
9   He refuses to say / anybody / anything

13.12
In which of the following sentences would you
normally leave out the conjunction **that**?
(Assume that they are spoken sentences.)

1   I told you that it was important.
2   I was told that you might be able to help me.
3   She mentioned to her colleagues that she
    was thinking of retiring.
4   He said that you were interested in joining
    our group.
5   We decided to go to Florence in spite of the
    fact that the autostrada was under repair.
6   He told them that he would go alone, and
    that they were not to worry about him.
7   It has been suggested that the opposition
    party might agree to a coalition.
8   I suppose that you will buy some souvenirs
    when you leave.
9   He did not realize that you were a relative of
    mine.
10 Did they explain to you that you have to
    pay your own expenses?
11 The delay is due to the fact that the rail
    strike is affecting deliveries.
12 Has everyone been told that the concert has
    been cancelled?
13 I forgot that I had an appointment at three.
14 I should like to make it clear that I do not
    approve of violence.

15 He proved to everyone's satisfaction that the drug was effective and harmless.

16 He agreed that he had no reason to complain.

17 Are you sure that you understand what that means?

18 I think that he realizes that he cannot do as he likes.

13.13

a Combine each verb with the appropriate adjective and complete the sentences. In sentences 4 and 6 more than one verb will fit. Make any necessary changes to the verbs.

Verbs: dye, get, grow, hold, keep, leave, make, paint, set
Adjectives: free, green, ill, long, open, shut, undone, wet, white

1 She has _____ her hair _____ : her head looks like a GO sign!

2 When I was younger, I _____ my hair _____ : it was down to my waist.

3 'How did you manage to _____ your clothes _____ ?' 'I fell in the river.'

4 Would you _____ the door _____ so that I can carry the food in?

5 If you eat any more, you will _____ yourself _____ .

6 I always _____ the top button _____ : it's more comfortable.

7 We _____ the windows _____ to keep the noise out.

8 The guerrillas attacked the prison and _____ their comrades _____ .

9 We wanted a bright kitchen, so we _____ it _____ .

b Use combinations from the table to complete the sentences. In some cases more than one alternative is suitable. Make any necessary changes.

find	it	remarkable
make		difficult
		clear
		obvious

1 I wish to _____ that I am not connected with the company.

2 I _____ that so few people are interested in nature.

3 She has _____ that she wants to have nothing to do with us.

4 He always _____ to express himself clearly.

5 Don't you _____ that nobody knows anything about the incident?

6 I am _____ to concentrate properly.

7 Can't you _____ to her that it is her job, not yours?

8 I don't _____ to understand why people want a change.

9 You are _____ to everyone that you don't really like them.

13.14

In the following sentences choose between the verbs **have** and **get** (or the verb form provided). In some cases, only one will fit. Where both are possible, choose the one which fits better the general meaning of the sentence, and say what difference of meaning or emphasis would be produced if you had chosen the other one.

1 How on earth did you manage to | have / get | your car repaired so cheaply?

2 We must | have / get | this place tidied up before mother and father come home!

3 He has | had / got | his driving licence endorsed by the police for dangerous driving.

4 My children | have / get | their teeth checked routinely every six months.

5 | Have / Get | your hair cut – it's a disgrace!

6 I | had / got | my binoculors stolen when I was in Barcelona.

7 We're trying to $\begin{vmatrix} \text{have} \\ \text{get} \end{vmatrix}$ the central heating repaired before the bad weather comes.

8 You really ought to $\begin{vmatrix} \text{have} \\ \text{get} \end{vmatrix}$ that cut examined: it looks infected to me.

9 I'm sorry I haven't written the report yet: I'll $\begin{vmatrix} \text{have} \\ \text{get} \end{vmatrix}$ it done right away.

10 I like to $\begin{vmatrix} \text{have} \\ \text{get} \end{vmatrix}$ the house repainted every five years.

11 Mind you don't $\begin{vmatrix} \text{have} \\ \text{get} \end{vmatrix}$ your fingers caught in the door.

12 Do you know where I could $\begin{vmatrix} \text{have} \\ \text{get} \end{vmatrix}$ a pair of shoes made cheaply?

13.15

What is the difference in meaning or emphasis between the following pairs of sentences? (One way to show the difference is to describe situations in which each might be said.)

1 i) *He was allowed not to* join the union.
  ii) *He was not allowed to* join the union.

2 i) *He went on talking* about his experiences for hours.
  ii) *He went on to talk* about his experiences in a busy London clinic.

3 i) *He let us* go out.
  ii) *He made us* go out.

4 i) *I heard her sing* One Fine Day.
  ii) *I heard her singing* One Fine Day.

5 i) I did not know *whether* John had called.
  ii) I did not know *that* John had called

6 i) *Do you intend to stay* here tonight?
  ii) *Do you intend staying* here all night?

7 i) 'Would you like a lift?' 'No, thanks, *I prefer to walk.*'
  ii) 'Although I have a car, *I prefer walking* to driving.'

8 i) I expect *he will come.*
  ii) I expect *him to come.*

9 i) *I began to study* the report very carefully.
  ii) *I began studying* French while I was still at school.

Just for fun

13.16 Bits and pieces

Below is a story about a spaniel (a kind of dog) and a hedgehog (a small animal with spines all over its body). Unfortunately, the sentences are out of sequence, and in some cases, the sentences themselves are in bits! Can you put them back together in the correct order? Look carefully at each piece of the 'jigsaw' – in each one there is something which you can relate to another piece, and so on, until the whole story is reconstructed.

1 , but again he got nothing put a painful jab in his flesh.
2 In the meantime, the hedgehog had curled up into a little ball,
3 He sniffed at the animal but leapt back with a cry of pain
4 One day, a spaniel was playing in the garden
5 The spaniel then pushed it with his paw in order to turn it over,
6 when he came across a strange animal with spines
7 as the creature's spines stuck in his nose.
8 so that you could no longer tell
9 it could be to make friends with a hedgehog.
10 all over its body.
11 which end was which.
12 He did not know what the strange creature was, but he soon found out how painful

Tip: pay attention to the punctuation as well as the words.

Unit 14 Sentence construction

14.1

a   The first part of each sentence expresses a proposed course of action. The second part expresses either the reason for taking that action; or the result of taking the action. Use one of the conjunctions **so that** or **in case** to complete the sentences according to the meaning of the second part.

Proposed action		*Reason or result*
1 Take an umbrella		you won't get wet. it rains.
2 Pack an overnight bag		you have to stay the night. you can stay the night.
3 Have something to eat		you won't feel hungry later. you can't get anything to eat later.
4 Let's have an early night	**in case**	we'll be fresh in the morning. we have to get up early tomorrow.
5 Take the files with you	**so that**	you need to refer to them. you can refer to them.
6 We must fill up with petrol		we'll have enough for the journey. the filling stations are closed.
7 Wear your heavy overcoats		the weather turns colder. you won't feel the cold.
8 Write everything down		you forget it. you have a record of what is said.
9 Book well in advance		you are sure of getting a seat. they sell out.

b   Rewrite the sentences you have made up in **a** saying what you did and why or with what result.
e.g. keep some money in reserve in case you need it.
= I kept some money in reserve in case I needed it.

14.2

a The first part of each sentence describes a situation. Complete each sentence with a clause beginning **because** or **even though** and using the words given in the second part. In sentences 4–9, we leave you to make any necessary changes to the second part.

1	The streets are wet		it has been raining. it hasn't been raining.
2	We got wet through		we didn't take an umbrella. we took an umbrella.
3	He failed his driving test		he didn't practice enough. he practised a lot.
4	She is fit and healthy	even though	not much exercise. a lot of exercise.
5	I'm hungry		not much for breakfast. a lot for breakfast.
6	Our team seldom wins		not very good players. very good players.
7	I run an expensive car	because	not afford it. afford it.
8	They often go to discos		not keen on dancing. keen on dancing.
9	He speaks Japanese fluently		never lived in Japan. lived in Japan.

b Use these nine conjunctions in the sentences. as far as, as if, as long as, considering, providing, (or provided), seeing (that), supposing, unless, wherever.

1 _____ you lost your job, what would you do then?
2 'Where's Joe working these days?' 'He's still at Sankey's _____ I know.'
3 _____ I go, I seem to bump into people I was at school with.
4 Don't use the car _____ it is absolutely necessary.
5 He looked _____ he had seen a ghost.
6 You can take books out of the library _____ you bring them back.
7 _____ you don't need your bicycle any more, do you think I could have it?
8 You can keep it _____ you like: I don't need it any more.
9 _____ how much he earns, I'm surprised he dresses so badly.

14.3

a Complete the sentences using the expressions
so . . . that or such (a) . . . that, in the 'SITUATION', and expanding the elements given in the 'consequence' column.

	Situation	Consequence
1	/crowded restaurant The restaurant was _____	/we/not/table/
2	/expensive hotel/ It is _____ hotel _____	/only the rich/afford/
3	/large feet/ He has _____	/not/shoes to fit/
4	/difficult exercise/ It was _____ exercise _____	/nobody/do it/
5	/beautiful hair/ She had _____	/everyone/admire)

6 /Russia big/   /eleven time zones/
   Russia _____
   country _____
7 /polluted air/   /your clothes/dirty
   The air is _____
8 /polluted river/   /no fish/live in it/
   It is _____ river
   _____
9 /good advice/   /able/save thousands
                     of pounds!/
   He gave me _____

b Match the expressions in the left hand column to the expressions in the right hand column, and complete the sentences using **so much/many/little** or the construction SO + ADVERB.

1 I have _____ work to do
2 He drove _____ fast
3 She has _____ intelligence
4 I have _____ letters to write
5 She has _____ admirers
6 He drove _____ slowly
7 I have _____ money left
8 She has _____ clothes
9 He drove dangerously

a) you rarely see her in the same dress twice.
b) I don't know where to begin.
c) it will take me ages to get through them all.
d) nobody could catch up with him.
e) he arrived half an hour late.
f) men are afraid of her.
g) his wife refused to ride with him.
h) she goes out with a different man every night.
i) I don't think I will be able to pay my bills.

14.4

Choose the conjunction which fits the meaning of the sentence. In some cases more than one will fit, so study the meaning of each conjunction carefully in relation to the rest of the sentence.

1 | As / As though / As soon as | it is getting late, I suggest we break off now.

2 Nobody is to leave | until / unless / since | I say so.

3 He arrived | just as / as long as / as far as | I was leaving.

4 She cried out | although / as though / as if | she had been stung by a wasp.

5 Call in and say hello | whenever / however / wherever | you are in town.

6 | Since / Seeing that / In case | nobody else seems to want these sandwiches, I'll eat them.

7 | As soon as / Since / Now that | you leave school, you'll be able to get a good job.

8 | As far as / So that / Once | I can see, he has no intention of paying the bill.

9 Stay in your flat | as far as / until / since | somebody sends for you.

10 | Once / Whenever / After | you have driven a Porsche, you will never want to drive any other car.

11 You will never make friends | if / when / unless | you go out and meet people.

12 We'll invite Chris and Mary, | considering / supposing / assuming | that they are interested.

13 | As / When / If | you think it is necessary, send him some more money.

14 Please don't talk | while / whenever / now that | the concert has begun.

15 I do not trust him | as though / even though / although | I do business with him.

| 16 What did you do | while
before
since | you met me? |

| 17 What were
you doing | while
as
after | I was
travelling around
Europe? |

| 18 What will
you do | after
once
now that | the course
is nearly over? |

14.5
Describe the difference in meaning or emphasis between the following pairs of sentences. One way to do this is to describe the different situations in which each might be said.

1 i) You must visit the National Gallery when you get a chance.
  ii) You must visit the National Gallery whenever you get a chance.

2 i) Give me a ring when you come to town.
  ii) Give me a ring if you come to town.

3 i) Once you have passed your test, you'll be able to get a car of your own.
  ii) Now that you have passed your test, you can get a car of your own.

4 i) They left when the party started to get a bit noisy.
  ii) They left just as the party was beginning to get a bit noisy.

5 i) Stand still or I'll hit you!
  ii) Stand still and I'll hit you! (2 meanings)

6 i) You can stay here *as long as* you like.
  ii) You can stay here *as long as* you don't make a noise.

7 i) As it was beginning to snow, we set off for home.
  ii) We set off for home just as it was beginning to snow.

8 i) Put winter tyres on your car in case it snows.
  ii) Put winter tyres on your car if it snows.

9 i) Don't start writing until you are told to.
  ii) Don't start writing unless you are told to.

10 i) Why don't you go and see them while you are in London?
  ii) Why don't you go and see them when you are in London?

11 i) I'll come if you want me to.
  ii) I won't come unless you want me to.

12 i) I didn't write to her because I was angry. (I calmed down later)
  ii) I didn't write to her because I was angry. (Although she may have thought so)

14.6
a Rephrase these sentences starting with the words given and using the conjunction in brackets where one is given. Make any necessary changes of verb form.

1 Eat that and you'll be ill!
  If . . .
2 Drink this and you'll feel better.
  Once . . .
3 Put it away or I'll take it off you.
  If . . . (not) . . .
4 She has gone back to Sicily and I am feeling sad.
  I . . . (because)
5 He put the lights on and we could see much better.
  He . . . (so that)
6 Do your homework or you won't learn anything.
  You . . . (unless)
7 He did his best for her, and she left him!
  She . . . (even though)
8 I don't know her very well, but I like her very much.
  I . . . (although)
9 Everyone else had gone, so they put out the lights and went to bed.
  It was not . . . (until)
10 The disco was crowded so we didn't go in.
  Seeing . . .
11 We are old but we enjoy life.
  We . . . (even if)
12 He speaks Japanese and he can read it as well!
  Not only . . . (but)

b Join the following pairs of sentences using the conjunction given in brackets. Remove the italicized adverbials, and make any other necessary changes. (Take special care with verb forms!)

1 He set his alarm for 6 a.m. *As a result*, he would not be late for work. (so that)
2 I worked hard. *Nevertheless* I didn't get anywhere. (even though)
3 She came running up to me. *At that moment* I was about to leave the office. (just as)
4 You seem to know so much about it. *For this reason*, I would like to hear your version of the incident. (since)
5 It might rain. *Therefore* you should take your umbrella. (in case)

6 The lesson had been cancelled. For this reason, all the students were sitting in the canteen. (because)
7 You can have the day off. *However*, you must work on Saturday instead. (as long as)
8 You may not feel like it. *All the same*, you must go and visit your aunt. (even if)
9 We could have a game of cards. *Unfortunately*, the Queen of Diamonds is missing. (if)

14.7
Report these direct questions starting with the words *He wants to know*... We have done the first one to help you.

	He wants to know	
1 'Why isn't she at work?'		why she isn't at work.
2 'Where are you living?'		_____ we _____
3 'What are they talking about?'		_____ they _____
4 'When will she come back?'		_____ she _____
5 'What happened?'		what _____
6 'Did anyone call?'		_____ anyone _____
7 'Can I talk to Joe?'		_____ he _____
8 'Have you always lived in Bern?'		_____ we _____
9 'Who looks after the record player?'		who _____
10 'How long have they been married?'		_____ they _____
11 'Do I have to do all these exercises?'		_____ he _____
12 'Shall I wait for the others?'		_____ he _____
13 'Why hasn't anyone done the washing-up?'		_____ nobody _____
14 'When does the new term start?'		_____ the new term _____
15 'Who do you like best?'		_____ we _____
16 'Who likes you best?'		who _____
17 'Would you like to come as well?'		_____ we _____
18 'Shall I need my overcoat?'		_____ he _____

14.8
a How many grammatically correct and meaningful combinations can you make by combining elements from the two columns?

1 He wanted to know
2 I'm trying to find out
3 She has just asked me
4 You ought to find out
5 He was beginning to wonder
6 We should try to discover
7 We should have asked earlier
8 I could not find out
9 I must find out
10 Nobody would tell us
11 It is your job to know
12 Can't you ask somebody

a) what is going on?
b) what was going on?

b Report the direct questions in Exercise 14.7 starting with the words
He wanted to know _____

14.9

Make meaningful and grammatical sentences by combining elements from each column.

1	He would like to know	a) when they are leaving.
		b) when they were leaving.
		c) when they will be leaving.
2	He was curious to find out	d) when they would be leaving.
		e) why she left.
		f) why she has left.
3	John said he wasn't sure	g) why she had left.
		h) how many people have been invited.
4	Try to find out	i) how many people had been invited.
		j) how many people were invited.
		k) how many people might be invited.

14.10

a Ask direct questions about the situations given below.

Example
Situation: He is looking at something.
Ask him *what*?
What are you looking at?

		Ask him
1	He is thinking about something.	What?
2	He is up to something.	What?
3	He gave it to someone.	Who?
4	He is going in one of the cars.	Which car?
5	He is looking for something.	What?
6	He went out with someone last night.	Who?
7	He has to save up a certain amount of money.	How much money?
8	He has saved up a certain amount of money.	How much?
9	He has been waiting for someone.	Who?
10	He belongs to several clubs	Which clubs?
11	He was talking to someone.	Who?
12	He is staying for some time.	How long?

b Report the questions you have made up in (a) beginning with the expressions
  i) I am curious to know . . .
  ii) I was curious to know . . .

14.11

a Report these statements or questions beginning with the words given.
(Make any necessary changes to verbs and to time expressions)

1	It's too late.	He told me . . .
2	'Aren't you worried about her?'	I'm surprised . . .
3	'You mustn't worry!'	He advised us . . .
4	'Haven't you finished?'	He seemed surprised that I . . .
5	'Give everyone a copy.'	He suggested that everyone . . .
6	'You must leave tomorrow.'	We were ordered . . .
7	'I saw her yesterday.'	He told me he . . .
8	'Everything must be ready by 6 tonight.'	The General told us . . .
9	'Why didn't you tell me before now?'	He said he wished I . . .

b The following passages report two conversations which took place. Rewrite them as a dialogue, i.e., give the speakers' exact words.

Begin:
Alan: 'Hello Cathy, what . . .

1 Alan asked Cathy what she was doing that day. She told him she had not got any plans, so he invited her to go swimming with him. She asked him to wait while she went and got changed. He said he would go and have a coffee while he was waiting, but she pointed out that he would not have time because it would only take her a second to get changed.

2 Alan wanted to know if he could help Cathy with her homework. She replied that she could use some help. He could see, he remarked, that she had a lot to do. He then told her that he had finished his own work some time before. She asked him how he had been able to do it so quickly. He replied with a grin that he had found a key to the

exercises, so he had simply copied out all the answers. She called him a cheat and told him to get out and not to bother her again.

14.12

a Join the two parts of these sentences. Only put in **whom** when it is necessary.

1	We need someone	knows about statistics.
2	I'm looking for a man	I can do business with.
3	They are a pop group	you do not hear very often.
4	Have you seen the girl	**who** usually sits here?
5	She is the last person	you would tell!
6	I am talking to those of you	have actually experienced poverty.
7	What about the ones	cannot fight for themselves?
8	Do you know the girl	**Ø** I was with the other night?
9	These are the sort of people	the company should employ.
10	He is the kind of man	really knows what is going on.
11	Do you know anyone	can play as well as he can?
12	He is the only one	the men will listen to any more.

b   Change the sentences between dashes (–) into relative clauses. Replace the dashes by commas, add a suitable pronoun and make any necessary changes.

1   Mr John Dawes – most of you have already met him – has agreed to take on the job as treasurer.

2   Ted Brett – most of you know his books – will be the guest speaker at our Annual Dinner.

3   The Advanced Passenger Train – you may have seen it on TV – will revolutionize public transport in this country.

4   We wish to thank Miss Dinah Harris – she wrote all the music for the festival.

5   The lead guitarist – everyone refers to him as 'Jezz' – is the only trained musician in the group.

6   The Beresford Gallery – admission to it used to be free – has had to introduce an entrance fee of £3.

7   Arthur Bowyer – his latest novel is already a best seller – gave up a well-paid job to become a writer.

8   His father John – we rarely see him now – used to appear regularly on television.

9   Abu Kammash is a huge chemical complex – the salt plant is only a small part of it.

10   The need for a further increase in postage rates – and I shall say more about that in a moment – is one more example of bad planning.

11   The factory was completed on time – and this surprised a lot of people.

12   The girls' dresses – a local firm supplied the material for them – were made by members of the Parents' Association.

14.13

a Join these sentences by adding a suitable relative pronoun (and commas where necessary). Make any other necessary changes.

e.g. I'd like to buy a tie. It will match my suit.
= I'd like to buy a tie *which/that* would match my suit.
This is my sister. She lives in Birmingham.
= This is my sister, *who* lives in Birmingham.

1	I went to see her flat.	She lived in it when she was a student.
2	I went to see the flat.	She lived in it when she was a student.
3	Come and meet the friends.	I told you about them.
4	Come and meet my friends.	You know most of them.
5	This the Director.	He founded the company.
6	There are several directors. This is the director.	He founded the company.
7	What we really need is a dam.	It would be big enough to supply the whole area with power.

8 I have a photo of   It supplies the whole
   the Kariba dam.   area with power.
9 I'd like to introduce   I used to work with
   Mr Bridge.   him.
10 Can that be the   I used to work with
   Mr Bridge.   him.
11 I have to study   I do not enjoy it.
   mathematics.
12 Statistics is the   I do not enjoy it.
   one part of maths.

b Complete each of the statements using a suitable relative pronoun, and inserting commas where they are necessary.

1 English people _____ go abroad for their holidays often develop a taste for a variety of different styles of cooking.
2 Each year Britain welcomes several million visitors (many) _____ never travel outside London, surprisingly.
3 Airline pilots _____ have a very stressful job must have regular health checks.
4 Young married couples _____ usually have very little money find it difficult to save enough to buy their own homes.
5 Left-handed people _____ are often very good at music and art make up only 10% of the population.
6 People _____ put on weight easily have to be careful what they eat.
7 Olympic sportsmen (many) _____ train for years to become successful have to be very dedicated.
8 Old people _____ bones break very easily have to be very careful when walking on snow and ice in winter.
9 Young babies _____ need to be kept warm can easily become ill if the temperature is too low.

14.14

What is the difference in meaning or emphasis between these pairs of sentences? (Describe a situation to which each one might refer.)

1 i) Nobody knew what the quarrel was about.
   ii) Nobody knew what the quarrel had been about.

2 i) I wish you would work a bit harder.
   ii) I wish you had worked a bit harder.

3 i) I thought you were leaving tomorrow.
   ii) I thought you were leaving the next day.

4 i) John said he'll see to the photocopying.
   ii) John said he would see to the photocopying.

5 i) My mother told me I should not waste my money on a new car.
   ii) My mother told me I should not have wasted my money on a new car.

6 i) He often wondered why she loved him so much.
   ii) He often wondered why she had loved him so much.

7 i) I think you might be a bit more honest with me.
   ii) I think you might have been a bit more honest with me.

8 i) The teacher told us that there were still cannibals in Borneo.
   ii) The teacher told us there are still cannibals in Borneo.

9 i) He said we must work harder.
   ii) He said we had to work harder.

10 i) I wish I knew all the facts.
   ii) I wish I had known all the facts.

11 i) I thought you didn't speak French.
   ii) I didn't think you spoke French.

12 i) He wondered if she had come back.
   ii) He wondered if she would come back.

Just for fun

14.15 Proverbs and sayings

Here are nine well-known English proverbs or sayings. Unfortunately, they have got very mixed up. Can you rebuild the proverbs from the elements in the three columns? (Put a suitable relative pronoun in place of the _____)*

All	_____ pays the piper	is not gold.
People	_____ laughs last	should not throw stones.
All's well	_____ prays together	.
He	_____ glitters	calls the tune.
He	_____ blows nobody any good	laughs best.
It's a long lane	_____ do not want to hear	.
It's an ill wind	_____ ends well	.
There are none so deaf as those	_____ live in glass houses	.
The family	_____ has no turning	stays together.

*You should be able to work the proverbs out from the meaning of the elements. If you are stuck, the following comments on each proverb might help you:

1 Do no judge things by their outward appearance.
2 Don't criticize others when your own behaviour is not very good.
3 Difficulties do not matter as long as you get the result you want.
4 The person with power gets what he wants.
5 Winning is what really matters.
6 Things always get better sooner or later.
7 Something good can come out of the worst situations.
8 People will deliberately ignore unpleasant facts if they choose to.
9 This is a notice which is encouraging families to go to church.

Answers

Unit 1

1.1
4 Miss Jones   6 Tuesday   7 the Duke of Kent   8 Easter Sunday   11 the *Moonlight Sonata*   13 the Daily Mirror   15 Tolstoy's *War and Peace*   17 New Year's Eve   18 the first Sunday in June

1.2
1 offices   2 loaf   3 losses   4 potato   5 roofs   6 mouse   7 solos   8 keys   9 tooth   10 sandwiches   11 cities   12 children   13 tomatoes   14 stepsons   15 woman   16 pence (pennies also possible but less likely)   17 foot   18 cupsful   19 sons-in-law   20 life   21 menservants   22 traffic wardens   23 spoonfuls (spoonsful is possible but less common)   24 passers-by   25 rabbits   26 species   27 sheep   28 salmon   29 trout   30 series

1.3
1 [s]   2 [z]   3 [ɪz]   4 [z]   5 [z]   6 [s]   7 [z]   8 [ɪz]   9 [z]   10 [s]   11 [ɪz]   12 [z]   13 [s]   14 [ɪz]   15 [ɪz]   16 [z]   17 [ɪz]   18 [s]   19 [z]   20 [s]   21 [s]   22 [z]   23 [z]   24 [z]

1.4
1 lines   – [z] ending, others all [ɪz] ending
2 roads   – [z] ending, others all [s] ending
3 grapes   – [s] ending, others all [z]
4 hearts   – [s] ending, others all [z]
5 months   – [s] ending, others usually [z] ending

1.5
1 cactus   2 analyses   3 stimulus   4 stratum   5 data   6 vertebra   7 bases   8 fungi   9 genus   10 indexes or indices   11 crisis   12 criterion   13 memorandum   14 stadia

15 museums   16 addendum   17 radius   18 dramas   19 geniuses or genii   20 appendix   21 axes   22 medium   23 albums   24 phenomenon

1.6
1 singular   2 plural   3 singular or plural   4 plural   5 singular or plural   6 plural   7 singular   8 plural   9 plural   10 plural (or singular if referring to the science of statistics)   11 usually plural, occasionally treated as singular   12 plural   13 singular or plural   14 singular or plural   15 singular or plural   16 singular or plural   17 plural   18 singular or plural

1.7
1 All mass nouns with no plural form
2 All can be treated as either singular or plural
3 All occur only in the plural
4 All mass nouns
5 All occur only in plural, and all have two parts

1.8
A blade of grass	A slice of meat
A loaf of bread	A sheet of paper
A speck of dust	A lump of coal
An item of news	A strand of hair
A grain of sand	
A drop of water	
A bar of soap	

1.9
A box of matches	A flock of birds
A a pack of cards	A tin of sardines
A crowd of people	A bunch of flowers
A herd of cows	A packet of cigarettes
A bottle of milk	A bundle of clothes

1.10
1 sister   2 father   3 husband   4 aunt   5 nephew   6 daughter

7 heroine   8 bachelor   9 waitress
10 duchess   11 empress   12 count or earl
13 king   14 lady   15 usherette
16 manageress   17 lad   18 Dear Madam,

1.11

Male	Female	Young
bull	cow	calf
boar	sow	piglet
buck	hind	fawn
stag	doe	fawn
fox	vixen	cub
dog	bitch	pup
gander	goose	gosling
drake	duck	duckling
stallion	mare	foal
cock	hen	chick

1.12

1 drummer   2 engineer   3 physicist
4 economist   5 surveyor   6 violinist
7 lawyer   8 chemist   9 dramatist
10 telephonist   11 supervisor   12 attendant
13 technologist   14 cellist   15 trumpeter
16 footballer   17 scientist   18 organizer
19 librarian   20 comedian   21 typist
22 trombonist   23 photographer
24 musician   25 instructor
26 accountant   27 flautist   28 democrat
29 athlete   30 gymnast

1.13

addition; agreement; amusement; apology;
appearance; association; assumption;
authorization; arrival; attendance or attention;
comparison; completion; conception;
concentration; conclusion; conference;
confusion; deception; decision; declaration;
defence; defiance; departure; difference;
disappointment; distinction; division;
employment; endurance; enjoyment;
entertainment; explanation; explosion;
exploration; failure; information; imitation;
interference; intervention; irritation;
judgement; multiplication; observation;
offence; permission; persistence; preference;
procedure; provision; reception; reference;
refusal; repetition; revision; signature;
simplification; solution; sympathy;
transmission; variation.

1.14

1 (i) a ´darkroom (ii) a dark ´room
2 (i) a ´lighthouse (ii) a light ´room   3 (i) a
country ´house (ii) a ´countryman   4 (i) a
´briefcase (ii) a brief ´meeting   5 (i) a gold
´watch (ii) a ´goldfish   6 (i) a ´schoolboy (ii) a
school ´building   7 (i) a paper ´bag (ii) a
´paperback (ii) a ´paperweight   8 (i) a cash
´offer (ii) a ´cashbox (iii) a ´cashbook   9 (i) a
working ´model (ii) working ´mothers (iii)
´working hours.

1.15

1 ´s   2 ´   3 ´s   4 ´   5 ´s   6 ´s
7 ´s   8 ´   9 ´s   10 ´   11 ´ or ´s
12 ´s   13 ´s   14 ´   15 ´s

1.16

1 The Duke of Edinburgh's scheme   2 The
managing director's office   3 My sister-in-
law's car   4 A boys' school
5 The railwaymen's union   6 Murphy's law
7 A fortnight's holiday   8 The nurses' home
9 Mr Brown's wife's car *or* Mrs Brown's car

1.17

1 [s]   2 [z]   3 [ɪz]   4 [z]   5 [z]
6 [s]   7 [ɪz]   8 [s]   9 [z]   10 [ɪz]
11 [z]   12 [ɪz]   13 [z]   14 [s]
15 [z]   16 [ɪz]   17 [s]   18 [s]

1.18

1 greengrocer's   2 dentist's   3 optician's
4 chemist's   5 ironmonger's   6 butcher's
7 hairdresser's   8 florist's   9 cleaner's

1.19

1 dog's   2 Thursday's   3 Life's
4 . . . day's . . . day's   5 sheep's
6 woman's   7 . . . man's . . . man's . . .
8 goodness'   9. Love's

1.20

1 George
2 Mary
3 Two, Frank and Alan
4 She is his sister-in-law
5 They are his grandchildren
6 Mildred
7 Janet

8   George
9   William and Mary
10   Susan
11   Three, Frank, Alan and Susan
12   Four, Helen and John, and Janet and
     Christopher

1.21 *Word Square*

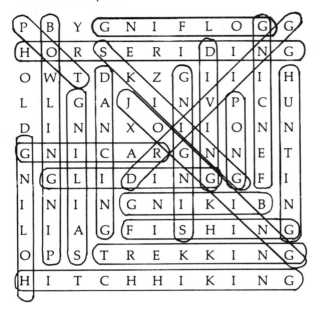

Unit 2

2.1

The Elephant and the Mouse

An elephant and *a* mouse fell in love and
decided to get married. When *the* elephant told
her father, he said: 'Don't be silly, *an* elephant
cannot marry *a* mouse.'

When *the* mouse told his mother, she said:
'Don't be silly, mice do not marry elephants.'

So *the* elephant, who was very musical,
became *a* pianist, and *the* mouse, who had *a*
good voice, became *a* singer. They toured *the*
world together for many years, giving concerts
and bringing pleasure to everyone who heard
them.

Moral: There is more than one way to live in
harmony.

2.2

2, 3, 6, 10, 11, 12, 13, 14, 18, 19, 21, 23, 25, 27,
28, 29, 30.

2.3

1   'Is this the book you were telling me about?'
    'Yes, it is about the life of Queen Victoria.'
2   It is an interesting book. It gives a
    wonderful picture of what life was like in
    Victorian times.
3   'Is there a newsagent's near here?' 'There are
    several; the nearest one is just down the
    road on the left.'
4   We always stay at the Palace Court Hotel
    because it is the only one with facilities for
    the disabled.
5   The Playhouse is an old theatre, but it puts
    on modern plays.
6   The Swiss Alps are a good place to go if you
    like skiing. There is usually plenty of snow
    during the winter months.
7   Just look at the snow! It seems to be just the
    right kind of snow for skiing.
8   English people are forever complaining
    about the weather, but in fact the British
    Isles have a reasonable climate on the whole.
9   This is the toughest steak I have ever eaten.
    It is the last time I eat in this restaurant.
10   The otter used to be a common animal, but
    it is now found only in the north of Britain.
11   In the old days, you used to see otters all
    over the place, but now you can only find
    them in certain parts of the country.
12   Robin Hood is a legendary hero that
    children learn about from story books. He
    used to take money from the rich and give it
    to the poor.
13   Martin King lives in a little village on the
    edge of the New Forest. He writes books
    about natural history in general, and about
    the natural history of the New Forest in
    particular.
14   I have just bought a copy of his latest book,
    A Close Look at Nature. It contains some of
    the finest photographs of wildlife subjects
    that I have ever seen.
15   Martins's book deals with a wide range of
    animal species, from blackbirds to rare
    animals like otters.

16 We have just been on holiday to the Lake District. At first we thought of camping, but then we decided to stay in hotels instead.

17 It is a wonderful part of England and the scenery reminds you of mountainous countries like Switzerland. As a matter of fact, we had such a good time that we have decided to have a holiday there again next year.

18 We also paid a short visit to Scotland. We went to Edinburgh to see the usual sights, including the Castle and Prince's Street. Then we spent a week in the Highlands.

2.4

1 What terrible weather! What a terrible climate!   2 What beautiful luggage! What a beautiful suitcase!   3 What elegant clothes! What an elegant dress!   4 What heavy rainfall! What a heavy shower!   5 What a healthy cow! What healthy cattle!   6 What awful rubbish! What an awful mess!   7 What clever people! What a clever person!   8 What a difficult job! What difficult work!   9 What fresh bread! What a fresh loaf!   10 What delicious food! What a delicious meal!   11 What a horrible tune! What horrible music!   12 What tough beef! What a tough steak!

2.5	
glass	a substance used, for example, in windows
a glass	a container for drinking out of
paper	material for writing on
a paper	*The Times* or the *Daily Mirror* for example
wood	the material obtained from trees with which we make furniture, for example
a wood	a group or clump of trees
iron	a metal, chemical symbol Fe, from which steel is made
an iron	a device for taking unwanted creases out of clothes; also the popular name for a kind of golfclub
string	something which you use for tying up parcels, for example
a string	the part of a guitar, for example, which you pluck in order to make a note
coffee	substance used for making a stimulating drink
a coffee	refers to a cup containing a drink made from this substance
cloth	material from which clothes are made, for example
a cloth	a piece of material used for wiping or cleaning things
rubber	material from which car tyres, for example, are made
a rubber	something which you use to get rid of a pencil mark
lamb	a kind of meat which we get from a young sheep
a lamb	an animal, the young of a sheep
language	the faculty or ability by which human beings communicate with each other
a language	English, Spanish, Arabic or Japanese, for example
tin	a metal, chemical symbol Sn, used in the manufacture of food containers
a tin	a container into which food is put before it is sold
study	the activity of learning
a study	a quiet room where you go to think or to work
light	a form of energy from the sun which enables us to see
a light	a device which we switch on in a room when it goes dark
air	the stuff we breathe in order to stay alive
an air	a tune or melody; also used to describe someone's manner or appearance
duck	meat from a particular kind of bird
a duck	kind of bird which lives on or near water
gold	a precious metal, chemical symbol Au
a gold	popular name for the medal awarded to the best performer in an Olympic event
play	an activity performed purely for pleasure; not work

a play   a story performed on stage by
actors
thought   a mental process
a thought   an idea

2.6

1 'I don't take sugar, thank you'.
2 Although brown rice is better for you, most
people prefer white rice.
3 Roger knows a lot about classical music. He
seems to like the string quartets of
Beethoven best.
4 I studied modern history at University. In
the last year I specialized in the history of
the American Civil War.
5 'What can you tell me about the history of
this town?'
'Well, I can tell you that the Cathedral was
begun in the twelfth century and that it is
supposed to be a fine example of early
Gothic architecture.'
6 Do you think that I could ever learn to
speak Japanese the way the Japanese speak
it?
7 They say that the Japanese language is
particularly difficult for Europeans.
8 The two kinds of dog that I detest most are
show dogs and lap dogs.
9 What an interesting piece of furniture! The
top is made of Spanish mahogany, and the
legs are made of iron.
10 Here is a picture of the village where I was
born. It is about ten minutes by car from
Wellington, the nearest big town.
11 I have just heard on the radio that the
Boltavian ambassador has asked the
American government for political asylum.
12 I have noticed that English people do not
seem to shake hands as much as people do
on the Continent.
13 They both joined the army at the same time.
After the war, they met quite by accident
when they were both on leave in Cyprus.
14 Because the sun was so strong, they decided
to sleep during the day and travel by night.
15 Did you know that English children start
school at the age of five? Those who want to
go on to university have to stay on at school
until they are eighteen.

16 Her husband is ill in hospital so she has to
stay at home to look after the children
instead of going to work.
17 It seems to me that worker participation in
industry is an excellent idea in theory, but it
is very difficult to put into practice.
18 She works in the hospital as personal
assistant to Mr Read, the Senior Registrar.

2.7

1i   2f   3p   4h   5c   6j   7b   8l
9a   10n   11m   12o   13d   14e
15r   16q   17k   18g

2.8

1 A screwdriver is a tool/device/instrument
for driving in screws.
2 A computer is a machine for processing
information.
3 A ruler is a tool/device for drawing straight
lines.
4 A telescope is an instrument/a device for
making distant objects appear bigger.
5 A butcher is a man/woman who sells meat.
6 A mechanic is a man/woman who repairs
cars and other machines.
7 A headmistress is a woman who runs a
school.
8 A valve is a device for controlling the flow
of gas or liquid.
9 A camera is an instrument/a
machine/device for taking photographs.
10 A saw is a tool/device/machine/an
instrument for cutting wood.
11 An accountant is a man/woman who
checks figures.
12 A drill is a tool/machine/device/an
instrument for making holes.
13 A pen is an instrument/a device for writing
with.
14 A tractor is a machine for pulling heavy
loads.
15 A clock is an instrument/a machine/device
for measuring time.
16 A thermometer is a device/an instrument
for measuring temperature.
17 An actress is a woman who acts in plays and
films.
18 A thermostat is a device/an instrument for
controlling temperature.

2.9

1 Please pay attention to what I have to say.
2 Her behaviour gave rise to a lot of gossip.
3 British Steel is a good company to do business with.
4 I think she took offence at what you said.
5 He has decided to change jobs.
6 Poor Martin! His wife is forever finding fault with him.
7 I have confidence in you.
8 The bridge gave way under the weight of the snow.
9 The other boys made fun of him.
10 He worked hard and made progress.
11 The protest meeting took place in the Caxton Hall.
12 I rarely have occasion to go to London nowadays.
13 We had fun at Edith's party.
14 He used to belong to the Labour Party, but he has now changed sides.
15 I've lost track of the number of times I have said this.
16 The Princess has given birth to a baby daughter.
17 It is a good idea to make friends with your neighbours.
18 I will try to make arrangements for your transfer to another section.

2.10

1 plural only   2 plural only   3 if singular, use the words *every car*   4 singular or plural   5 singular or plural, but if singular, use the words *No Russian citizen can*   6 singular or plural   7 plural, because it means every year; if singular, say *An examination will take place. . .*   8 singular or plural   9 plural is better. If singular, say *any student who has not received his or her . . .*

2.11

The chapel is on the left
just before the newsagent's
next to the newsagent's
opposite the Red Lion.
*near the pub

The newsagent's is on the left
just after the chapel
just before the grocer's
next to the grocer's/chapel
opposite the telephone booth
*near the grocer's

The grocer's is on the left
between the chapel and the butcher's
just after the newsagent's
just before the butcher's
next to the newsagent's/butcher's
opposite the bus stop
*near the newsagent's
between the newsagent's and the butcher's

The butcher's is on the left
just after the grocer's
just before the village hall
next to the grocer's/village hall
opposite the post office
*near the village hall
between the grocer's and the village hall

The village hall is on the left
just after the butcher's
just before the church
next to the butcher's/church
opposite the bank
*near the church
between the butcher's and the church

The church is on the left
just after the village hall
next to the village hall
opposite the police station
*near the butcher's

The Red Lion pub is on the right
just before the telephone booth
next to the telephone booth
opposite the chapel
*near the telephone booth

The telephone booth is on the right
just after the pub
just before the bus stop
next to the pub/bus stop
opposite the newsagent's
between the pub and the bus stop
*near the pub

The bus stop is on the right
just after the telephone booth
just before the post office
next to the telephone booth/post office

opposite the grocer's
near the post office*
between the telephone booth and the post office

The post office is on the right
just after the bus stop
just before the bank
next to the bus stop/bank
opposite the butcher's
*near the bank
between the bus stop and the bank

The bank is on the right
just after the post office
just before the police station
*next to the post office/police station
opposite the village hall
near the post office
between the post office and the police station

The police station is on the right
just after the bank
next to the bank
opposite the church
*near the bank
*suggested answers

In full, the names are:
without **the**
Big Ben, Charing Cross, Harrow, Hyde Park,
Marble Arch, Piccadilly Circus, Saint Paul's
Cathedral, Soho Square, Stepney.

with **the**
The City, The East End, The Serpentine, The
Strand, The Tate Gallery, The Thames, The
Tower, The Tube, The West End.

The unused letters form the word EUSTON
(Station).

Unit 3

3.1
There was once a very serious rabbit. He was
not handsome or clever but he worked hard and
saved *a lot of* his money. The beautiful lady
rabbit who lived near him was a widow, and she
had *a lot of/several* admirers, but he knew that
none of them was as rich as he was.
   The widow had *several/a lot* of children, so
each/every time he visited her, he brought a
different present for *each* child.
   One day, a handsome stranger came to town.
Soon, *every* female rabbit was in love with him.

3.2
1 a few   2 little   3 few   4 a little
5 few   6 little   7 a few   8 a few
9 a little   10 a little   11 few (note verb
change to *have*)   12 little

3.3
1 some time   2 every one   3 any one
4 anyone   5 everyone   6 some time
7 not one   8 sometimes   9 anyone
10 everyone   11 any one   12 sometimes

3.4
1 [səm]   2 [sʌm]   3 [sʌm]   4 [sʌm]
5 [səm]   6 [səm]   7 [sʌm]   8 [səm]
9 [sʌm]   10 [səm]   11 [sʌm]   12 [səm]

3.5
1 any   2 some   3 some any   4 any
some   5 some   6 any   7 any
8 some   9 any some   10 any   11 any
12 some   13 any   14 any   15 some
16 some   17 any   18 any some
You could leave both out in sentences 3, 4, 6, 12,
13.

3.6

1 anywhere   2 somewhere
3 something   4 anything   5 some time
6 anybody   7 Somebody   8 anywhere
9 anybody   10 somewhere   11 some
time   12 anything   13 something
14 anywhere   15 somewhere
16 anything   17 something   18 something

3.7

1 I like both these objects   2 I like both of
them.   3 I like all these objects.   4 I like all
of them.   5 I do not like either of these
objects.   6 I do not like either of them.
7 I do not like any of these objects.   8 I do
not like any of them.

5 I like neither of these objects.   6 I like
neither of them.   7 I like none of these
objects.   8 I like none of them

3.8

1   I do not take as much medicine as I used to.
2   You should try to eat fewer potatoes.
3   There aren't many jobs for young people
     nowadays.
4   Too many hours are wasted on unimportant
     things.
5   How much money is there in the cashbox?
6   I need a little more time.
7   We are having far less trouble with the new
     computer.
8   Many of the things you say make sense to me.
9   There are very few nightclubs in this place.
10   We own a large amount/great deal of
     property around here.
11   We could do with a few more facts.
12   There have been a great many meetings
     about it.
13   A large amount/great deal of material is
     missing.
14   We are no longer getting much news from
     abroad.
15   There is very little furniture in the room.
16   He has had plenty of chance of getting married.
17   We were just having a few laughs.
18   Anna sends you lots of love.

3.9

1 both   2 the whole of   3 everyone
4 everything   5 all, none   6 all the

7 all   8 each   9 all   10 each   11 both,
neither   12 all of   13 both   14 the whole
of   15 either both   16 a whole
17 both   18 the whole

3.10

1 He gave every one of them a hundred
pounds.   2 He goes to London every other
Thursday.   3 I get angry every time I think of
it.   4 Everyone is invited.   5 I see her every
day.   6 Every member of staff was
interviewed.   7 He gave everything he had to
the poor.   8 Every passenger was given a free
meal.   9 We have circled every fourth number.

3.11

1   (i) suggests that I expect that he gave you
     money; (ii) is a simple question and I have
     no idea whether the answer will be yes or
     no.
2   (i) means that there isn't anyone who knows
     exactly what happened; (ii) means 'it does
     not matter who you ask, because everyone
     knows and can tell you what happened.'
3   (i) emphasizes that I have spent a geat deal
     of time, (ii) is just a simple statement of fact
4   as for question 1, i.e., (ii) is really saying
     that I know that somebody has borrowed it,
     I want to know who; (i) is a simple question
     – it is also possible that I have lost it, or left
     it at home, etc.
5   (i) suggests that I have a particular time in
     mind, (ii) says that it does not matter what
     time we meet.
6   (i) is a simple statement of fact,
     (ii) emphasizes my ignorance about politics
7   (ii) is a simple statement of fact, (i) suggests
     a certain impatience, 'I have no idea who
     she was, but I do not believe that she is
     important'
8   (i) is with *I'd like* and means *a few*; (ii) is
     with *I like* and means *some, but not all*.
9   (ii) is a simple statement of fact,
     (i) emphasizes that I have read not just
     some, but *all* of them, a fact which I expect
     you to find amazing.
10   (ii) emphasizes that he spoke to each child
     separately (i) does not tell us whether he
     spoke to them one at a time, or all at once.

11 It depends which fact you find important or
    amazing: (i) suggests that more people
    ought to know it, (ii) suggests simply it is a
    little-known fact.
12 (i) is a simple statement of fact,
    (ii) emphasizes that it is very easy to make
    an omelette because everyone, it does not
    matter who, can do it.

3.12

1 F	6 E
2 C	7 D
3 H	8 I
4 J	9 B
5 A	10 G

Unit 4

4.1

1 hungry   2 cowardly   3 noisy
4 childish   5 childlike   6 foolish
7 truthful   8 fatherly   9 lively
10 funny   11 snobbish   12 leisurely
13 youthful   14 princely   15 plentiful
16 filthy   17 boyish   18 skilful

4.2

1 useful, useless   2 wonderful   3 hopeful,
hopeless   4 shameful, shameless
5 thoughtful, thoughtless   6 beautiful
7 helpful, helpless   8 forgetful
9 senseless   10 successful   11 reckless
12 awful   13 harmful, harmless
14 ruthless   15 truthful   16 playful
17 priceless   18 frightful.

4.3

1 reddish   2 daily   3 silvery
4 worthless   5 businesslike   6 greasy
7 homely   8 breathless   9 powerful
10 plentiful   11 elderly   12 lifelike
13 peaceful   14 oldish   15 careless
16 wintry   17 nosy   18 handy

4.4

brother – fraternal; woman – feminine; friend –
amicable; god – divine; fun – comic(al); year –
annual; mother – maternal; man – masculine;
cat – feline; dog – canine; mind – mental; brain –
cerebral; sight – visual; touch – tactile; hand –
manual; house – domestic; earth – terrestrial;
east – oriental.

4.5

1 nocturnal   2 diurnal   3 pedestrian,
town   4 country an urban   5 dental
6 salty   7 saline   8 law   9 legal
10 optical   11 eye   12 domestic
13 lunar   14 oral, a mouth, tooth
15 starry, ground   16 stellar   17 juvenile,
a senior   18 marine, Maritime

4.6a

1 predictable   2 believable
3 changeable   4 deniable   5 despicable
6 recognizable   7 regrettable
8 reliable   9 transferable   10 valuable
11 variable   12 workable
13 obtainable   14 curable
15 advisable   16 translatable
17 forgettable   18 describable.

b 1 unpredictable   2 unbelievable
4 undeniable   6 unrecognizable
8 unreliable   9 untransferable
10 invaluable   11 invariable
12 unworkable   13 unobtainable
14 incurable   15 inadvisable
16 untranslatable   17 unforgettable
18 indescribable

4.7a

1 adaptable   2 contemptible
3 respectable   4 viable   5 terrible
6 irritable   7 debatable   8 feasible
9 memorable   10 avoidable
11 hospitable   12 eligible
13 responsible   14 fallible   15 capable
16 probable   17 desirable   18 flexible

b 10 unavoidable   11 inhospitable
12 ineligible   13 irresponsible
14 infallible   15 incapable
16 improbable   17 undesirable
18 inflexible

4.8a

1 destructive 2 excessive 3 extensive
4 responsive 5 deceptive 6 impulsive
7 explosive 8 possessive 9 repulsive
10 progressive 11 productive
12 persuasive 13 attractive
14 receptive 15 representative
16 permissive 17 repetitive 18 retentive

b

1 persuasive 2 attractive 3 receptive
4 representative 5 repetitive
6 retentive 7 progressive
8 productive 9 permissive

c

10 responsive
11 impulsive 12 deceptive
13 repulsive 14 explosive
15 excessive 16 destructive
17 extensive 18 possessive

4.9a

1 illiterate 2 affectionate 3 adequate
4 private 5 deliberate 6 temperate
7 elaborate 8 appropriate 9 delicate

b

10 stationary 11 temporary
12 elementary
13 contemporary 14 imaginary
15 satisfactory 16 compulsory
17 introductory 18 necessary

4.10a

1 magnificent 2 indecent 3 important
4 hesitant 5 sufficient 6 decent
7 pregnant 8 affluent 9 indignant
10 silent 11 violent 12 current
13 immigrant 14 tolerant
15 permanent 16 consistent 17 recent
18 migrant.

b

1 realistic 2 technical 3 alphabetical
4 biological 5 fantastic 6 romantic
7 practical 8 specific 9 critical
10 antibiotic 11 public 12 atomic
13 medical 14 scientific 15 clinical
16 mathematical 17 automatic
18 radical

c

1 ambitious 2 dangerous 3 ambiguous
4 obvious 5 miscellaneous
6 ridiculous 7 various 8 strenuous
9 outrageous 10 jealous 11 courteous
12 superstitious 13 virtuous
14 enormous 15 spontaneous
16 arduous 17 simultaneous
18 tremendous

4.11a

1 (i) true (ii) truthful 2 (i) childish
(ii) childlike 3 (i) youthful (ii) young
4 (i) uneatable (ii) inedible 5 (i) illegible
(ii) unreadable 6 (i) historic (ii) historical
7 (i) economic (ii) economical 8 (i) electric
(ii) electrical 9 (i) sensible (ii) sensitive

b

1 (i) She has been a friend of ours for a long
time
(ii) He is a man of great age.
2 (i) He is an industrious worker.
(ii) Do you think this exercise is difficult?
3 (i) Have you met the people who have
recently moved into the neighbourhood?
(ii) I like the dress you've just bought.
4 (i) He smokes a lot.
(ii) This parcel is quite a weight!
5 (i) I am sure that this book used to belong to
me.
(ii) There is a particular person I'd like you to
meet whose name is Mr Smith.
6 (i) The person who is Foreign Secretary now
is better than the last one.
(ii) Is everybody here?
7 (i) Why do you have such a worried
expression on your face?
(ii) I wish to speak to all the people who have
anything to do with the matter.
8 (i) This is the wrong (inappropriate) time to
talk about money.
(ii) I mean the town itself, i.e. the central
area, not the suburbs.
9 (i) I don't want to hear a long complicated
explanation.
(ii) The police took statements from
everyone who had something to do with the
accident.

4.12

1 disturbing   2 surprising
3 interesting   4 thrilled   5 bored
6 satisfied pleased   7 relaxing relaxed
8 embarrassed   9 tiring exhausted
10 entertained exciting   11 fascinating
12 disappointed satisfied.

4.13

1 a half-hour programme   2 a five-hour
drive   3 a 15-ton lorry   4 a 3½-hour
flight   5 a 12 inch ruler   6 a 3½-litre
engine   7 a five-year-old child   8 a six-foot
man   9 an eight-mile walk   10 a 16-gallon
tank   11 a 300-millimetre telephoto lens
12 a 4-star hotel   13 a second-year student
14 a third-floor flat   15 a second-generation
computer   16 a last-minute decision   17 a
first-class meal   18 a third-rate production

4.14

1 a Hungarian, Hungarian   2 a Saudi
Arabian, Arabic   3 A Dane, Danish
4 a Pole, Polish   5 an Englishman, English
6 a Spaniard, Spanish   7 a Dutchman,
Dutch   8 a Turk, Turkish   9 a Portuguese,
Portuguese   10 a Japanese, Japanese
11 a Norwegian, Norwegian   12 a Russian,
Russian   13 a Czech, Czech   14 a Chinese
('a Chinaman' is old-fashioned) Chinese
15 a Finn, Finnish   16 an Israeli, Hebrew
17 a Greek, Greek   18 a Thai, Thai

4.15

1 Several lovely old English tables.
2 a lot of pretty young French girls.
3 These last few valuable Regency dining-
  room chairs.
4 His first three really important
  Impressionist paintings.
5 All my best dark blue shirts.
6 Many young German factory workers.
7 All these old-fashioned marble-topped oval
  wash stands.
8 All Mike's latest black and white wildlife
  photographs.
9 A few carefully-chosen plain hand-woven
  cotton dresses.
10 A number of brand-new French-made non-
  stick frying pans.

11 The first really important national
  government-sponsored survey.
12 His last exhausting one-month European
  tour.

4.16

1 tinier, the tiniest   2 handsomer, the
handsomest   3 livelier, the liveliest
4 drier, the driest   5 pleasanter, the
pleasantest   6 simpler, the simplest
7 mellower, the mellowest   8 better, the
best   9 worse, the worst   10 farther, the
farthest *or* further, the furthest   11 sadder,
the saddest   12 heavier, the heaviest
13 greyer, the greyest   14 later, the latest
15 quieter, the quietest   16 politer, the
politest   17 clever, the cleverest   18 bigger,
the biggest   19 fatter, the fattest   20 wider,
the widest   21 foggier, the foggiest
22 abler, the ablest   23 iller, the illest
24 commoner, the commonest   25 sooner,
the soonest   26 thinner, the thinnest
27 calmer, the calmest   28 healthier, the
healthiest   29 truer, the truest   30 wider,
the widest   31 earlier, the earliest
32 narrower, the narrowest   33 freer, the
freest   34 rarer, the rarest   35 flatter, the
flattest   36 prettier, the prettiest

4.17

1 Anna is older than Louise.
2 Girls are cleverer than boys.
3 The sun is brighter than the moon.
4 Northerners are more friendly or friendlier
  than southerners.
5 Rome is more beautiful than Milan.
6 Cats are more intelligent than dogs.
7 Dior dresses are more elegant than
  Balmain's.
8 Men are more sensible than women.
9 The English are wittier than the Americans.
10 Some people are more honest than others.
11 Physics is harder than chemistry.
12 Boys are more sensitive than girls.

4.18

1 English is easier than Japanese.
2 Japanese is more difficult than English.
3 Japanese is not as/so easy as English.

4 Health is more important than money.
5 A change is as good as a rest.
6 Blackbirds are commoner/more common than eagles.
7 You are as welcome as flowers in May.
8 Programmes are less interesting than they used to be.
9 Thirst is worse than hunger.
10 Half a loaf is better than no loaf at all.
11 Things are not as (so) good as they used to be.
12 Jogging is healthier than smoking.
13 Cigarettes are less harmful than cigars.
14 Pluto is farther away than Mars.
15 Pluto is more distant than Mars.
16 Mars is less distant than Pluto.
17 She is worse than she was yesterday.
18 The towns are noisier than the villages.

4.19
1 the most incredible   2 the brightest
3 more comfortable   4 the deepest
5 more self-confident   6 The tallest
7 easier   8 better off   9 the saddest
10 the most powerful   11 better   12 more irritating   13 shorter and more direct
14 older . . . younger   15 finer   16 the oldest . . . older   17 tidier . . . better-organized   18 better-looking . . . better

4.20
1 short-tempered   2 bow-legged
3 broad-minded   4 narrow-minded
5 blue-eyed   6 good-natured   7 thick-skinned   8 left-handed   9 cross-eyed
10 broad-shouldered

Unit 5

5.1
One summer's day, a duck decided to go to the river for a picnic. *She* took a lot of food with *her*, and was really looking forward to eating *it*. *She* sat down on the river bank, and spread the food out in front of *her*.

'*You're* not going to eat all that food *yourself*, are *you*?' said a small voice.

She looked up and saw a frog sitting at the water's edge. 'Please give *me* some of *yours*,' pleaded the frog, wiping a tear from *his* eyes.

She gave *him* a sandwich. To *her* surprise, *he* did not eat *it*, but simply put *it* on the ground beside *him*.

'Won't *you* give *me* something else? After all, my need is greater than yours.'

Bit by bit, the duck handed over most of *the* food. Soon, the frog had a huge pile of food in front of *him*. With an effort *he* picked *it* all up and started to swim across the river.

But the food was so heavy that *both* the frog and *his* load sank like a stone and the duck never saw *either* of *them* again.

Moral: When it is hard to say 'no', say 'no'.

5.2
1 I did   2 I am   3 I don't   4 I didn't
5 I have   6 I can   7 I won't
8 I haven't   9 I do   10 I didn't
11 I would   12 I did   13 I don't
14 I could   15 I do   16 I didn't
17 I haven't   18 I do; I have to

1 He/She did   2 He/She is   3 He/She doesn't   4 He/She didn't   5 He/She has
6 He/She can   7 He/She won't   8 He/She hasn't   9 He/She does   10 He/She didn't   11 He/She would   12 He/She did   13 He/She doesn't   14 He/She could
15 He/She does   16 He/She didn't
17 He/She hasn't   18 He/She does/has to

1 They did   2 They are   3 They don't
4 They didn't   5 They have   6 They can   7 They won't   8 They haven't
9 They do   10 They didn't   11 They would   12 They did   13 They don't
14 They could   15 They do   16 They didn't   17 They haven't   18 They do/have to

5.3a
1 It was so cold that the river froze over.
2 It was raining when I left the house.
3 If it's raining (*or* If it rains) we will stay in.
4 It's warm today – you do not need an overcoat.
5 You cannot take good photographs when it is cloudy.

6   Do you think it's freezing at the moment?
7   I do not like to go sailing when it is too windy.
8   It's very late – I must go now.
9   It was three miles to the nearest petrol station, and I had to walk all the way.

b
10   There are some people waiting to see you.
11   There was very little left to eat.
12   There isn't much I can do about it.
13   There are some letters here for you.
14   There is a bit of cheese in the refrigerator.
15   There is a lovely smell in here.
16   There is nothing I'd like better than to stay here with you.
17   There's something I want to tell you.
18   There's nothing broken.

5.4

NB The word *that* can be left out, except for question 8, i.e., after *to me*.
1   It is difficult to speak another language fluently.
2   It is important (that) everyone should keep quiet about it.
3   It is hard to believe (that) he was once a school principal.
4   It is vital (that) everything is finished on time.
5   It is not easy to do a full-time job and run a home.
6   It is interesting to just sit and watch other people.
7   It is curious (that) nobody else noticed the mistake.
8   It is incredible to me that he failed his examination.
9   It is unnecessary for you to be able to speak other languages.
10   It is better to leave while it is still light.
11   It is better (that) you and I aren't seen together.
12   It is pleasing to learn (that) everyone passed the test.
13   It is not necessary for you to read every page.
14   It is surprising (that) you didn't notice anything wrong.
15   It is not worthwhile for you to repeat the course.
16   It is funny (that) you should say that.
17   It is impossible for him to know the name of every pupil.
18   It is essential for me to work overtime.

5.5

Adjectives 1, 6, 9 and 12 are followed by **of**
Adjectives 4, 5 and 11 are followed by **for**
Adjectives 2, 3, 7, 8 and 10 can be followed by **for** or **of**, but with a change of meaning. For example: *It was wrong of you to join the society* means *You did something wrong or bad; It was wrong for you to join the society* means *It did not bring you any benefit: it is the wrong kind of society for you.*

5.6

1 You/you   2 they/they   3 They/they
4 We/we   5 You/you/you   6 they
7 your/you/you/you/you   8 They/we
9 They/us/we   10 we/our/we/us
11 You/you   12 they

5.7

1 Hand them to him.   2 Hand them to John.   3 Teach them the alphabet *or* Teach the alphabet to them.   4 Teach it to the children.   5 Buy her the flowers *or* Buy the flowers for her.   6 Buy them for Mary
7 Buy them for her.   8 Get him the paper *or* Get the paper for him.   9 Get it for father.
10 Fetch her her briefcase *or* Fetch her briefcase for her.   11 Fetch it for her.   12 Tell them the truth *or* Tell the truth to them.   13 Tell it to them.   14 Send it to George.   15 Send him the money *or* Send the money to him.
16 Tell it to everyone.   17 Bring it to me.
18 Show them to him/her.

5.8a

1   They told me/him/you/every contestant/John/us/the people/her a strange story/the truth/how to meditate They told you how to defend yourself.
2   They gave me/him/you/every contestant/John/us/the people/her a fortnight's holiday/a sealed envelope/a number of questions. They gave me/him/you/every contestant/John/us/her first prize. They gave me/him/you/John/us/the people/her a pay increase/the truth/a job. They gave me/him/you/John/us/her another flat.
3   They will teach me/him/you/every contestant/John/us/the people/her the truth. They will teach you how to defend yourself.

4 They handed me/him/you/every contestant/John/us/her a sealed envelope/first prize.

5 They have awarded me/him/you/every contestant/John/us/the people/her a fortnight's holiday. They have awarded me/him/you/every contestant/John/us /her first prize. They have awarded me/him/you/John/us/her a pay increase.

6 They promised me/him/you/every contestant/John/us/the people/her a fortnight's holiday/a sealed envelope/the truth. They promised me/him/you/every contestant/John/us/her first prize. They promised me/him/you/John/us/the people/her a pay increase/a job. They promised me/him/you/John/us/her another flat.

7 They will ask me/him/you/every contestant/John/us/the people/her a number of questions/how to meditate. They will ask you how to defend yourself.

8 They have not told me/him/you/every contestant/John/us/the people/her the truth/how to meditate. They haven't told me/him/you/every contestant/John/us /her a strange story. They haven't told me/you/him/John/us/her the people anything. They haven't told you how to defend yourself.

9 They have offered me/him/you/every contestant/John/us/the people/her a fortnight's holiday/a sealed envelope. They have offered me/him/you/John/us/her a strange story. They have offered me/him/you/every contestant/John/us /her first prize. They have offered me/him/you/John/us/the people/her a pay increase/another flat/a job.

10 They will show me/him/you/every contestant/John/us/the people/her a sealed envelope/the truth/how to meditate. They will show me/him/you/John/us/the people/her anything/another flat. They will show you how to defend yourself.

11 They have found me/him/you/every contestant/John/us/the people/her a job. They've found me/him/you/John/us/her another flat.

12 They are not telling me/him/you/every contestant/John/us/the people/her a strange story/the truth/how to meditate. They are not telling me/him/you/John /us/the people/her anything. They are not telling you how to defend yourself.

b

1 I was told a strange story.
2 He was given a fortnight's holiday.
3 You will be taught how to defend yourself.
4 Every contestant was handed a sealed envelope.
5 John has been awarded first prize.
6 We were promised a pay increase.
7 You will be asked a number of questions.
8 The people haven't been told the truth.
9 We have been offered another flat.
10 You will be shown how to meditate.
11 She has been found a job.
12 We aren't being told anything.

5.9
1 her . . . her 2 your . . . my 3 the 4 my . . . the 5 his . . . his . . . his . . . his 6 the . . . her . . . her 7 the . . . his 8 the . . . his . . . my 9 your . . . your . . . your 10 the 11 your . . . your 12 the 13 their . . . their 14 your . . . your 15 your . . . your . . . your 16 the . . . his 17 the . . . the . . . his 18 my . . . my

5.10
1 my own 2 yours 3 me 4 of my father's 5 herself 6 her own 7 my father's, me 8 yours, your wife's 9 his 10 my 11 Yours 12 mine . . . Anna's

5.11
1 him . . . himself 2 yourself . . . you 3 each other 4 yourselves 5 each other 6 himself 7 ourselves 8 herself 9 me . . . ourselves 10 them . . . them 11 dress himself 12 had a wash . . . got dressed 13 me . . . their own 14 themselves 15 himself 16 yourself . . . yourself . . . me 17 each other 18 Ø

5.12
1 made it myself. 2 gave it to me himself *or* himself gave it to me. 3 was made by

Stradivarius himself.   4 organized it
themselves *or* themselves organized it.
5 itself was boring . . .   6 don't like them
myself   7 taught herself   8 writes them
herself   9 go by myself   10 it yourself
11 investigated it themselves *or* did it
themselves   12 wash and dress himself

5.13
1 who   2 (which)   3 which
4 (which)   5 whose   6 who   7 who
8 whose   9 which   10 (who)   11 (which)
12 who   13 whose   14 whose   15 which
16 who   17 whose   18 (which)

5.14
1 who   2 (whom)   3 who   4 who
5 who   6 (whom)   7 (whom)   8 who
9 who   10 (whom)   11 who   12 (whom)

5.15a
NB Where either is possible, we have put the
more likely one first.
1 which   2 which *or* what   3 which
4 which *or* what   5 which   6 which *or*
what   7 which *or* what   8 what *or*
which   9 which
b
10 what   11 which   12 which
13 which *or* what   14 what   15 which
16 which   17 which *or* what   18 which
. . . which

5.16a
1 somewhere else   2 somebody else
3 something else   4 anything else
5 anyone else   6 nowhere else   7 anything
else   8 somebody else   9 nobody else
b
10 somebody else's   11 anybody's
12 everybody's *or* everybody else's
13 nobody's   14 everybody's
15 nobody's *or* nobody else's   16 everybody
else's   17 nobody else's   18 somebody
else's

5.17
I   me   my   you   your   yours   he   him
his   she   her   hers   it   its   we   us   our
ours   they   them   their   theirs   this
those   thou   thy

5.18
1 kill   2 enjoy   3 blame   4 ask
5 help   6 please   7 take   8 make
9 give   10 pull   11 let   12 behave

Unit 6

6.1
Farmer Jones was very lonely and bored. He
lived *by* himself *in* an old house *on* the edge *of*
the village and rarely talked *to* anyone. The
villagers thought that he ought to have a pet *for*
company, but the only pet they could find was a
dog *with* only one ear.

When the farmer saw it, he shouted, 'Get *out*
of my house.' The dog, *to* his surprise,
responded *by* doing exactly the opposite. It
wagged its tail and went *into* the house.

The farmer stared *at* the funny dog *for* a while
and then said finally, 'Ah well, you might as
well stay, I suppose. Come and sit *next to* me.'

The dog wagged its tail, but walked *away*
from the man, and went to sit *on* the other
side *of* the room.

'Sit on the chair,' said the farmer. The one-
eared dog promptly sat *under* it.

The farmer took the dog outside and pointed
up the road: the dog immediately turned round
and went *down* the road!

'Why do you always do the opposite *of* what I
tell you to do?' he asked. The dog just looked up
at him *with* his head *on* one side, and his solitary
ear sticking up *like* a radio aerial.

6.2
1 down   2 below   3 out   4 over
5 inside   6 behind   7 under(neath), *or*
beneath   8 to   9 away from
10 without   11 off   12 before
13 past   14 excluding   15 out of
16 far from   17 unlike   18 for

6.3
1   A to; B towards; C past; D through; E in;
F from; G away from
2   A on to; B off; C over; D across; E on;
F under; G next to near. (G and H could be
near and *next to*, depending on your point of
view)

3 A out of; B into; C inside; D in front of;
E behind
4 A up; B above; C round; D below; E down

6.4a
1 above, below   2 above, below, on,
over   3 above, below   4 on, under
5 over, under   6 above   7 under
8 over, under   9 above, below, on, under
b
10 at, by   11 during, in   12 during, in
13 at, by   14 during, in   15 by, during, on
16 on   17 by, on   18 at, by, during in

6.5 *Suggested answers*
1 over the horizon; at seven o'clock   2 above
sea level   3 below freezing point; in the
summer; during the summer   4 under the
table; at night   5 under 16   6 under
suspicion   7 under protest   8 under £200
9 on the ground   10 at night; on Mondays
11 on the night   12 during the summer; in the
summer; in September   13 at seven o'clock;
in September; on 7th October; on Monday; in
the summer; during the interval   14 during
the night/the summer/September/the interval;
in September   15 by 7 o'clock/September/
7th October/summer/Monday
16 at/during the night!; on Mondays   17 on
7th October   18 during the interval

6.6
a 1 at   2 on; in   3 at   4 on   5 on
6 at   7 in   8 at   9 in   10 on
11 at   12 in
b 13 since   14 for   15 since   16 for
17 for   18 for
c 19 during   20 while   21 during
22 while   23 while   24 during

6.7
1 at present   2 in time   3 at times
4 on my birthday   5 on holiday   6 at the
time   7 in the past   8 at frequent
intervals   9 in the future   10 on this
occasion   11 at one time   12 in recent
years   13 since the middle of last year
14 for a number of years   15 since she got
married   16 for ages   17 for several
hours   18 for the last six months
19 during the interval   20 while the children

are in bed   21 during the summer
22 while the sun is shining   23 while we have
time   24 during the present crisis

6.8a
1 in   2 to   3 at   4 in . . . at   5 to
6 at   7 at   8 to   9 at   10 in
11 to   12 in
b
13 by   14 until   15 by   16 By
17 until   18 by
c
1 at   2 to   3 to   4 at   5 to   6 at
7 to   8 at   9 to   10 at   11 at   12 to

6.9a
1 with   2 with   3 by   4 by
5 with   6 by   7 with   8 by   9 by
b
10 of   11 of   12 by (A picture *of* Degas
would mean that someone had painted a picture
which showed Degas).   13 of   14 of . . .
by . . . from   15 from   16 of, by, of
17 from, by   18 of

6.10
1 on; about   2 about   3 on; about
4 about   5 on   6 about   7 on
8 about   9 on; about   10 about, on
11 on; about   12 about

6.11
A 1 a/b/c/d/e; A 4 b/e; A 6 c; A 7 c;
A 8 c/d/e   B 1 a/b/c/d/e; B 4 b/e;
B 6 c/d; B 7 c/d; B 8 c/e   C 2 c;
C 3 c; C 5 c; C 9 c   D 4 e; D 6 d;
D 7 d;   E 1 b/c/d/e; E 2 e; E 3 b/e;
E 4 c/e; E 5 b/d/e; E 8 b/c/d/e; E 9 b/e

6.12
1 a   2 a   3 b   4 a   5 b   6 b
7 c   8 d   9 c   10 c   11 d   12 c

6.13
1 D a/b/c/d/f/g/h/i; 1 E a/b/c/d/e/f/g/h/i;
1 G a/b/c/d/e/f/g/h/i; 2 A b; 2 B c/e/h/i; 2 C
a/b/c/d/f/h/i; 2 F c/i; 3 D a/b/c/d/f/g/h/i; 3 E
a/b/c/d/f/g/h/i; 3 G a/b/c/d/f/g/h/i; 4 D
a/b/c/d/e/f/g/h/i; 4 G a/b/c/d/e/f/g/h/i; 5 A
b/e; 5 B c/e/i; 5 C a/b/c/d/f/g/h/i; 6 C
a/b/c/d/e/f/g/h/i; 7 D a/b/c/d/e/f/g/h/i; 7 E
a/b/c/d/e/f/h/i; 7 G a/b/c/d/e/f/g/h/i; 8 E

a/c/d/h/i; 9A b/e; 9B c/e/h; 9C
a/b/c/d/e/f/i; 9F a/b/c/d/e/f/g/h/i

6.14

1 I would never resort to telling lies!
2 Because I am accustomed to (*or* used to) getting up early.
3 You'll soon get used to driving on the left.
4 We should confine ourselves to warning him not to do it again.
5 Because I definitely object to being told what to do.
6 You'll have to resign yourselves to taking a holiday at home.
7 We are really looking forward to going to Spain.
8 Perhaps it is because he isn't used to getting up early.
9 I don't think she is accustomed/used/looking forward to working in an office.

6.15a

1 I'm no good at typing.
2 I'm afraid of making mistakes.
3 He is interested in joining the debating society.
4 She left without saying goodbye first.
5 He is tired of working in an office.
6 Switch off the lights before leaving.
7 They had a crash through driving too fast.
8 He is involved in running the youth club.
9 She went on her own instead of waiting for the others.
10 I am accustomed to getting up while it is still dark.
11 She is bad at remembering people's names.
12 We can only improve by working harder.

b

13 Thank you for phoning.
14 He was discouraged from going.
15 They prevented me from addressing the meeting.
16 The police accused him of driving without due care and attention.
17 He is thinking of changing jobs.
18 Concentrate on getting good grades in your examinations.
19 Everybody congratulated Jeremy on passing his driving test.
20 They were suspected of cheating.

21 She would not dream of asking a man to dance with her.
22 I believe in living a day at a time.
23 I'm looking forward to visiting you next summer.
24 He talks a lot about emigrating to America.

6.16a

1 from	2 for	3 to	4 of	5 of
6 from	7 to	8 for	9 of	10 for
11 to	12 of			

b
13 for	14 of	15 to	16 from
17 for	18 of	19 of	20 to	21 for
22 from	23 of	24 to	

6.17a

1 on	2 from	3 against	4 for
5 of	6 to	7 for	8 from	9 for
10 of	11 to	12 about	

b
13 from	14 on	15 of	16 for
17 to	18 for	19 for	20 against
21 about	22 of	23 from	24 to

6.18a

1 Fresh air is good for you/me.
2 My uncle is good/bad at mathematics/remembering names.
3 I am good/bad for you. I am good/bad at mathematics/remembering names. I am good/bad to you.
4 Too much smoking is bad for you/me.
5 Most people are good/bad for you/me. Most people are good/bad to you/me. Most people are good/bad at remembering names/mathematics.

b

6 His face is familiar to me.
7 Don't get familiar with me. Don't get annoyed with me/the way things turned out. Don't get annoyed about the results/the way things turned out. Don't get angry with me/the way things turned out. Don't get angry about the results/the way things turned out.
8 He was very familiar with me. He was very annoyed with me/himself/the way things turned out. He was very annoyed about the results/the way things turned out. He was very angry with me/himself. He was very angry about the results/the way things turned out.

c

9 She is very sensitive to people's feelings/her. She is very sensitive about her failure. She is very sorry about her failure/her. She is very sorry for her failure/her.

10 He said he was sensitive to people's feelings/her/what other people had said/her. He said he was very sensitive about her failure/what other people had said/her. He said he was very sorry about people's feelings/her failure/what other people had said/her. He said he was very sorry for her.

6.19

1 All those in favour of going . . .
2 According to the papers . . .   3 On behalf of the committee . . .   4 In view of the number of absences . . .   5 In spite of the deep snow everywhere . . . *or* In spite of there being deep snow everywhere . . .
6 Everyone on the staff, apart from Simon, liked the idea.   7 We dealt with all the prepositions which express relationships other than those which refer to time and space.
8 Instead of waiting for the others . . .   9 In addition to visiting her in hospital, they looked after her bungalow for her.   10 Tonight's play has been cancelled owing to (a) lack of interest.   11 The fire in the oil well was put out by means of explosives.   12 In case of fire, sound the alarm.

Unit 7

7.1

The farmer *stared* down at the dog. He simply *could* not *understand* such peculiar behaviour.

'Perhaps it *is* because the poor thing *has* only one ear,' he *thought* to himself. Anyway, he began to spend all his spare time *training* the dog, until eventually it *did* everything he ordered – as long as he *said* the opposite of what he *wanted*.

A horse, which *had been watching* these strange events, finally *asked* the dog: "Why do you always do the opposite of what he *tells* you to *do*? Is it because you *have* only one ear?"

'Of course not,' replied the dog. 'I *started* to *do* it because I *don't think* he would *be* interested in an ordinary dog, do you?'

And, indeed, the farmer *was* no longer lonely or bored: he now *had* very interesting company.

Moral: There *is* nothing peculiar about being peculiar

7.2

a 1b, 1c, 2b, 2c, 3b, 3c, 4a
b 1c, 2b, 2c, 3a, 4b, 4c
c 1b, 1c, 2a, 3a, 4a

7.3

a 1c, 2b, 3a, 4c, 5b
b 1a, 1d, 2a, 3c, 4a
c A1b, A1d, A3a, A4c, B1a, B1d, B2a, B3a, B4c

7.4

a 1a, 2a, 3d, 4c
b 1aC, 1cB, 2aA, 3aA, 3bB, 4aC, 4cB
c 1c, 1d, 2a, 2c, 3b, 4a, 4c, 4d

7.5

a 1a, 1c, 2a, 2c, 3d, 4d
b 1b, 2d, 3b, 4d
c 1a, 1b, 2a, 2b, 3c, 3d, 4a, 4b

7.6a

1 A delay was announced.
2 A delay has been announced.
3 You are wanted on the phone.
4 These cars are made in Japan.
5 A new factory is being built here.
6 It couldn't be moved.
7 Has the dog been fed?
8 Are you being picked up tonight?
9 The money must be kept in the safe.

b
10 Someone has stolen my car.
11 Last year thieves stole my car.
12 I will have to sell the car.
13 The police are watching him very closely.
14 You do not need any special skills to operate this machine, *or* You need no special skills to operate this machine.
15 They say that money cannot buy happiness.
16 His story didn't fool me.

17 Nobody could persuade him to leave.
18 The secretary told me to wait outside.

7.7a
1 can   2 be able to   3 been able to
4 could   5 be able to   6 could
7 be able to   8 cannot can/are able to
9 being able to
b
10 has to   11 must/have to   12 have to
13 had to   14 must   15 having to
16 mustn't   17 have to   18 have had to

7.8
1 goes [z]   2 helps [s]   3 says[z]
4 watches[ɪz]   5 operates [s]   6 laughs
[s]   7 emphasizes [ɪz]   8 belongs [z]
9 likes [s]   10 replies [z]   11 worries [z]
12 fixes [ɪz]   13 halves [z]   14 amuses
[ɪz]   15 climbs   16 flies [z]
17 judges [ɪz]   18 bathes [z]

7.9a
1 liked [t]   2 lived [d]   3 wanted [ɪd]
4 refused [d]   5 laughed [t]   6 persuaded
[ɪd]   7 tried [d]   8 played [d]   9 reached
[t]   10 offered [d]   11 benefited [ɪd]
12 landed [ɪd]   13 photographed [t]
14 separated [ɪd]   15 panicked [t]
16 realized [d]   17 exploded [ɪd]
18 vanished [t]
b
1 housed [d]   2 fixed [t]   3 decided [ɪd]
4 searched [t]   5 rubbed [d]   6 reminded
[ɪd]   7 slipped [t]   8 remembered [d]
9 allowed [d]   10 picnicked [t]
11 profited [ɪd]   12 insisted [ɪd]
13 worried [d]   14 giggled [d]
15 occurred [d]   16 developed [t]
17 fitted [ɪd]   18 preferred [d]

7.10
1 heard heard   2 bind bound   3 ride
rode   4 set set   5 fall fallen   6 find
found   7 became become   8 tear torn
9 slide slid   10 caught caught   11 eat
eaten   12 shut shut   13 fed fed   14 seek
sought   15 hurt hurt   16 bit bitten
17 sell sold   18 break broke   19 spread
spread   20 lie lain   21 laid laid   22 drive
driven   23 dealt dealt   24 drink drank
25 beat beaten   26 showed shown
27 stick stuck   28 lead led   29 struck
stricken   30 fly flew   31 lose lost
32 shake shook   33 met met   34 forbade
forbidden   35 meant meant   36 cost cost

7.11
1 They misled us.
2 . . . is often misspelt.
3 . . ., you are mistaken.
4 I have mislaid my calculator.
5 The weatherman forecast more snow.
6 We could not have foreseen how much . . .
7 Nostradamus foretold the French
   Revolution.
8 The council overcame people's objections
   . . .
9 I was close enough to overhear what they
   were saying.
10 The car which overtook us on the
    motorway . . .
11 . . . so I reset the timeswitch,
12 . . ., The Finnish team withdrew from the
    race.
13 The authorities withheld the facts about the .
    disaster.
14 The soldiers underwent a hard training
    programme.
15 Martin undertook to provide the slides . . .
16 This place is overrun with rats!
17 . . .: her performance outshone everyone
    else's.
18 . . . and rebuilt several times during its
    history.

7.12
1 There aren't any apples in the pantry.
2 She doesn't like spaghetti bolognese.
3 I don't know anything about it.
4 He isn't being examined this week.
5 I'm not used to being left alone.
6 Hasn't the dog had anything to eat?
7 They can't go by car.
8 You mustn't do any really hard physical
   work.
9 The concert will not finish at ten o'clock*.
10 Won't you need to take some warm clothes
    with you?
11 Shan't I see you again?

12 He wouldn't have done it without payment.
13 Hasn't your car been serviced recently?
14 She didn't put anything in her handbag.
15 We weren't very happy with the arrangements.
16 You oughtn't to have said anything to him.
17 I haven't been feeling particularly well recently.
18 The best form is *He never used to be* because it avoids the problem of *usedn't* (which sounds unnatural or old-fashioned) or *didn't use(d)* (which is rather inelegant, if not actually incorrect).

(*This is a written or formal spoken announcement. Informally, someone could mention to you: "I hear the concert *won't* finish at ten o'clock after all.")

7.13a
1 Can you swim? You can swim, can't you? You can't swim, can you?
2 Do you know the answer? You know the answer, don't you? You don't know the answer, do you?
3 Have you answered his letter? You've answered his letter, haven't you? You haven't answered his letter, have you?
4 Are you coming with us? You're coming with us, aren't you? You aren't coming with us, are you?
5 Do you like my book? You like my book, don't you? You don't like my book, do you?
6 Did you go to the bank? You went to the bank, didn't you? You didn't go to the bank, did you?
7 Have you got enough money? You have got enough money, haven't you? You haven't got enough money, have you?
8 Will you be able to come? You will be able to come, won't you? You won't be able to come, will you?
9 Have you been drinking? You've been drinking, haven't you? You haven't been drinking, have you?

b
1 But I do want to go out with you!
2 But she does drive!
3 But I do practise!
4 But she does like mathematics!
5 But I did tell you!
6 But I do really love you!

7 But he does like card games!
8 But I did pay the bill!
9 But I do practise.

7.14
Only with -**ise**: 3, 6, 7, 8, 10, 15, 23, 25, 27 and 29

All the rest may be written with -**ise** or -**ize**. (If you always use -**ise**, you will always be right!)

7.15a
1 [eɪt]   2 [ət]   3 [ət]   4 [eɪt]   5 [eɪt]
6 [ət]   7 [ət]   8 [ət]   9 [ət]   10 [eɪt]
11 [eɪt]   12 [eɪt]

b
1 aggravate   2 assassinate   3 tolerate
4 concentrate   5 segregate   6 stimulate
7 indicate   8 evaluate   9 demonstrate

7.16a
1 quantify quantity   2 computerize computer   3 electrify electricity
4 minimize minimum   5 stylize style
6 personify person   7 personalize person
8 liquify liquid   9 diversify diversion
10 idolize idol   11 solidify solid/solidarity   12 liquidize liquid
13 moralize moral/morality   14 falsify falsification   15 indemnify indemnity
16 testify testimony   17 intensify intensification   18 mobilize mobile/mobility

b
1 identify   2 mystified   3 qualified
4 justify   5 magnification   6 notified
7 classify   8 modified   9 clarified

7.17a
1 reheated   2 overcharged
3 undercooked   4 unpacked
5 miscalculated   6 overthrew   7 repaid
8 overslept   9 misinterpreted

b
10 unbuttoned   11 disconnected
12 rewritten   13 coexist (*or* co-exist)
14 outgrown   15 untied   16 overshot
17 outweighed   18 disappeared

7.18

admit; ascribe; assent; attain; attend; confer; conform; confuse; commit; compose; compress; consent; conserve; contain; contend; deduce; defer; deform; defuse; depose; depress; describe; deserve; detain; differ; diffuse; dispose; dissent; distain; distend; eject; emit; expose; express; extend; induce; infer; inform; infuse; inject; impose; impress; inscribe; intend; offer; object; oppose; oppress; observe; obtain; prefer; prescribe; present; preserve; pretend; produce; proffer; project; propose; proscribe; reduce; refer; reform; refuse; reject; remit; repose; repress; resent; reserve; retain; suffer; suffuse; subject; submit; suppose; suppress; subscribe; subserve; subtend; transfer; transform; transfuse; transmit; transpose; transcribe; perform; permit; pertain

---

Unit 8

8.1

The three bears *had been working* (or *had worked*) hard and were looking forward to a nice bowl of soup when they got home. What they *did not know was* that, while they were out, a pretty girl called Silverlocks *had got* into their cottage. She *(had) tried* the soup in each dish, and *had drunk* (or *drank*) up the soup in the smallest one. Then, because she was *feeling* (or *felt*) very tired after her meal, she *went* into the other room, where there *were* three comfortable chairs. She *tried* them all, but *chose* the smallest one *to curl up* in, because it *had* the softest cushions.

She *was* still there, fast asleep, when the three bears *came* back.

The bears *noticed* at once that someone *had been* in.

'Who has *been drinking* my soup?' *shouted* the big and the middle-sized bears at the same time.

'Someone *has drunk* all my soup!' *squeaked* the small bear.

Then they *went* into the next room, where the comfortable chairs *were*.

'Who *has been sitting* in my chair?' *said* the two bigger bears simultaneously.

The small bear *looked* down at his chair, which *was* in the darkest corner of the room. He *said* nothing, but *waited* patiently for the other two bears to go away.

Moral: Two's company; four's a crowd.

8.2

1 Where do you come from?   2 Do they get more rain in northern than in southern Europe?   3 Are you learning to play the guitar?   4 What do you do for a living?   5 Why are you measuring that?   6 How much do you weigh?   7 Why is everybody getting so angry?   8 How do you make a date and nut loaf?   9 What are you doing with that electric drill?   10 What time does the post come?   11 Why is the post arriving so late at the moment?   12 Is Janet coming to the party?   13 Why aren't you working?   14 Does Janet come to your lectures?   15 What do you get when you add magnesium to water?   16 How many Christmas cards are you sending this year?   17 How much petrol does the tank hold?   18 Are you playing tennis this week?

8.3a

(i)   1a; 1c; 2a; 2c; 3b; 3d; 4a; 4c; 5b; 5d
(ii) 1a, b, d complains; 2a, c, d complaining
(iii) 1a, b, c gave me presents; 2b, c giving me presents

8.4

1 (i) am expecting (ii) expect;   2 (i) are considering it (ii) consider;   3 (i) see (ii) are you seeing?   4 (i) holds (ii) are holding;   5 (i) are you thinking? (ii) do you think?   6 (i) is tasting (ii) tastes;   7 (i) am depending (ii) depends;   8 (i) am seeing (ii) see;   9 (i) am I hearing? (ii) hears;   10 (i) have (ii) are having;   11 (i) stands (ii) are standing;   12 (i) does not apply (ii) are you applying?;   13 (i) am hoping (ii) hope;   14 (i) are you having? (ii) do you have?;   15 (i) does it cost? (ii) costs;   16 (i) think (ii) am thinking;   17 (i) appears (ii) is appearing;   18 (i) does it look? (ii) am looking

8.5

a   1a, 1b, 2b, 2c

b   3e, 3f, 3h, 4f, 4g, 4h, 5f, 5g, 5h, 6e, 6f, 6h

c   7i, 7j, 8i, 8j, 9k

8.6

a   10 'He went there for a week.'   11 'Yes, he has been there since Easter.'   12 'He went there a week ago.'   13 'He has been there for a week' *or* 'He has been there since Easter.'

b   14 'What did you do last night/today/this morning?'   15 'What did you do today/this morning?' *or* 'What have you done today/this morning?'   16 'Have you been working hard today/lately/this morning?'   17 'Did you work hard last night/today/this morning?'

c   18 'What were you doing when the teacher came into the room?'   19 'What did you do when the teacher came into the room?'   20 'What were you doing before you joined ICI?'   21 'What did you do before you joined ICI?'

8.7a

1 since   2 since   3 for   4 for
5 since   6 since   7 for   8 since
9 for   10 since   11 for   12 since
13 for   14 for   15 since Easter *or* for Easter, (depending on whether you are referring to Easter as a point of time, or a period of time i.e. the holiday of Easter.)   16 for
17 since   18 for

b

1 Joe studied at Teeside Polytechnic for seven years.

2 He got his BSc degree in 1977.

3 After leaving Teesside, he worked in Saudi Arabia for five years.

4 He has been a science graduate since 1977.

5 He left Saudi in 1982, and he has been working for ICI since then.

6 He has been interested in football for many years, but he hasn't played football since he was at school.

7 Bill lived in London for 12 years.

8 He has worked/has been working at British Leyland since 1970.

9 He has always had the same job, and he has never thought about changing.

10 He got married in 1981, i.e. he has been married for X years.

11 They bought a new house X years ago.

12 Bill's wife is called Angela. They met while they were at school: they have known each other for over 15 years.

13 When was she at college?

14 How long has she worked/has she been working for/at the travel agency?

15 When did she join the travel agency?

16 How long has she been (a/the) manager?

17 How many children has she had since she got married?

18 When did she become interested in amateur dramatics?

8.8

a   1b; 2b; 3a; 3c; 3d; 4a, 4b.

b   5g; 6e; 6h; 7f; 8e; 8h

c   9 5g, . . .   10 3a, 3c, or 3d.
11 6e or 6h.   12 1b   13 7f
14 8e, 8h   15 4b.

8.9

a   1c; 2d; 3b; 4a

b   5f; 6h; 7e; 8g

c   9k; 10i; 11l; 12j   13 10i   14 6h
15 2d   16 9k   17 1c   18 7e

8.10a

1 Let's go, shall we?

2 Let's have a look.

3 Don't let her see what you're doing.

4 Let them leave (go) when they've finished.

5 Don't let them leave until they've finished.

6 Let's have a party, shall we?

7 Let the dog have the bones.

8 Don't let me forget to take the files with me.

9 Let me do that for you.

b *Suggested answers*

10 Do make it tidier!

11 Do drive carefully! Do drive slowly!

12 Do phone me any time. Do feel free to phone me any time.

13 Do be more careful in future!

14 Do bring him to the party.

15 Do let me look. Do let me have a look.
16 Do make an appointment. Do get an appointment.
17 Do tell us what happened.
18 Do get your car seen to.

8.11

1(i)   They have been given a day off.
 (ii) We've given them the day off.
2(i)   They asked me to make a statement.
 (ii) I was asked to make a statement.
3(i)   My parents always told me the truth.
 (ii) Yes, I was always told the truth.
4(i)   Well, we were promised an increase.
        or Well, we have been promised an increase.
 (ii) He has promised us an increase.
5(i)   Everybody will be shown her photo.
 (ii) They will show her photo.
6(i)   She is giving us our new timetables.
 (ii) We are being given our new timetables.
7(i)   My secretary handed me a note.
 (ii) I was handed a note.
8(i)   You will be sent a letter.
 (ii) Don't worry, someone will send you a letter.
9(i)   We were taught a new song.
 (ii) She taught us a new song.
10(i) Yes, I have been offered another job.
 (ii) No, in fact they offered me another job.
11(i) We were shown how to make an omelette.
 (ii) He showed us how to make an omelette.
12(i) She told me to wait outside.
 (ii) We were told to wait outside.

8.12a

(i) *Report of a chemical experiment*
You can use Avagadro's law to give information about the equations for reactions involving gases. You can investigate the reaction between NH_3 and HC^1 by connecting two syringes. You open the tap between the two syringes and you push one gas into the other syringe. When the reaction is over, you measure the volume of any remaining gas.

(ii) *Instructions on how to clean a tape recorder head*
From time to time you should clean parts which are in contact with the tape. You should use a soft cloth which you should moisten with cleaning spirit. Before cleaning, you should disconnect the tape recorder from the mains and remove the batteries.

b *Suggested answers*
1 All our staff speak English.
2 We buy and sell books.
3 You can get keys cut here.
4 We do not accept cheques unless you have a bank card
5 We need someone to help us.
6 You may/must not bring dogs into the shop.

c *Suggested answers*
7 The recent storms have cut some villages off.
8 An unknown gunman has assassinated (killed) a senior official.
9 The police are holding a man for questioning about a murder.
10 The kidnappers will free the hostages soon *or* The kidnappers will let the hostages go free soon.
11 Is it true that they are going to ration petrol?
12 The Rail Union has officially declared a strike.

8.13a

1 Girls are said to mature earlier than boys.
2 Charles Dickens is believed to have had a hard childhood.
3 White rhinos are reported to be getting scarcer.
4 Northerners are supposed to be friendlier than southerners.
5 Girls are expected to help their mothers in the house.
6 The Chinese are known to have discovered gunpowder.
7 Mohammed Ali is acknowledged to have been the greatest boxer of all time.
8 Women are said to be able to stand pain better than men
9 Men are said to be able to go for weeks without sleep.

b

10 It was the first one (one of the first) to be printed.
11 Me? I'm always the last person to be told.
12 No, but I would like (or I would have liked) to have been invited.
13 Well, I would like to be invited.
14 It is the first to be held abroad.
15 Of course. I don't want to be left out.
16 No, they are not to be eaten yet.
17 No, they are not to be opened until Christmas.
18 The doctor said you cannot (or must not) be given anything to eat till tomorrow.

Unit 9

9.1

A cat and a tortoise were having an argument.

'I *am* very fast, and you *are* very slow,' said the cat.

'All right,' *replied* the tortoise, 'we *will have* a competition.'

'I'll *win*/I'm *going to win*,' *said* the cat at once.

'We'll *see*,' *replied* the tortoise, *smiling* to himself. 'I *bet* you that I *can* travel 100 metres in the same time as you.'

The cat *agreed*, sure that he *could/would be able to* travel much faster than any tortoise. They *shook* hands, and the tortoise *led* the cat to the top of a tall tower. You see, the tortoise *had learned* about the law of gravity at school. One day, his teacher *had spoken* about gravity.

'What *does that mean*?' the tortoise *had asked*. (He was not usually curious about things, but gravity *sounded* to him like something a tortoise *could/would be able to* make use of.)

'It *means*,' had said the teacher, 'that two bodies of different mass *will fall* at the same speed, and *reach* the ground at the same time.

The cat looked down anxiously at the ground far below them. 'What *do we have to do/must we do*?' he asked in a small voice.

'We *jump* when I *count* three. 1 – 2 – 3, go!'

They *jumped* and, thanks to the law of gravity, they *fell* together and *hit* the ground at exactly the same moment. The cat *landed* on his feet, but the tortoise *landed* on his back,

breaking his shell and most of his bones. He *was* in hospital for a long time afterwards.

Moral: Gravity is strictly for cats.

9.2a

1(i) won't you   (ii) don't you.
2(i) will you do   (ii) will you be doing
3(i) won't   (ii) wants to
4(i) I will go   (ii) I want to go
5(i) I'll get   (ii) I get
6(i) He won't work   (ii) He doesn't work
7(i) I'll come   (ii) I'm coming
8(i) won't be going   (ii) won't go
9(i) Will   (ii) Won't

b

10 are you doing   11 are you doing
12 will you do   13 will you be
14 will you be doing   15 are getting
16 Will you come   17 will be opening
18 won't you tell

9.3

a 1b; 2a; 3a; 4c.
1 is to   2 leaves   3 will be leaving
4 will be leaving   5 leaves   6 will leave
b 1aA; 1bB; 2aC; 2cB; (1bC and 2cC are possible: *drive* can be a vt as in *Let me drive you to the station*)   7 We'll drive instead   8 they'll have been driving for
9 we'll be driving   10 we'll have been driving   11 They'll drive   12 we'll have driven

9.4

1 receive . . . will be   2 are . . . will start
3 hear . . . will let   4 will not . . . ask
5 Will . . . go   6 calls . . . will be   7 won't
. . . has arrived   8 will begin . . . is given
9 hear . . . will take place   10 go . . . will
11 get   12 don't . . . will eat   13 don't
hurry . . . will be . . . get   14 Will . . . has
come   15 is still moving   16 won't . . . are
given   17 will deliver . . . are able   18 will
. . . have had.

9.5

1(i) are they going to do (ii) will do
2(i) won't eat (ii) You're not going to eat those cakes, are you?

3(i) are going to pull it down (ii) will pull it down
4(i) I'm not going to lend you mine (ii) Will you lend me
5(i) I won't tell you (ii) I'm not going to tell you
6(i) Is he going to marry Susan? (ii) will marry
7(i) won't start (ii) isn't going to start
8(i) I'm going to buy (ii) I'll buy
9(i) I'm going to take (ii) I'll take

9.6a
1 He will be in his office at this time of day.
2 He will be having his lunch about now.
3 I will be seeing her on Friday.
4 He won't be back yet.
5 He will be coming to the funeral, I'm sure.
6 They will be arriving at any moment.
7 You will be feeling hungry.
8 You will be wanting something to eat.
9 Will you be going to the dance tonight?
b
10 He won't eat.   11 The car won't start.
12 Will you come to the theatre tonight?
13 Won't you come with us?   14 I'll make the beds if you'll do the washing up.   15 He will eat between meals!   16 My pen won't write.   17 Won't you come home, Bill Bailey?   18 She won't listen to anyone.

9.7 *Suggested answers*
1 I'll have to go by train.
2 I won't need to/have to buy one.
3 won't be able to have a picnic.
4 you will have to get a taxi.
5 you will need a car of your own/will have to have a car. . .
6 will have to/need to apply for a visa.
7 won't be able to hear a thing.
8 will have to/need to set off early.
9 I'll have to/need to get a new one.
10 I'll have to borrow someone else's.
11 You'll have to/need to get an international driving licence . . .
12 The children won't be able to get in.
13 I'll need to/have to get my eyes tested first.
14 won't be able to see you tomorrow.
15 I'll have to try again later.
16 But won't they have to/need to get their parents' permission first?
17 You will soon be able to play as well as Segovia!

18 will have to let her know you are coming.

9.8
1f; 2i; 3a; 4j; 5b; 6h; 7e; 8g; 9l; 10c; 11d; 12k
13 The students are having a test, aren't they?
14 You will be careful, won't you?
15 It'll be all right to park the car here, won't it?
16 Your parents won't mind, will they?
17 You won't forget, will you?
18 Susan isn't going to marry him, is she?

9.9
1 yellow   2 red   3 blue and red
1 The red light will come on if you close switches 3 and 5.
2 Both the red light and the blue light will come on if you close switches 3, 4 and 6.
3 Both the red light and the yellow light will come on if you close switches 1, 2, 3 and 5.
4 All the lights will come on if you close switches 1, 3, 3, 4 and 6.
5 If you want the red light to come on, you will have to close switches 3 and 5.
6 If you wanted all the lights to come on, you would have to close switches, 1, 2, 3, 4 and 6.
7 The red light will not come on unless you close switches 3 and 5.
8 The red light would not come on if you didn't close switches 3 and 5.
9 Neither the red light nor the blue light would come on if you didn't close switches 3, 4 and 6.

Unit 10

10.1
There was once a hippopotamus who *was* a mathematical genius. He *could do* any calculation in his head, and he always *got* the right answer. One day, he *was lying* in his mudhole, *humming* to himself and working out π to 300 decimal places, when he *felt* a terrible pain behind the eyes.

'It *must be* all this calculating that *is giving* me such a headache,' he *thought*, 'I really *ought to go* and have my eyes *tested*.'

To tell you the truth, the hippo *was* very short-sighted, but he *refused* to *admit* it, even to himself. The optician *gave* him a strong pair of glasses, and *said* (because he *did not want* to *hurt* the hippo's feelings):

'You *need not wear* them all the time, but I *think* you *should wear* your glasses whenever you *feel* like *doing* any sums in your head.'

The hippo *caught* sight of himself in the mirror, and *thought* how intelligent he *looked* in his glasses, so he *kept* them on, stopping to *admire* himself in every pool as he *walked* back to his mudhole. On the way he *spotted* a notice nailed to a tree. Thanks to his wonderful new glasses, he *could make* out what *was written* on it. It *said*, quite simply, 2 + 2 = 5!

10.2

a 1 Can/Could   2 can't/couldn't
3 can't   4 Can   5 can/could/will be able to   6 couldn't   7 can't
8 could   9 can/am able to
b 10 might be able to   11 have to be able to translate   12 Apart from being able to type   13 useful to be able to   14 hasn't been able to   15 need to be able to
16 shall be able to   17 used to be able to
18 not being able to

10.3

a 1a; 2a; 3b; 4a; 5d; 6d; 7c
b 1 might have to   2 used to have to/would have to   3 would have had to   4 has had to   5 would have to   6 has had to
7 will have to   8 might have to
9 without having to

10.4

a 1 don't have to   2 mustn't
3 mustn't   4 doesn't have to
5 mustn't   6 don't have to   7 don't have to   8 mustn't   9 don't have to
b 10 didn't have to   11 weren't allowed to   12 didn't have to   13 weren't allowed to   14 weren't allowed
15 didn't have to   16 didn't have to
17 weren't allowed to   18 didn't have to

10.5

a 1e; 2d; 3b; 4a; 5f; 6c; 7j; 8i; 9l; 10k; 11g; 12h

b 13 1e/2d/3b   14 6c   15 2d/4a
16 8i;   17 10k   18 9l/12h

10.6a

1 You must be joking!
2 It can't be Simon.
3 Oh, she must be in her late fifties I would think.
4 Oh, she can't be more than thirty at the most.
5 It must have lasted more than two hours.
6 She can't have been lying.
7 It must have been a very unpleasant experience for you.
8 It can't have been a very nice experience for you.
9 It must have been travelling at 100 mph!

b
10 She had enough, so she didn't need to ask him.
11 She needn't have borrowed the money after all.
12 I needn't have bothered to tell him.
13 I didn't need to tell him.
14 She needn't have retyped it after all.
15 Fortunately, she didn't have to retype it.
16 You needn't have done all the housework *or* You didn't need to do all the housework.
17 I didn't need to get an international licence for France.
18 I needn't have paid so much.

10.7a

1 There should be a dot over the third letter
2 The word *French* should be written with a capital letter
3 The RED light should be at the top, and the GREEN light should be at the bottom.
4 The word *come* should be written with/should have a capital letter, and there should be a comma after *in*
5 There should be a hyphen between *well* and *educated*.
6 The word *ladies* should go/be written before the word *gentlemen*.
7 The car should not have been travelling at 85 mph/km/h
8 The woman should not have been smoking.

9 The words *thank* and *you* should not be joined. They should be written as two words.

b

10 He should not have been driving so fast.
11 He should have been in school.
12 You shouldn't be sitting there.
13 Shouldn't he be at school today?
14 She should see/go to/call a doctor right away.

Suggested answers:

15 You should mend them!
16 You shouldn't go to bed so late/work so hard.
17 They should get divorced/stop talking to each other.
18 You shouldn't have drunk so much last night!

10.8

a 1 may/can/could   2 might/may
3 can   4 may/might/could
5 might/may   6 can/may   7 may
8 can   9 can

b 10 may not   11 may not   12 cannot
13 may not   14 cannot   15 may not
16 cannot   17 may not   18 cannot

10.9

a 1a; 1b; 1c; 1d; 2b; 2d; 2f
b 1a, 1f;   2b, 2e;   3b, 3c, 3e;
4b, 4d, 4e, 4f;   5b, 5e;   6d, 6f
c 1 If my father lends me the car, I can take you with me.
2 If my father lent me the car, I could take you with me.
3 If I had enough money, I would buy a new car.
4 If I have enough money, I might buy a new car next year.
5 If you are free, I want you to come as well.
6 If you were not so busy, you could come with us.

10.10a

1 bB; 2 aA; 3 aA; 3 bB

b

1 The soup wouldn't be tasteless if enough salt had been added during the cooking.
2 The meat wouldn't be dry if it hadn't been under the grill for so long.
3 The vegetables wouldn't be soggy if less water had been used.
4 The engine wouldn't be so noisy if it had been properly serviced.
5 It wouldn't run so badly if they had changed the oil.
6 It would start properly if they hadn't forgotten to set the timing.
7 Claire wouldn't be angry with Julian if he hadn't borrowed her radio without asking.
8 Julian wouldn't be angry with Claire if she had given him something for his birthday.
9 She wouldn't be so upset if he hadn't been rude to her friend Jacky.
10 She wouldn't still have a cold if she had gone to the doctor's in the first place.
11 She wouldn't be ill if she hadn't ignored your advice.
12 She wouldn't have a very sore throat if she hadn't continued to smoke.

10.11

1 The soup wouldn't have been tasteless if enough salt had been added.
2 The meat wouldn't have been so dry if it hadn't been under the grill for too long.
3 The vegetables wouldn't have been soggy if too much water hadn't been used.
4 The engine wouldn't have been so noisy if it had been properly serviced.
5 It wouldn't have run so badly if they had changed the oil.
6 It would have started properly if they hadn't forgotten to set the timing.
7 Claire wouldn't have been angry with Julian if he hadn't borrowed her radio without asking.
8 Julian wouldn't have been so angry with Claire if she had given him something for his birthday.
9 She wouldn't have been so upset if he hadn't been rude to her friend Jacky.
10 She wouldn't have still had the cold after three weeks if she had gone to the doctor's in the first place.

11 She wouldn't have been ill if she hadn't ignored your advice.

12 She wouldn't have had such a sore throat if she hadn't continued to smoke.

10.12a *Suggested answers*

1 . . . will have to give them up.

2 . . . may have to use smaller cars.

3 . . . will be able to visit the other planets.

4 . . . will need to make more nature reserves.

5 . . . should be able to get to France more easily.

6 . . . won't need to depend on oil.

7 . . . will not be able to find work.

8 . . . will have to find other kinds of fuel.

9 . . . people won't be able to afford to go by train.

b *Suggested answers*

10 . . . would be able to communicate with each other.

11 . . . would have to make our own amusements.

12 . . . would have to earn a lot of money.

13 . . . would have to walk a lot more.

14–18 You're on your own!

10.13

1 (i) says he had the chance to get in, (ii) says that he definitely got in

2 (i) is more direct, (ii) is more polite.

3 (i) expresses surprise or anger that the train has not arrived, whereas (ii) simply says that you are expecting it to arrive very soon.

4 (i) means 'I expect they have finished'; (ii) quite definitely expresses the annoyance you feel because they have not finished.

5 (i) forbids you to go out, (ii) tells you that you are not obliged to go out, but that you can if you want to.

6 (i) expresses, for example, your feeling of guilt or shame because your uniform is dirty, (ii) suggests that someone in authority has told you to get it cleaned.

7 (i) suggests that it is probable, (ii) that it is possible, i.e., *may* expresses a stronger likelihood than *might*

8 (i) expresses permission (ii) expresses ability

9 (i) expresses the idea that the person saying this is passing on an instruction, i.e., 'Mr Brown has told me to tell you that you must . . .'

10 (i) means it is not possible, perhaps because someone forbids it: (ii) quite definitely says that someone forbids it.

11 (i) could be a suggestion (Why don't you . . .?'); (ii) is more likely to mean that you are obliged to do it.

12 The difference is very slight. In both cases you are told that it is not necessary to do something. (i) suggests that the speaker is giving you the freedom (i.e. it is his idea that it is not necessary); (ii) suggests that he is simply reporting to the facts of the situation (i.e., he is telling you that the situation does not require whatever it is you are doing or were about to do).

10.14a *Table 1*

1 If I had mixed red and yellow, I would have got orange.

2 If I had mixed blue and yellow, I would have got green.

3 If I had used more blue, I would have got dark green.

4 If I had used less blue, I would have got light green.

Table 2

5 If I had divided 12 by 3, the answer would have been 4.

6 If I had added 3 to 12, the answer would have been 15.

7 If I had subtracted 3 from 12, the answer would have been 9.

8 If I had multiplied 12 by itself, the answer would have been 144.

Table 3

9 If I had wanted black coffee with sugar, I would have pressed 4 and A.

10 If I had wanted chocolate with milk and sugar, I would have pressed 5 and A.

11 If I had wanted tea with milk and sugar, I would have pressed 1 and A.

12 If I had wanted black coffee without sugar, I would have pressed 4 and B.

b

13 You will only get purple if you mix red and blue.

14 If you mixed blue and yellow, you would get green.

15 If you added more yellow, you would get a lighter shade of green.

16 You should get orange if you add red and yellow.

17 If you (then) divided 48 by 16, the answer would be 3.

18 If you multiplied 3 by itself, the answer would be 9.

19 If you multiplied 9 by itself, the answer would be 81.

20 If you subtracted your age from 81, the answer would be . . .

21 You would not press A, unless you wanted sugar in your drink.

22 You would not press A with 3, unless you wanted coffee with sugar.

23 If you didn't press A, you would not get sugar in your drink.

24 You would not have got chocolate without milk or sugar if you had pressed 5 and A (*or* if you had not pressed 6 and B)

Unit 11

11.1

The hippo *looked at* the notice board once again. 2 + 2 = 5??? He *scratched* his head and *began* to mutter *to* himself, 'That can't be right. There must be some mistake.'

He *sat down* and *tried to work out* for himself how 2 + 2 *could* possibly *make* 5. He *thought* too *about* the person who had written the expression *up on* the board. Somebody *had written* it, and they *must have had* a good reason for *doing* so. There must be something in it. Finally, he *got* very angry, *tore* the notice *down*, and *took* it with him. He *put it on* the ground and *continued to stare at* it for days on end, no longer *bothering to eat* or *drink*. 2 + 2 = 5???

He *took off* his glasses to *wipe off* some mud. Immediately the board and the crazy expression *became* a blur — he *could* no longer see the figures; nor could he *make out* the plus or equal signs. Suddenly he *began to feel* much better, as if a big weight *had been lifted from* his shoulders. He smiled, rolled *about* in the mud, and *began singing*. He no longer *had* a problem. After that, he *gave up* maths, and *took up* singing instead.

Moral: If you want to see things really clearly, take your glasses off.

11.2

carry out/on/across/off; catch out/on/up; come out/on/up/to/across/off; get out/on/up/across/off; hold out/on/up/to/off; work out/on/up/to

11.3

a 1 come to 2 Come on 3 catch up 4 come out 5 came up 6 caught on 7 carry on 8 came across 9 carry out

b 10 work out 11 get up 12 got on 13 held up 14 got out/off 15 getting it across 16 work up 17 Hold on 18 hold out

11.4

break away/down/in/off/up; cut away/across/down/in/off/up; give away/in/off/up; keep away/down/in/off/up; fall away/across/down/in/off; see in/off.

11.5

a 1 broke off 2 cut down 3 broke down 4 break in/cut in 5 fallen off 6 broke up 7 cuts across 8 falling down 9 cut off

b 10 gave up 11 keep up 12 keep away 13 see me off 14 give in 15 giving them away 16 sees in 17 keep off 18 gave off

11.6

1 Give up 2 take up 3 hold up 4 pulled up 5 turns up 6 doing up 7 making up 8 bring up 9 set up 10 cut down 11 take down 12 turn down 13 break down 14 get down 15 come down 16 look down on 17 put down 18 lie down.

11.7
1 filling in   2 drop in   3 break in
4 standing in for   5 be turning in   6 come
in   7 call in   8 fit in with   9 live in
10 try out   11 died out   12 give out
13 put out   14 watch out   15 make out
16 pass out   17 stands out   18 turned out

11.8
a 1 to   2 on the news/with the car in
front   3 on   4 with   5 to   6 to
7 with   8 to   9 to   10 for
11 with   12 to a bully/for what you
believe in

b 1 to details/with influenza   2 to
3 on   4 to   5 with   6 on   7 on
8 for   9 on   10 for   11 with
12 with

11.9
a 1 do away with   2 falling behind with
3 get away with   4 looks back on
5 looking forward to   6 run out of
7 been up to   8 go back on
9 fall back on
b 10 comes   11 go   12 come
13 go   14 come   15 went
16 came   17 come   18 go

11.10
a 1 B   2 A   3 A   4 B   5 A
6 B   7 B   8 B   9 A

b 10 gave the game away   11 put everything
away   12 gave away all her money/gave all
her money away   13 put away what you
don't need;   14 brought the house down
15 put John and Mary up   16 put up next
year's calendar/put next year's calendar up
17 take out a year's subscription to Punch
18 think things over.

11.11
1 talk it over; walk over it   2 live off it; laugh
it off   3 live in it; fill it in   4 blow down it;
pull it down   5 talk about it; throw it
about   6 climb up it; pump it up   7 look
behind it; leave it behind   8 lie on it; switch it
on   9 hand it over; look over it   10 get
across it; get it across   11 live by it; put it

by   12 see through it; see it through
13 walk up it; bring it up   14 get round it;
hand it round   15 stand under it; hold it
under

11.12
1 go out   2 get away   3 looked down
4 get across   5 take off   6 get back
7 put off *or* turn off/turned off   8 turn
down/turned down   9 go on   10 brought
up   11 stand for   12 put off

11.13
a 1d;   2b;   3e;   4a;   5–;   6k;   7c;   8l;
9j;   10f;   11h;   12g;   13i;   14–;   15–.
b 1 dozed off   2 ended up   3 butt in
4 hanging about   5 brush it up   6 wind
up   7 clear off   8 shut up   9 split up
10 slipped up   11 told off   12 wore off
13 show off   14 explain away   15 patched
up

11.14
Group 1 1d;   2f;   3i;   4c;   5a;   6h;   7b;
8g;   9e
Group 2 10o;   11j;   12q;   13m;   14r;
15l;   16n;   17p;   18k

Unit 12

12.1
1 Frankly/deeply in love/just the same
2 by chance one afternoon during the rainy
season/from a
storm/immediately/generally
3 greatly/never/Naturally/soon/even/
seriously
4 so easily/too tightly/anxiously/equally
5 Anyway/very/sensibly/though/
passionately/too hard
6 even/only/silently/at that moment

12.2
a 1f; 2c; 3g; 4b; 5i; 6h; 7d; 8e; 9a
b 10r; 11q; 12n; 13o; 14l; 15j; 16p; 17m; 18k

12.3
a 1a; 2a, 2b; 3a, 3b; 4c; 5c; 6d; 7b; 8c; 9a, 9d;
10c; 11a, 11d; 12a, 12b, 12d 1d and 2d are
possible when *off* = away from work, on
holiday

b 13 18c and 5c;   14 6d;   15 10c;
      16 1a and 2b;   17 4c;   18 7b and 7a

12.4

1 (i) there;   (ii) here;   2 (i) here;   (ii) there;
3 (i) here;   (ii) there;   4 (i) there; (ii) here;
5 (i) there;   (ii) here;   6 (i) here;   (ii) there;
7 (i) there;   (ii) here;   8 (i) here;
(ii) there;   9 (i) there;   (ii) here

12.5

a   1 BAC;   2 BCA;   3 BAC;
        4 BCA;   5 BAC;   6 BAC/BCA;
        7 BAC;   8 BCA/BAC; 9 BAC/BCA
b   10 BCA;   11 BCA/BAC;
        12 CBA/BAC;   13 BCA;
        14 BCA/BAC;   15 BAC/BCA;
        16 BAC/ACB;   17 CBA/BAC;
        18 BCA

12.6

a 1a; 1d; 2c; 2f; 2g; 3b; 3e
b 1a; 1b; 1c; 1d; 1e; 1f; 1g; 2a; 2e; 2g; 3b; 3c;
       3d; 3f

12.7

a 1B; 2B; 3B; 4A; 5B; 6B; 7B; 8A; 9B
b 10 I always do!   11 I never would!
       12 I have never done it before.   13 I never
       have done.   14 I have usually had too
       many other things to do.   15 I have often
       wanted to.   16 I always used to.
       17 I am usually too busy.   18 I usually
       am too busy!

12.8a

 1 Do you still work at Bowmaker's?
 2 Have you finished your exams yet?
 3 They will still be here when you get back.
 4 He hasn't come back yet.
 5 He still hasn't come back!
 6 He won't be back for some time yet.
 7 Are you still here? I thought you were
    leaving.
 8 Hasn't the mail arrived yet?
 9 It isn't still raining, is it?

b
10 Because she doesn't love him any more.
11 No, we don't employ him any longer.

12 Because I still find them very comfortable.
13 But you still haven't told me which one you
    want!
14 Yes, I decided I couldn't afford it any longer.
15 I just haven't got around to it yet.
16 I've been thinking about that question for
    months, and I still haven't decided.
17 I rarely go there any more.
18 I haven't even finished writing it yet!

12.9

a 1 funnily   2 freely   3 gratefully
       4 musically   5 sadly   6 easily
       7 economically   8 publicly
       9 happily   10 privately   11 legally
       12 noisily   13 ironically
       14 uselessly   15 usefully   16 finally
       17 politically   18 gaily

b 1a; 2b; 3b; 4a; 5a; 6a; 7a; 8a; 9b; 10b; 11a;
       12a

12.10

a 1c/e;   2h;   3f/i;   4g/d;   5d;   6b/f/h;
       7a/c/e/i;   8a/d;   9i
       10o/l/n;   11n;   12m/q;   13l;
       14m;   15p;   16j/p;   17k/r;   18n/r
       19z;   20u;   21v;   22w;   23α;
       24x;   25y;   26t;   27s

12.11

1 faster   2 in a friendly manner(way)
3 hard   4 fast   5 well   6 more slowly
. . . better   7 well   8 worse   9 in an
unfriendly way (manner)   10 loudly . . .
more quietly   11 quickly   12 quicker
13 fast   14 faster   15 well . . . badly
16 more beautifully   17 fast   18 in a
fatherly way.

12.12

 1 For several hours they had been patiently
    waiting outside the cinema.
 2 I generally like to get home by five o'clock.
 3 She always sleeps badly in a strange bed.
 4 In the evening he usually spends a long time
    at his desk.
 5 She dozed peacefully in her armchair until
    teatime.
 6 I would never go to work by car.

7 With a sharp knife she carefully cut the bread into thin slices.
8 This term he has really done well in history.
9 In London we seldom go out at night.
10 I always used to work much better before lunch.
11 In summer people frequently go abroad for their holidays.
12 For hours we continued to climb steadily towards the summit.
13 Frankly, I don't really care in the least.
14 For the moment we simply had to stand absolutely still at our posts.
15 Unfortunately, I rarely get a chance to sit quietly and read.
16 As a matter of fact, he quite often tells me confidentially what happens at board meetings.
17 Actually, you can hardly blame her for reacting violently.
18 Apparently, he has just been abroad on business.

12.13

1 Under no circumstances should you go away.
2 Never in my life have I felt so angry.
3 Rarely do you see so many Russian ships in the harbour.
4 Not only does she play, but she also composes well.
5 Not until then did I realise how much she wanted to go.
6 Only much later did I realize what he was trying to achieve.
7 Scarcely had he had time to take his coat off when the phone rang.
8 No sooner had we said yes than they ran upstairs to pack.
9 Only recently have I begun to think about politics.
10 Seldom have I heard such rubbish.
11 Not until the others had left could we talk.
12 Only in special circumstances will you be able to extend your visa.

12.14

1 (i) John and nobody else (ii) only Arabic, not any other language
2 (i) I wish to tell you frankly that I cannot . . .; (ii) I can speak to her but not frankly, I have to be careful what I say to her

3 (i) states a fact, (ii) means that it is late and I am a bit annoyed about it
4 The difference is slight. It depends whether you are proud of the company (i), or whether you are talking about working conditions, etc., of employees (ii).
5 (i) *Soon* refers to the decision, (ii) *soon* refers to the time of leaving
6 (i) *Earlier* refers to when I told you, (ii) *Earlier* refers to the time of your coming
7 (i) *Earlier* refers to the time when I had this desire, and suggests that I no longer want him to have it: (ii) means that he has it now, but that he should have had it before now.
8 (i) means that I prefer expensive restaurants when I am in London; (ii) is ambiguous because of the word *only*, which could mean *only expensive restaurants* or *only in London*.
9 (i) He cheats a lot but it is difficult to catch him doing it; (ii) he doesn't cheat very often.
10 (i) is a simple statement of fact; (ii) is a response to something like 'Why aren't you interested in politics?' 'I never have been.'
11 The difference is slight. Putting an expression at the end of the sentence draws our attention to it more (i) means 'Don't forget about Friday'; (ii) means 'Don't forget to be there at nine thirty'.
12 (ii) draws our attention to the way she put them away; (i) is a simple statement of fact, where *carefully* seems part of the verb: she carefully-put . . .

12.15

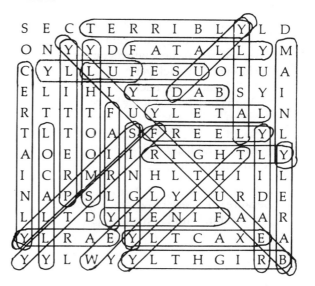

Unit 13

13.1
a 1 lasted 2 cost 3 took 4 lost
5 gained 6 weigh 7 rose
8 dropped 9 measures
b 10 does 11 holds 12 totals
13 sleeps 14 covers · 15 register
16 spend 17 contains 18 seat

13.2
a 1e; 2g; 3b; 4i; 5a; 6f; 7h; 8c; 9d
b 10 get better 11 go stale 12 turn
brown 13 look tired 14 tastes
funny 15 remain silent 16 stand
still 17 make sure 18 ring true

13.3
a 1 crawling 2 switch on; walk
3 cutting down 4 burning
5 moving 6 playing 7 tap
8 trying 9 get . . . pull
b 10 has gone fishing 11 Did you go
dancing . . .? 12 are going sailing
13 have gone hiking 14 have been
surfing 15 goes horse-riding
16 would go cycling 17 go skating
18 would/could go skiing

13.4
1 replying 2 we went 3 stay 4 in
arguing 5 to get 6 go 7 to help
8 to have 9 to have 10 you started
11 complaining 12 to see 13 to be
feeling 14 servicing 15 go 16 of
worrying 17 to ask 18 leave

13.5
1 to do 2 adding 3 giving 4 to
post 5 to talk 6 to meet 7 smoking
8 to stay 9 meeting 10 to give
11 wondering 12 to prepare
13 changing 14 to interrupt
15 watching 16 to cook 17 getting
up/going 18 meeting

13.6
a 1 Fancy (marrying) 2 try (saying)
3 recollect (seeing) 4 mind (helping)
5 puts off (going) 6 regret not

(staying) 7 finish (reading/typing)
8 suggest (leaving) 9 keep (reminding)
b 10 imagine having to 11 miss being able
to 12 dislike seeing 13 consider
emigrating 14 resist phoning
15 practise saying 16 avoid travelling
17 enjoyed talking 18 deny telling

13.7
a 1a; 2b; 3a/b; 4b; 5b; 6b; 7a; 8a; 9b/a
b 1a; 2b; 3a; 4b/a; 5b; 6b
c 1a; 2b; 3b; 4b; 5a; 6a; 7b; 8b; 9a

13.8
a 1 me 2 to me 3 me 4 to me
5 to me 6 me 7 to me 8 me
9 to me
b 1b; 2a/c; 3a; 4b; 5b; 6a/c; 7a/c 8b; 9a

13.9a
2 She begged him to wear a tie.
3 (S)He advised him/her not to tell the police
anything.
4 He warned them to keep away from the
Grotto disco.
5 She told them not to talk to strangers.
6 He didn't (or wouldn't) allow her to go out.
7 She reminded him to book a table at
Luigi's.
8 He asked her not to be late.
9 She expected them to be back by ten thirty.

b
2 He was begged to wear a tie.
3 (S)He was advised not to tell the police
anything.
4 They were warned to keep away from the
Grotto disco.
5 They were told not to talk to strangers.
6 She wasn't allowed to go out.
7 He was reminded to book a table at Luigi's.
8 She was asked not to be late.
9 They were expected to be back by ten thirty.

13.10
a 1 make 2 making 3 let 4 made
5 let 6 letting 7 made 8 make
9 let
b 2 We'll get Joe to see to it. 3 We'll get
Mike to deliver it. 4 I got Julia to

interview him.   5 She can get the children to do it.   6 They got him to confess (to having committed the crime).   7 I'll get Alan to go through it.   8 Perhaps we can get Mr Smith to contribute.   9 Why don't you get Mrs Woodhouse to train it?

13.11

a   1a; 2b; 3b; 4b; 5a; 6b; 7a; 8a; 9b

b   1 Give him your share   2 Buy them a drink   3 Do him/her a favour. 4 Reserve me a table.   5 Leave them all your money.   6 Save him a place. 7 Offer him/her a job.   8 Pass him/her the draft.   9 Spare us something.

c   1 He announced his resignation to the press.
2 She explained the situation to her colleagues.
3 He forgot to mention the matter to his boss.
4 I shall have to report this to the authorities.
5 He teaches young people mathematics.
6 Don't tell the others anything.
7 I have promised the children a party.
8 Would you like to read the story?
9 He refuses to say anything to anybody.

13.12

1; 2; 4; 6; 7; 8; 9; 10; 12; 13; 16; 17; 18

13.13

a   1 dyed; green   2 grew; long   3 get; wet   4 hold (leave/keep); open 5 make; ill   6 leave (keep); undone 7 keep; shut   8 set; free   9 painted; white

b   1 make it clear   2 find it remarkable 3 made it obvious/clear   4 finds it difficult   5 find it remarkable 6 finding it difficult   7 make it clear 8 find it difficult   9 making it obvious/clear

13.14

1 get   2 get   3 had   4 have; (*get* would suggest that they had to make the appointment themselves or that it was their idea)   5 get 6 had   7 have; (use *get* if you want to suggest that there may be some difficulty about it, e.g., all the plumbers are very busy at this time of year)   8 have or get, the difference is slight 9 *have* means that someone else, not the speaker, will do the report; *get* could mean that the speaker himself was going to do it.
10 have   11 get   12 get; *have* is less likely, because the question suggests that it is not easy to find a place that makes shoes at a reasonable price.

13.15

1(i) He did not want to join and they said it was all right not to join. (ii) He wanted to join but they would not let him join.
2(i) He spent all the time talking about it; (ii) he finished one subject and then started talking about his experiences in the clinic.
3(i) He allowed us to do it. (ii) He obliged us to do it.
4(i) I heard the whole song. (ii) I heard part of the song.
5(i) Did he call? I am not sure. (ii) He called, but I did not know at the time that he had called.
6 The difference is slight. (i) is more a simple question for information '*What are you going to do?*'; (ii) suggests that the person's intention is clear, but that you are telling him/her that you do not like it: *It seems to me that you intend to stay here all night. I think you should leave now.*
7(i) On this occasion, I want to walk; (ii) In general walking is better than driving.
8(i) I feel sure that he will come. (ii) I think that he ought to come (it is his duty).
9 The difference is slight. (i) suggests that the studying started a long time ago and is still going on (*began studying*); (ii) refers to the act of starting to study (in the sense of '*to read*'), but does not suggest that the reading is still going on at the time of speaking.

13.16

Order of sentences: 4 6 10 12 9 3 7 2 8 11 5 1

Unit 14

14.1a
1 Take an umbrella so that you won't get wet. Take an umbrella in case it rains.
2 Pack an overnight bag in case you have to stay the night. Pack an overnight bag so that you can stay the night.
3 Have something to eat so that you won't feel hungry later. Have something to eat in case you can't get anything to eat later.
4 Let's have an early night so that we'll be fresh in the morning. Let's have an early night in case we have to get up early tomorrow.
5 Take the files with you in case you need to refer to them. Take the files with you so that you can refer to them.
6 We must fill up with petrol so that we'll have enough for the journey. We must fill up with petrol in case the filling stations are closed.
7 Wear your heavy overcoats in case the weather turns colder. Wear your heavy overcoats so that you won't feel the cold.
8 Write everything down in case you forget it. Write everything down so that you have a record of what is said.
9 Book well in advance so that you are sure of getting a seat. Book well in advance in case they sell out.

b
1 I took an umbrella so that I wouldn't get wet. I took an umbrella in case it rained.
2 I packed an overnight bag in case I had to stay the night. I packed an overnight bag so that I could stay the night.
3 I had something to eat so that I wouldn't feel hungry later. I had something to eat in case I couldn't get anything to eat later.
4 We had an early night so that we would be fresh in the morning. We had an early night in case we had to get up early the next day.
5 I took the files with me in case I needed to refer to them. I took the files with me so that I could refer to them.
6 We filled up with petrol so that we would have enough for the journey. We filled up with petrol in case the filling stations were closed.

7 We wore our heavy overcoats in case the weather turned colder. We wore our heavy overcoats so that we wouldn't feel the cold.
8 I wrote everything down in case I forgot it. I wrote everything down so that I had a record of what was said.
9 I booked well in advance so that I was sure of getting a seat. I booked well in advance in case they sold out.

14.2a
1 The streets are wet because it has been raining. The streets are wet even though it hasn't been raining.
2 We got wet through because we didn't take an umbrella. We got wet through even though we took an umbrella.
3 He failed his driving test because he didn't practise enough. He failed his driving test even though he practised a lot.
4 She is fit and healthy even though she doesn't get much exercise. She is fit and healthy because she gets a lot of exercise.
5 I'm hungry because I didn't have much for breakfast. I'm hungry even though I ate a lot for breakfast.
6 Our team seldom wins even though they have some very good players. Our team seldom wins because they don't have any very good players.
7 I run an expensive car because I can afford it. I run an expensive car even though I can't afford it.
8 They often go to discos even though they aren't keen on dancing. They often go to discos because they are keen on dancing.
9 He speaks Japanese fluently because he has lived in Japan: He speaks Japanese fluently even though he has never lived in Japan.

b 1 Supposing 2 as far as
  3 Wherever 4 unless 5 as if
  6 providing (or provided) 7 Seeing that 8 as long as 9 Considering

14.3a
1 The restaurant was so crowded that we couldn't get a table.
2 It is such an expensive hotel that only the rich can afford it.

3   He has such large feet that he can't get shoes to fit him.
4   It was such a difficult exercise that nobody could do it.
5   She had such beautiful hair that everyone admired it.
6   Russia is such a big country that it has 11 time zones
7   The air is so polluted that your clothes always feel dirty.
8   It is such a polluted river that no fish live in it any more.
9   He gave me such good advice that I was able to save thousands of pounds!

b
1b I have so much work to do (that) I don't know where to begin.
2d He drove so fast (that) nobody could catch up with him.
3f She has so much intelligence (that) men are afraid of her.
4c I have so many letters to write (that) it will take me ages to get through them all.
5h She has so many admirers (that) she goes out with a different man every night.
6e He drove so slowly (that) he arrived half an hour late.
7i I have so little money left (that) I don't think I will be able to pay my bills.
8a She has so many clothes that you rarely see her in the same dress twice.
9g He drove so dangerously that his wife refused to ride with him.

14.4
1 As   2 until/unless   3 just as   4 as though/as if   5 whenever   6 since/seeing that   7 as soon as   8 as far as   9 until
10 once, after   11 unless   12 assuming
13 if, when   14 now that   15 even though/although   16 before   17 while
18 now that

14.5
1   (i) You should pay a visit there the next time you get an opportunity to do so. (ii) means *every time* and advises you to go as often as you can.

2   (i) means that you are definitely coming to town. (ii) The suggestion is that you might come to town.
3   (i) means that you have not yet passed your test, i.e. *once* is similar to *as soon as*. In (ii) you have passed your test.
4   (i) *When* suggests that they left *because* the party was beginning to get noisy; (ii) simply states a fact about the coincidence of two events.
5   (i) means *If you don't stand still, I will hit you* (ii) probably means *If you stand still, I will hit you*, but it could be a kind of invitation or suggestion *Would you like me to hit you? If so, stand still.*
6   *As long as* means *for the length of time that* in (i), and *providing* in (ii).
7   *As* means *because* in (a), and *when* in (b)
8   (i) means do it now, before the snow comes. (ii) means do it when the snow comes.
9   (i) You will be told to write (ii) You might have to write but only do it if someone tells you to.
10 The difference is slight. (i) suggests that you are in London, and this would be a good opportunity to go and see them; (ii) probably means go and see them *the next time* you are in London.
11 They are two sides of the same coin. (i) expresses my willingness to come; (ii) expresses my intention not to come, except in special circumstances (i.e., if you ask me to come).
12 (i) I did not write to her. I was too angry to write. (ii) I wrote to her, but not because I was angry.

14.6a
1   If you eat that, you'll be ill.
2   Once you've drunk this, you'll feel better.
3   If you don't put it away, I'll take it off you.
4   I am feeling sad because she has gone back to Sicily.
5   He put the lights on so that we could see much better.
6   You won't learn anything unless you do your homework.
7   She left him even though he had done his best for her.

8 I like her very much although I don't know her very well.

9 It was not until everyone else had gone that they put out the lights and went to bed.

10 Seeing that the disco was crowded, we didn't go in.

11 We enjoy life even if we are old.

12 Not only does he speak Japanese, but he can also read it.

b

1 He set his alarm for 6 am so that he would not be late for work.

2 Even though I worked hard, I didn't get anywhere.

3 She came running up to me just as I was about to leave the office.

4 Since you seem to know so much about it, I would like to hear your version of the incident.

5 You should take your umbrella in case it rains.

6 All the students were sitting in the canteen because the lesson had been cancelled.

7 You can have the day off as long as you work on Saturday instead.

8 Even if you don't like it, you must go and visit your aunt.

9 We could have a game of cards if the Queen of diamonds weren't missing.

14.7

1 He wants to know why she isn't at work.

2 He wants to know where we are living.

3 He wants to know what they are talking about.

4 He wants to know when she will come back.

5 He wants to know what happened.

6 He wants to know if anyone called.

7 He wants to know if he can talk to Joe.

8 He wants to know if we have always lived in Bern.

9 He wants to know who looks after the record player.

10 He wants to know how long they have been married.

11 He wants to know if he has to do all those exercises.

12 He wants to know if he should wait for the others.

13 He wants to know why nobody has done the washing up.

14 He wants to know when the new term starts.

15 He wants to know who we like best.

16 He wants to know who likes us best.

17 He wants to know if we would like to go too.

18 He wants to know if he will need his overcoat.

14.8

a 1b; 2a; 2b; 3b; 4a; 4b; 5b; 6a; 6b; 7b; 8b; 9a; 9b; 10b; 11a; 12a; 12b

b

1 He wanted to know why she wasn't at work.

2 He wanted to know where we were living.

3 He wanted to know what they were talking about.

4 He wanted to know when she would come back.

5 He wanted to know what had happened.

6 He wanted to know if anyone had called.

7 He wanted to know if he could talk to Joe.

8 He wanted to know if we had always lived in Bern.

9 He wanted to know who looked after the record player.

10 He wanted to know how long they had been married.

11 He wanted to know if he had to do all the exercises.

12 He wanted to know if he should wait for the others.

13 He wanted to know why nobody had done the washing up.

14 He wanted to know when the new term started.

15 He wanted to know who we liked best.

16 He wanted to know who liked us best.

17 He wanted to know if we would like to go too.

18 He wanted to know if he would need his overcoat.

14.9

1a, 1c, 1e, 1f, 1h, 1j, 1k;   2b, 2d, 2e, 2g, 2i;
3b, 3d, 3e, 3g, 3i, 3j, 3k;   4a, 4c, 4e, 4f, 4h, 4j,

4k. The combinations 2j, 2k and 3f are possible, but would only be said in very unusual circumstances.

14.10a
1 What are you thinking about?
2 What are you up to?
3 Who did you give it to?
4 Which car are you going in?
5 What are you looking for?
6 Who did you go out with last night?
7 How much money do you have to save up?
8 How much money have you saved up?
9 Who have you been waiting for?
10 Which clubs do you belong to?
11 Who were you talking to?
12 How long are you staying (for)?

b
1 I am curious to know what you are thinking about.
2 . . . what you are up to.
3 . . . who you gave it to.
4 . . . which car you are going in.
5 . . . what you are looking for.
6 . . . who you went out with last night.
7 . . . how much money you have to save up.
8 . . . how much money you have saved up.
9 . . . who you have been waiting for.
10 . . . which clubs you belong to.
11 . . . who you were talking to.
12 . . . how long you are staying (for).

14.11a
1 He told me it was too late.
2 I'm surprised you aren't worried about her.
3 He advised us not to worry.
4 He seemed surprised that I hadn't finished.
5 He suggested that everyone be given a copy.
6 We were ordered to leave the following day.
7 He told me he had seen her the day before.
8 The General told us everything had to be ready by 6 that night.
9 He said he wished I had told him before.

b 1 *Suggested answer*
ALAN Hello Cathy, what are you doing today?
CATHY Nothing special [*i.e. I haven't got any plans.*]
ALAN Well, would you like to come swimming with me?

CATHY Mmm . . . Can you wait a minute while I go and get changed?
(Would you mind waiting . . .)
ALAN Okay. I'll go and have a coffee while I'm waiting.
CATHY You won't have time (or I don't think you'll have time). It'll only take me a second to get changed.

2 *Suggested answer*
ALAN Can I help you with your homework?
CATHY Yes, I can (or could) use some help.
ALAN I can see you have a lot to do. I finished mine some time ago.
CATHY How were you able to do it so quickly?
ALAN I found a key to the exercises, so I simply copied out all the answers.
CATHY You're a cheat (or Cheat!) Get out, and don't bother me again!

14.12a
1 We need someone who knows about statistics.
2 I'm looking for a man I can do business with.
3 They are a pop group you don't hear very often.
4 Have you seen the girl who usually sits here?
5 She is the last person you should tell.
6 I am talking to those of you who have actually experienced poverty.
7 What about the ones who cannot fight for themselves?
8 Do you know the girl I was with the other night?
9 These are the sort of people the company should employ.
10 He is the kind of man who really knows what is going on.
11 Do you know anyone who can play as well as he can?
12 He is the only one the men will listen to any more.

b
1 Mr John Dawes, whom most of you have already met, has agreed to take on the job as treasurer.

2   Ted Brett, whose books most of you know, will be the guest speaker at our Annual Dinner.

3   The Advanced Passenger Train, which you may have seen on TV, will revolutionize public transport in this country.

4   We wish to thank Miss Dinah Harris, who wrote all the music for the festival.

5   The lead guitarist, whom everyone refers to as 'Jezz', is the only trained musician in the group.

6   The Beresford Gallery, admission to which (*or* to which admission) used to be free, has had to introduce an entrace fee of £3.

7   Arthur Bowyer, whose latest novel is already a best seller, gave up a well-paid job to become a writer.

8   His father John, whom we rarely see now, used to appear regularly on television.

9   Abu Kammash is a huge chemical complex of which the salt plant is only a small part.

10 The need for a further increase in postal rates, about which I shall say more in a moment, is one more example of bad planning.

11 The factory was completed on time, which surprised a lot of people.

12 The girls' dresses, for which a local firm supplied the material, were made by members of the Parents' Association.

14.13a

1   I went to see her flat, which she lived in when she was a student.

2   I went to see the flat that/which she lived in when she was a student.

3   Come and meet the friends that I told you about.

4   Come and meet my friends, most of whom you know.

5   This is the Director, who founded the company.

6   There are several directors. This is the director who founded the company.

7   What we really need is a dam which would be big enough to supply the whole area with power.

8   I have a photo of the Kariba Dam, which supplies the whole area with power.

9   I'd like to introduce Mr Bridge, who I used to work with.

10 Can that be the Mr Bridge (who) I used to work with?

11 I have to study mathematics, which I do not enjoy.

12 Statistics is the one part of maths which I do not enjoy.

b

1   English people who go abroad for their holidays often develop a taste for a variety of different styles of cooking.

2   Each year Britain welcomes several million visitors, many of whom never travel outside London, surprisingly.

3   Airline pilots, who have a very stressful job, must have regular health checks.

4   Young married couples, who usually have very little money, find it difficult to save enough to buy their own homes.

5   Left-handed people, who are often very good at music and art, make up only 10% of the population.

6   People who put on weight easily have to be careful what they eat.

7   Olympic sportsmen, many of whom train for years to become successful athletes, have to be very dedicated.

8   Old people, whose bones break very easily, have to be very careful when walking on snow and ice in winter.

9   Young babies, who need to be kept warm, can easily become ill if the temperature is too low.

14.14

1   (i) This suggests that a quarrel was going on at the time and nobody knew what it was about. (ii) The quarrel was over and nobody knew what it had been about.

2   (i) You don't work hard enough. (ii) You didn't work hard enough.

3   (i) You are leaving tomorrow, aren't you? (ii) When I saw you last Tuesday, I thought you were going to leave on the following day, i.e. Wednesday, but I now know that you left on a different day.

4   (i) This is said immediately after John made his promise. (ii) This reports what he said at an earlier time.

5 (i) actual words 'Don't waste your money'
(ii) actual words 'I see you have bought a
new car. What a waste of money!'
6 (i) 'She loves me. I wonder why.' (ii) 'She
loved me. I wonder why.' – either she
stopped loving him, or she is no longer
alive.
7 (i) You are not honest with me. (ii) You were
not honest with me.
8 (i) This reports his words, but does not
suggest whether they were true or not;
(ii) This suggests that the words are true it is
a fact that there are still cannibals there.
9 The difference is slight. (i) This means that
the command 'Work harder.' is still in force.
(ii) This reports the command but does not
necessarily suggest that it is still in force.
10 (i) I don't know them. (ii) I didn't know
them when I needed to.

11 (i) Somebody told me that you didn't speak
French. I am surprised to find out that you
do in fact speak French; (ii) A statement: I
see that you speak French. I always thought
that you only spoke German.
12 (i) 'Has she come back?' (ii) 'Will she come
back?'

14.15
All that glitters is not gold.
People who live in glass houses shouldn't throw
stones.
All's well that ends well.
He who pays the piper calls the tune.
It's a long lane that has no turning.
It's an ill wind that blows nobody any good.
There are none so deaf as those who do not want
to hear.
The family that prays together stays together.